LET'S GO CRUISING!

A GUIDE TO FAMILY BOATING

BOOKS BY JOY SMITH

Let's Go Cruising!

The Perfect First Mate

Kitchen Afloat

Oh, No, They're Engaged!

The Empty Nest Cookbook

Green Fire

Seagulls Don't Eat Worms

LET'S GO CRUISING!

A GUIDE TO FAMILY BOATING

JOY SMITH

JSB

JSBooks Publications

LET'S GO CRUISING!
A Guide to Family Boating

Copyright 2016 by Joy Smith

JSBooks Publications
www.jsbookspublications@weebly.com
jsbookspublications@gmail.com

Credits:
Can Stock Photo csp8696565 - EPS Vector
Cover art: Raman Bhardwaj
Illustrations: Raman Bhardwaj, Mary Valencia
Editing: Jane Haertel at Crazy Diamond Editing Services

ISBN: 978-0-9862422-67
First Edition published July 2016

TABLE OF CONTENTS

INTRODUCTION

Ahoy, Captains and First Mates! Welcome to Marinaland, where every day is Saturday, and the clock stops ticking. Whether you are a new boater or an old hand, the water awaits you. Once in vacation mode, it won't matter whether you are cruising down a river, motoring on a lake, or battling the ocean because you will be doing what you want to do. Aboard your boat, you are the boss, the captain—whether or not you have an official captain's license. Your time and your life are your own. Toss out a fishing line and catch dinner, cruise to another harbor, or simply hang out in the cockpit reading your favorite novel.

You may have cruised your local waters on a small day craft and found it limiting. Now you're ready for more. For the purposes of this book, we'll focus on power and sail boats with stay-aboard facilities that will allow you to travel to other harbors and spend the night sleeping under the stars, listening to waves crash against the shore.

If you don't own a boat but dream of owning one, make smart decisions by evaluating your needs and knowing your personal and environmental limitations. As the saying goes, a boat is a hole in the water you pour money into. Ideally, you have chosen (or plan to buy) a boat that won't strain your household budget. Factor in trips to the marine "candy" store to buy safety gear and other boat paraphernalia, as well as to boat shows to ogle larger boats. Yes, bigger boats, ones with more power, more amenities, because once you and your family have been hooked, you'll always long for something more.

Recreational, or pleasure boating (as I prefer to call it), challenges us in many ways. Operating a boat is much more than driving on water. It requires navigational skills as well as operational expertise. While running a marine engine is similar to driving a car, your hills will be waves and your roads will be channels set into waterways. You will learn how to contend with the elements—rain, fog, sun, wind, and the sea—and befriend marine weather predictions.

If you own a sailboat, controlling the wind may be your first challenge. From there you may go onto racing. In Marinaland, races among sailboats, as opposed to powerboats, are most common because of the skill required to compete.

Perhaps you love to fish. Your boat can ferry you to the best fishing grounds, where you can snag dinner or compete in a tournament for the biggest catch.

Your entry into boating will not only require you to embrace a new set of criteria and the necessity for learning new skills, but it will also give you the ability to be part of a community of folks who enjoy the same kinds of boating activities you do. On the water, everyone becomes equal as the woes of the work week are replaced by boatspeak: Where's a good anchorage? How do you fix . . . ? Did you catch any fish?

If it suits you, join the local yacht club, travel in a flotilla with other boaters, or get together at the end of a day for drinks or dinner. It's always five o'clock somewhere.

So, what are you waiting for? Read on for the information you need to make the boating experience for you and yours a good one!

PART ONE: BUY SMART

Hey there, boat buyer, come aboard and learn the ropes—or should I say "lines," because any functional "rope" on a boat is called a line. Oh? You say you have a boat and know most of this stuff, but you're looking to upgrade? If that's the case, reviewing this section will get you in tune with the latest in boat technology and refresh your memory on the details of the buy. Now, if you've just bought a boat or are happy with the one you have, skim over this section and move on to the remainder of the book for lots of great info.

CHAPTER 1

Choose the Right Boat

Owning a sizeable boat means committing to a lifestyle that will permeate everything: your work ethic, your home, and, especially, your relationships. By its very nature, cruising suggests heading out on the water to new destinations, much the same as if you were going on a vacation in your car. For the price of a tank of gas, less if you are a sailor, you can take your family on a mini vacation. On a nice weekend afternoon, you may run into boat traffic, but it will be nothing like the logjam on the highway to reach a beach or popular vacation spot, such as Cape Cod. Once on the water, you can get away with shutting off your cell phone, with a no-signal excuse to your boss. An old friend of mine named his boat *Sails Call*, which says it all.

Boating is like camping in that the expectations of comfort are low and the rewards are great. Few things are more enjoyable than sipping coffee in your cockpit as the sun rises out of the water or lying on the bow on a starlit night picking out the constellations. While boating isn't a cheap sport, it can bolster your self-confidence, provide quality bonding time with your loved ones, and extend your land life as far out to sea as you dare go. If you can conquer the ocean, you can pretty much do anything.

Once boating gets into your blood, you can't shake it off. Your heart rate slows from Mach speed, the muscles in your back unkink, and the daily clutter flees from your mind.

You can think, get a new perspective. You are refreshed and ready to take on the rest of the day. Having to concentrate on managing the helm or the sails allows you to refocus, to mind-shift from the pressures of job performance or personal problems you may be experiencing in your life. As you master your boating operational and navigational skills, your accomplishments will improve your readiness to accept challenges presented by your job and family situations. Can't-do becomes can-do as confidence in your ability to perform opens new pathways to success.

As a side benefit, cruising boosts family bonding time. In a confined area away from everyday distractions, there is little else to do but interact with each other. As long as you make cruising fun and don't pull the tyrant act, your kids will look forward to going on the boat and will even ask to bring their friends. Be sure your loved ones are on board with your commitment to boating to avoid spending lonely times at the marina washing your boat instead of taking the gang out for a spin.

So are you in? Let's check out your options.

DECIDE ON A BOAT

Buying a boat is a major financial commitment. The fancier the boat, the greater the expense. But, hey, it's only money. You can't put a price tag on pleasure, as the saying goes. Before you lay down big bucks for a new boat—or to upgrade to a model with more power or more creature comforts—take time to think about the kind of boat that is best suited to your cruising area, one that will give you the type of ride you and your family will enjoy without having to sell your firstborn child. As part of your decision process, take a hard look at your fixed family expenses. Decide how much more per month you can afford to add in as a boat payment, and then double this amount to estimate the expenses that go along with ownership.

The size and type of boat that you will need is equivalent to what you would need in a vacation home. You'll want it to be comfortable, convenient, problem–free, and, most important, affordable. Begin the boat-selection process by deciding the type of boat best suited to your cruising style, intended waterway, and family interests.

Ask yourself these questions:

> What kind of ride do I want, fast or leisurely?

> How many folks will normally be aboard?

> Will I also use my boat for sports like fishing or racing?

> Where do I plan to use my boat, in a lake, river, ocean?

> Where will I store my boat?

The cruiser category includes any boat, sail or power, equipped with stay-aboard accommodations. Most people begin cruising with a low-end boat and move up to those with more amenities. Startup options are varied, so examine each style boat with your comfort in mind. For example, if you choose a small cruising boat with only a cuddy cabin for sleeping accommodations, you'll be fine for the occasional one-nighter but limited by its close quarters to sleeping one average-sized person or two skinny ones. Most cruising boats, power or sail, are designed to accommodate four to six people. The average cruising sailboat will be 26 feet or more in length, whereas a powerboat with sleeping accommodations and an external engine may be as small as 21 feet.

DECIDE ON POWER OR SAIL

For some, the decision of whether to buy a powerboat or a sailboat is a no-brainer. If you lust for speed, you'll likely opt for power. If your idea of boating is spending relaxing time on the water, you're a sailor at heart. Any boat that needs an engine to move is considered a powerboat, with the exception of a sailboat. Although a sailboat may be equipped with an engine, it doesn't need an engine to navigate. With either category, hull design, layout, and the means of propulsion dictate the type of ride you can expect, how easy the boat will be to steer, and how expensive it will be to operate.

The larger the boat, the more spacious the berths, galley, head, and saloon. Boats 40 feet or longer, called yachts, can be sail or power and not only offer the essentials, but may also have sophisticated navigation electronics, equipment to keep boat systems powered when anchored, heat, air-conditioning, and more. With a properly equipped yacht, you can be on the water for days in total comfort without needing to plug into shore power.

Read on to learn the basics about the types of power and sail boats available to you.

POWER CRUISERS

We'll begin with the most complex, which are powerboats. The type of powerboat you might select for family cruising is sometimes referred to as a cabin cruiser. Living space is usually spread out over two to three decks with helm stations inside the cabin as well as on the flybridge, which is an open deck on a cabin cruiser located above the bridge on the cabin roof. It usually has a duplicate set of navigating equipment.

The classic powerboat has a planing hull, which means the bow tips upward as it speeds ahead. The more rounded the hull, the better it will handle the seas. A boat with a squared-off stern and flat-bottomed hull may ride like a barge in calm waters, but it will jump around uncomfortably when the seas come up. Powerboats have undergone a few modern changes that have made them go faster, using less fuel. One such technology is called Air Step.

Each type of boat hull has its unique means of supporting a boat's ability to travel over the water.

Planing hull: A planing-hulled boat uses the pressure of the water underneath the hull (much the same as airplane wings are supported by air pressure) and the power of its engines to lift the vessel up and over the water.

Displacement hull: A displacement-hulled boat travels through the water at a limited rate that is defined by the waterline length. The hull is supported exclusively or predominantly by buoyancy.

Semidisplacement hull: A semidisplacement-hulled boat develops some lift, like the planing-hulled boat can, but most of its weight is still supported by buoyancy.

Air Step: An Air Step-hulled boat draws air into the boat via a ducting system around the perimeter of the hull. The air circulating under the boat causes it to lift, or plane, thereby requiring less fuel due to less drag.

ENGINE STYLES

The more powerful the engine, the faster the boat will travel—thus consuming more fuel, a cost issue to keep in mind, especially with today's rising fuel prices. The standard powerboat has twin engines, which may be gasoline or diesel fueled. Because of the type and location of the engine, powerboats are often referred to as outboard, inboard, or sterndrive cruisers.

Outboard: An outboard engine assembly is external to the stern of the boat. Because outboard engines do not take up interior space, there is usually enough room to provide overnight cruising facilities in small powerboats.

Inboard: An inboard engine connects to the rudder and steerage assembly through a driveshaft in the bottom of the hull. Inboard power cruisers run upward of 30 feet in length. Cruising powerboats equipped with an inboard engine are usually 30 feet or larger.

Sterndrive: A sterndrive, also referred to as an inboard/outboard (I/O) engine, combines the benefits of both an inboard and an outboard engine. In a sterndrive, an inboard engine is connected to a steerable drive unit that is accessed through a cutout in the transom of the boat. Sterndrive-powered boats range from 24 to 40 feet in length and are popular on inland waters.

POWERBOAT MODELS

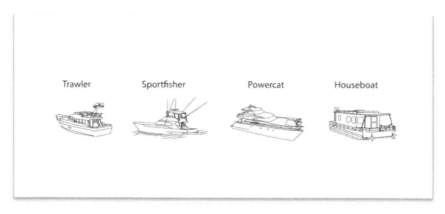

Trawler   Sportfisher   Powercat   Houseboat

Like ice cream, powerboats come in many flavors, each suited to a different boating style. Here, the major differences are living space, comfort of the ride, maneuverability, and range of speed. The powerboat category includes the sport fishing boat, the multihull powerboat, the trawler, and the houseboat or pontoon boat.

SPORT FISHING BOATS

If you are an avid angler and want to combine deep water or big game fishing with family cruising, a sport fishing boat could be for you. In addition to creature amenities, these cruisers are equipped with fish-finding electronics, live wells with circulating water to keep fish fresh, insulated fish lockers to ice your catch, and rod holders. Sizes range from 26 to over 100 feet in length.

MULTIHULL POWERBOATS

Multihull powerboats, a form of catamaran also called power cats, are the new kids on the block. These two-hulled, beamy boats ride better than a traditional powerboat. The twin hulls focus the buoyancy around the outside of the boat, which creates greater stability. In addition, the two narrow hulls offer less resistance underway, which means less fuel is consumed.

As the twin engines are farther apart due to hull placement, a power cat is easier to maneuver than a monohull or a traditional powerboat. The wide overall beam of these boats provides a lot of living space, making them ideal for family cruising or entertaining. The upper level looks similar to a trawler with an enclosed cabin and has many creature comforts.

TRAWLERS

The traditional trawler, a style lazy sailors turn to for their next boat, is a single-engine, displacement-hulled boat that combines the stability and cruising range of a sailboat with homelike comfort. With an average speed of 8 knots, they are fuel efficient. A large fuel capacity allows trawlers to travel great distances without refueling. Built for long-term cruising or living aboard, the most popular models range from 35 to 65 feet in length.

Be sure to test-drive trawler models configured with flattened aft sections. These are especially hard to steer when the wind and seas are against you. This style of stern creates an imbalance, which shifts the boat off course.

The need for increased speed has led to the popularity of twin engine models, known as fast trawlers. You will come across a tug version, such as Nordic Tug, which is a hybrid. The tug style has a semidisplacement hull, which combines the benefits of a displacement hull at low speeds with the power of a planing hull at higher speeds. Cruising speed for a tug ranges from 14 to 20 knots.

HOUSEBOATS

Whenever I see a houseboat, I think of Sophia Loren in the very old movie of that name and imagine what it must be like to live on such a boat. When we think of cruising, a houseboat may not be the first boat that comes to mind, yet such boats bear consideration. A slew of styles have emerged from the houseboat's humble, homey beginnings.

Often used on lakes and rivers, these beamy boats offer comfortable cruising with overnight facilities. Sizes range between 20 and 75 feet in length. Small versions can be trailerable. Twin gasoline or diesel engines are most common on these extra-wide boats, because they provide better maneuverability. However, single-engine or inboard/outboard sterndrive is also used.

The pontoon houseboat is the most popular because it's safe, easy to operate, needs little maintenance, and is reasonably priced as compared to a cruiser or a yacht. This style of boat is best suited to a fairly calm river or lake because its low freeboard allows it to easily take on water. The pontoon houseboat is available in two-pontoon or three-pontoon configurations. The added pontoon is used for heavier loads.

Other versions include the planing houseboat, which looks and rides much like a cruising powerboat, and the more stable, fuel-efficient catamaran (twin-hulled) houseboat. For shallow waters, the barge and full-hulled styles are very beamy and roomy, as well as stable. The displacement-hulled houseboat is popular for economical, long-distance traveling or rough waters.

SAILBOATS

The term sailboat covers a wide variety of sailing craft, each with its own characteristics and styles. In general, sailboats are distinguished by size, hull configuration, keel type, number of sails, use, and purpose. The most common sailboat is a single hull (or monohull), but beamy multihulls like catamarans or trimarans are popular in areas where speed and comfort matter more than bulk. Most sailboats over 18 feet long have an inboard gasoline or diesel auxiliary engine as backup, should the wind be uncooperative.

The beauty of a sailboat is you can enjoy the water without spending a lot of money on fuel. Due to its elliptical displacement hull, a sailboat travels easily over the water, expending no power to rise above the waves. Sails transform and control the power of the wind to move and steer the boat.

Learning to control the wind is a skill you can teach your children.

While sailors who singlehand their boats make it seem effortless, most captains travel with a small crew to help hoist and tweak the sails while the helmsman steers. Sailing is team building, or it should be. If you have sailed a hobie cat or sunfish, you already have the skill to move on to a larger sailboat. The larger the boat, the more stable and forgiving it will be when confronting gusty weather and confused seas.

A sailboat gives you a smoother ride than a powerboat, which leaps over the waves rather than flows with them. The combination of a deep keel and tall mast acts like a fulcrum, keeping the boat upright. Its rounded hull moves from side to side with the waves like a ball. While the boat will heel, a nautical term for tipping to one side, it will only tip so far before it rounds up to the wind and rights itself (under normal sea and wind conditions).

Because a sailboat is limited to the set of the sails and its hull speed, its average speed is usually between 5 and 10 knots. Boats with displacement hulls can go only as fast as an ocean wave matching its length. A narrow, light hull can move faster than a beamy, heavy one, which is why multihulls are speedier than most monohulls. The larger the boat, the greater the hull speed. Our 27-foot Buccaneer sailboat seldom budged above 6 knots, no matter how we tweaked the sails; but our 50-foot Farr sailboat has shot up to 11 knots in the right wind and sea conditions.

SAIL PLANS

The number and type of sails will also impact speed and maneuverability in winds ranging from light to heavy. The classic sailboat has at minimum a main sail and a foresail, which may be a jib (triangular sail) or a genoa style. Optional sails may include a spinnaker for light wind, a storm sail for heavy wind, or a mizzen for balance.

You may encounter these style sailboats:

Catamaran: A catamaran has two hulls, either identical or mirror images of each other, that are joined by a frame.

Catboat: A catboat has one mast set well forward with a single sail, regardless of boat size.

Cutter: A cutter is similar to a sloop except its mast may be set farther back and it includes two or more headsails, and often a bowsprit.

Ketch: A ketch is a two-masted boat where the mizzenmast—a smaller, shorter mast—is set in front of the helm.

Schooner: A schooner is a multimasted sailboat with triangular sails. The leading mast is always shorter than the other masts.

Sloop: A sloop is rigged with one mast, a single jib, and a mainsail.

Trimaran: A trimaran has three hulls: a large central hull for crew quarters and two smaller outer hulls.

Yawl: A yawl has two masts, one of which is a mizzenmast located behind the rudder post.

Sailboat configurations

Like powerboats, sailboats come in a variety of layouts and styles. Living space for all styles is belowdecks and includes berths or cabins, a galley, a saloon with a dining area, and a head. Sailboats run on 12 volt DC power, although European models may be 24 or 32 volts. Dockside AC electrical power, inverters, and generators to produce electricity are either optional or standard, depending on boat size and luxuriousness.

The basic cruising sailboat has an aft or center cockpit, which includes a steering station. A center cockpit sailboat, called a wedding cake because the design creates a tiered effect, usually has an ample berth located under the cockpit. A pilothouse yacht offers an enclosed steering station, which might be in addition to the standard outdoor helm, and provides fixed shelter from rainy, windy, and chilly weather.

A multihull sailboat, such as a catamaran or trimaran, is double or triple the width of a single-hulled vessel, which adds to its stability and buoyancy. At a marina, you will need either a double slip or one situated on the outer T-edge of the dock. Those suited for cruising (as opposed to racing) have the same amenities and cruising range of a sleep-aboard sail or powerboat of comparable length. The area between hulls offers extra living space, with a large cockpit and saloon, and mesh netting located between the hulls at the bow—ideal for sunning.

ADD A SPORT TO YOUR CRUISE

If you want to do more than cruise, add racing or fishing to your cruising plans. Each has a challenging learning curve that will get you and yours out on the water to test your collective skills.

GO RACING

When we think of racing, we think speed, so it may seem odd that the majority of boat racing occurs in the sailboat category. Because sailing is a skill, competition takes the form of matching tactics with other boats of the same type. Sailboats used specifically for racing—think America's Cup—are mere hulls with few creature comforts and a specialized sail plan.

Powerboat racing is offered by the American Power Boat Association (APBA). It requires specific kinds of boats and is regulated, much like NASCAR racing is for autos. For more information, log on to www.alpha-racing.com.

Any sailboat is eligible for yacht races, also called regattas. Yacht racing involves not only sailing the boat, but also choosing a class consisting of similar boats. Finding and training a crew and becoming expert in such things as boat- and sail-handling techniques, racing rules, strategies, tactics, and weather conditions will keep you busy.

Most likely you will begin by checking out races being held in your local cruising area via yacht clubs and marina personnel. In my cruising area, for example, a group of local sailors hold races every Wednesday evening throughout the boating season.

Yacht races held in local waters involve navigating a course around strategically placed buoys (or markers) and are geared toward small and midsized craft. Larger boats equipped with sleeping accommodations can participate in open ocean racing. Should you become a racing nut, you can move up to offshore races that extend to foreign ports, such as the Newport to Bermuda race, and take place over several days or weeks. Because a sailboat only requires wind power to move, with a seaworthy boat you can travel for months without needing to pull into port to refuel.

If powerboat racing appeals to you and family cruising is not on your agenda, consider a racing-style powerboat like a hydroplane or hydrofoil. Racing grounds for such boats are typically lakes or rivers. A hydroplane travels so fast that much of the force supporting its weight is created by air pressure. This allows it to plane, or skim, across the surface of the water rather than push through it as do traditional powerboats. Hydrofoil boats, on the other hand, have "water wings" that create lift while immersed, and they support the hull above water.

GO FISHING

There's no reason you can't use any boat for fishing. Heck, you can cast off from a dock or a shore. If fishing is your primary game, the exact boat you choose should accommodate the type of fishing you want to do and the places where you want to do it. Some cruising boats are designed to accommodate serious fishing and are equipped with live wells, ice chests, and the like. The ultimate is the sportfishing boat we discussed earlier, which is well suited to Great Lakes and deep-ocean fishing. And, of course, you can fish from a sailboat as long as you aren't also manning the helm.

If the type of fishing you enjoy involves motoring to shallow coves where your cruiser cannot travel, you might consider buying a second, smaller boat you can tow behind your cruiser and also use as a dinghy to reach shore. Some folks own a totally separate trailerable boat designed specifically for fishing, which they can drive to their favorite fishing ground. I can almost hear you chortling, "Right. One boat is enough trouble, thank you."

Despite what you may think, people *do* own two boats, even more. They use the cruiser for vacationing with the family and take the fishing boat out for the day. Many of these smaller boats are perfect for towable water sports like tubing, skiing, and wakeboarding. Keep in mind that any boat used for saltwater fishing should be sturdy enough to withstand finicky tidal waters and be resistant to corrosion. The vastness of the Great Lakes, such as Lake Erie, makes their waters as feisty as an ocean, so choose a seaworthy boat for fishing these kinds of waters, too.

Choose your Cruising Area

The style, size of boat, and type of ride you prefer are linked to the cruising area you choose. Most boaters select a waterway within reasonable driving distance of their homes, so first consider your local waters. Do you live near a lake, a river, or an ocean? If that lake down the road is too limiting for the kind of boating you have in mind, are you willing to drive an hour or more to reach a more expansive waterway or the ocean? Boaters from other states store their boats at our marina in Mystic, Connecticut for easy access to Long Island Sound, Cape Cod, Maine, and the Intracoastal Waterway (ICW) toward Florida.

While you are thinking about the kind of cruising you want to do and where you'd like to do it, stop by the area and check out how people are launching and storing their boats when they are not using them. Most boats used on a small lake need to be trailerable, so they can be towed, launched, and hauled for each use. Large lakes, rivers, and coastal areas are peppered with marinas offering slips and moorings, where you have the convenience of leaving your boat in the water for an entire season or launching it each time.

Rivers and Lakes

A lake is a controlled environment that is typically surrounded by foliage and residences. Check with local authorities for any laws regulating the use of the lake, as well as regulations regarding boat size and horsepower. Noisy jet skis, for example, may be taboo in certain harbors. Printed charts detailing depth, configuration, and preferred traveling routes of larger lakes and those with channels extending into other waterways are often available through marine stores.

Heavy rains and winds can flood the waters with debris, so when cruising near the shore it's important to keep a sharp eye out for a floating branch that could do a nasty number on your propeller. With any lake or treed waterway, expect shoaling. Shoaling is the reduction of depth due to a sandbank. It is caused by silt that has drifted from the shoreline. With sailboats having fixed keels, going aground due to low water is a concern. A small lake may not have an official chart detailing the layout of its bottom, so you may have to rely on local knowledge.

The larger the lake, the more its waters will be affected by weather conditions. While there may not be tidal concerns, you could be fighting choppy waters—short, bouncy waves resulting from boat traffic or heavy winds.

Lakes smaller than 5 miles across are best suited to small runabouts or daysailers. An example of this is Lake Pocotopaug in East Hampton, Connecticut. If you're thinking sleep-aboard, look for a larger lake, perhaps one with inlets to other waterways, where you can travel a bit and see the sights. One such lake is Lake Mendoza in Madison, Wisconsin. My husband and I sailed its waters with close friends. We dropped anchor in front of the University of Wisconsin and prowled the town before heading back to the boat. We might have overnighted in that hopping spot had we not needed to return to shore that day.

OCEANS AND THE GREAT LAKES

The larger a body of water is, the larger the boat needs to be to navigate and manage it. The Great Lakes have the same attributes as an ocean, with tidal concerns and fluctuations in sea states caused by weather changes. Choose a protected boat 28 feet or longer for heavy-duty coastal cruising. Should you plan to head out into the open ocean, which is offshore in big-boat lingo, you would be better served by a sturdy boat at least 35 feet in length that is built to weather all conditions comfortably and safely.

Chapter 2

Shop Smart

Congratulations! You have reached the shopping stage. You have thought through the kind of boat you want, and where and how you will use it. Now it's time to narrow down your choices and to understand how to evaluate various models, as well as to create a budget for the expenditure.

BEGIN SHOPPING

Be sure to involve your spouse and kids in the buying process. Discuss options, tour boats, and take them to dealers and boat shows. Make the prospect of cruising an adventure *everyone* looks forward to. Once you've got the family hyped about boating to the point where your wife doesn't mind giving up that trip to Europe and your son is okay with skipping summer baseball for a cruising vacation, you're home free.

As you and your family begin your search for the perfect boat, keep in mind you are not buying a car; you are buying a vacation home. In addition to considering the obvious features like speed and styling, envision yourselves living on your boat, sleeping in a berth, cooking in the galley, and lounging on the deck.

Even if your plan is to buy a used boat, shop new to check out the latest technology, decide which makes and models you like, and get a grasp on pricing. Keep your purchase on track by being realistic about the true cost of owning a boat, staying within your means, and finding manufacturers and dealers you can trust. As you sift through manufacturers, focus on those that are certified by the National Marine Manufacturers Association (NMMA). Their boats are built according to industry safety and construction standards.

Chat with Other Boaters

Boaters love to talk about their "babies." If boating season is in full swing, stop by the marina or harbor you have selected as your primary cruising ground and chat up captains of the kind of boat you are considering. Ask what they like best about their boats. Any problems with handling or manufacturer's support and such are apt to come out in normal conversation. Would they buy another product from that manufacturer? If not, why not? While you are there, find out where they bought their boat and if they would recommend the dealer.

Flip Through Magazines

If you haven't done so already, peruse boating magazines and pay special attention to boat tests and reviews as well as ads. You may find the most popular magazines at local bookstores. For a larger selection, stop by the nearest boating supply store. Most hard copy boating magazines have website counterparts, which are chock-full of articles and information.

Boating magazines target specific types of boats. Here's a short list of publications to get you started:

> ➢ Powerboats: *Boating, Boating World, Motor Boating, Powerboat*

> Sailboats: *Cruising World, SAIL, Sailing, Sailing World, Cruising Outpost, Blue Water Sailing*

> Yachts (the big boys): *Power & Motor Yachting, Yachting*

In addition, you will find specialized publications, such as *Wooden Boat, Passagemaker* (trawlers), and *Houseboat.* A store in your local cruising area will also carry boating publications specific to a location, such as *Southern Boating, Great Lakes Boating,* and *Sea* (Western boating).

As you scan through boating magazines and online boating sites, you will gravitate toward the *For Sale* section. Use this information to get a feel for prices of the kind and size of boat you think you want. But please don't jump in headfirst and buy a boat until you've checked out the validity of the ad and the boat being offered.

Shop Online

No doubt you have already perused a mind-boggling number of online boating sites. Sites such as BoatQuest (www.boatquest.com) are especially helpful for getting an idea of pricing for the type of boat you have targeted, both new and used, and for finding dealers in your area. Beware of online sites offering hard-to-believe pricing, and check for scams and fraudulent practices.

The Better Business Bureau is a traditional source for tracking down issues, but you will also find them detailed in boating forums. If a particular boating site seems to be on the level, phone the dealer to find out when the boat was first listed, if it's used, and what condition it is in at that moment. (Those photos may be older than dirt.)

Attend Boat Shows

Locate boat shows by searching online, perusing boating publications, or asking a dealer in your area—who might even provide you complimentary tickets. Attending boat shows is an efficient way to see and compare a variety of powerboats and sailboats, and will help you create a short list of the traits and features you need. As a side benefit, many shows offer how-to seminars. Oftentimes, a manufacturer's rep will be aboard one of the models to support the local dealer and answer specific questions and concerns. My husband and I made it a winter hobby to attend boat shows in various cities. This is a great way to involve the family and combine boat buying with a mini vacation.

Don't neglect looking at used (also called previously owned) boats. You may find the exact model you want at a steal. A used boat may come equipped with critical instruments and safety gear you might have had to pay extra for had you purchased it new.

In addition to displaying a variety of boats, shows offer a slew of vendor booths, where you can find almost any product related to boating from magazines to watermakers.

Visit Your Local Boat Dealer

The way boat dealerships work is that a manufacturer gives exclusivity to handle its product to specific dealers on a regional basis. Check out local boat dealers, for they usually carry the types of boats that are compatible with nearby waters. For example, you won't find large, seagoing yachts offered if the nearest waterway is a small to midsized lake or river. Usually, a dealer will have at least one boat of a particular brand on the lot as a demo. Even if the selection does not include the exact size boat you think you'd like, ask for a walk through so when you get back home and review the brochure, you will be better able to evaluate it.

CHARTER A BOAT

Combine family boating fun with the shopping process by chartering the type and model of boat you are interested in buying. To do this, you need to demonstrate your competence, usually by filling out a questionnaire about your on-the-water experience behind the helm. While renting operations tend toward basic models, you and yours will have a sampling of the type of ride to come. It may be possible to take a chosen boat out for a spin or an overnight excursion.

You may find charter companies in your local cruising ground, but if you are planning a vacation in a warm place, why not charter in exotic waters? Think Tahiti, Alaska, the Mediterranean, the Caribbean, and more. When my husband and I were thinking of upgrading, we gathered a few friends and planned a winter vacation in the Caribbean. Because of its consistent winds and beautiful waters, the Caribbean has always been a playground for sailors, however many of the companies also offer powerboats, power cats, and trawlers for charter.

Discounted prices for such charters are often offered at boat show booths along with the opportunity to tour boats in the fleet. For the cost of an airplane ride you can cruise waters anywhere in the world.

MAKE SENSE OF THE GLOSSY BROCHURE

You've walked your feet off at boat shows and your eyes are bleary from looking at boats on your computer screen. Now you sit home with a bunch of web printouts or hard copy brochures from various manufacturers and try to connect them to the boats you may have toured and discussed with dealers and manufacturers' reps.

If you are a true newbie at this, smarten up. Becoming savvy about the details will earn dealers' respect and help you decide which boat manufacturer and options are for you.

Let's analyze the basic boat brochure, which is composed of exterior and interior photos, a write-up on how wonderfully the boat performs and why, critical specifications, and a listing of standard and optional features. If you showed particular interest, the dealer may even have slipped in a price sheet, which could be in American dollars or Euros. Understand that the photos of the boat and its interior are meant to present the boat at its best. The boat is shown moving on the water, bow up and planing over waves or in full sail. Because of the way a photo is shot, a berth, for example, may appear spacious, while in reality it's barely large enough to accommodate an average-sized adult.

Most important to understand are the specifics—or, should I say, the specifications. Every boat, new or used, has a listing of its critical features available. For a used boat, you may be presented the original brochure. Secondary to specs are the features. Some brochures list only key features, whereas others offer a laundry list of every single item, standard and optional.

Let's go through the majority of items and terms you will come across, so you will be armed to compare various manufacturers' boats for value and functionality. This information will help you come across as knowledgeable once you are prepared to make a deal.

BOAT SIZE

The length overall (LOA) and weight of a boat affect how you will dock it as well as where you can travel. The LOA and beam of your boat dictates the size of the slip you will require at a marina. A deep-drafted boat, like a sailboat, is restricted by the depth of the water, and a tall-masted boat needs to be careful about traveling under fixed bridges. The weight of the boat is related to displacement, which is how far into the water the hull will sink. The heavier a boat, the more drag, thus the more fuel or sail power it will need to move through the water.

When reviewing a brochure, you are apt to encounter these terms:

Air draft (or bridge clearance) = the measure of the boat from the waterline to its highest fixed point, such as the top of the mast of a sailboat.

Overall length = the total length of the boat from stem to stern.

Draft = the amount of hull that is under water.

Hull beam = the width of the boat at its widest part.

Hull length = the length of the boat when measured at the waterline.

TANK CAPACITIES

Boats have three basic types of tanks: fuel, freshwater, and possibly one to hold toilet discharge. The capacity of each tank is indicated in liters or gallons. When reviewing the capacity of a tank, consider the usage rate. For example, how many gallons of fuel are needed to travel two hours at moderate speed? A powerboat requires a larger fuel tank than a sailboat. Cube shaped and usually of marine-grade aluminum or polyethylene, tanks are built into out-of-sight areas and accessed via a thru-hull opening for intake and discharge.

SPEED AND MANEUVERABILITY

The horsepower of the engine is an indicator of potential boat speed. The more horsepower an engine has, the faster a boat can travel under ideal conditions. Boat brochures often provide the potential speed, average speed, or cruising range of boats. If your brochure does not specify a speed range for a particular boat, your dealer should be able to provide the information, or you can use an online calculator to figure out the complex relationship between horsepower and boat speed.

Depending on the make and model, the engine can be dual (twin) or single, outboard or inboard, or sterndrive. On a new boat you may have the option to upgrade to a more powerful engine. The helm station may have a tiller or a wheel; the wheel is typical of larger boats. Steering may be single or double (twin) screw. A twin-screw engine makes maneuvering into tight spots a piece of cake. Usually an option, a bow thruster, built-in or mounted to the bow or stern, improves a boat's steerage and is especially helpful on boats with single-screw engines when docking or fighting currents or heavy winds.

You may be offered a choice of a gasoline or a diesel engine. Gasoline engines are cheaper, quieter, and emit less fuel odor than diesel engines, but they are not as long-lasting. If you can afford the larger upfront cost, a diesel engine will outperform its gasoline cousin in terms of fuel consumption and overall maintenance, and it will hold its value when it comes time to sell the boat.

POWER

Most pleasure boats have 12-volt battery systems consisting of banks of one to four batteries, connected in parallel. Larger boats, particularly European models, may have 24- or 32-volt systems. The capacity of the battery charger relates to the number and type of batteries in use. The batteries charge the engine as well as any other house systems, such as lighting and refrigeration.

Inverter: An inverter, which connects to the battery banks to convert DC power to AC electrical power, may be standard or optional.

Generator: A generator, a worthwhile option, is an external battery unit that converts mechanical energy into electrical energy. Having the ability to switch to generator power means you can hang out at your favorite fishing spot for days and keep all systems fully charged. Instead of running the engine to charge the batteries, you would run the generator. Even though a generator requires fuel, it consumes much less than your engine would.

Dockside Power: Dockside power should be standard on any boat. Double-check to be sure because you will need the ability to connect to shore power when at dock so you will be able to provide electricity to the boat and keep boat batteries charged.

EXTERIOR HULL MATERIALS

The material used for the hull of the boat should be light and durable, which is why fiberglass and aluminum are the most popular boat-building materials. Fiberglass, a glass fiber-reinforced plastic, has moved far ahead of aluminum because it is easy to mold into various hull designs. From a boat owner's standpoint, fiberglass is durable and easy to maintain. Since fiberglass is inert, it is not subject to the electrolysis or corrosion typical of aluminum boats. Because fiberglass is strong, a hull is not as prone to denting, common to aluminum boats. Other hull materials are wood and steel.

WOOD

Wooden boats have traditional beauty and feel more solid in the water, thus safer, because they are heavier than a fiberglass or aluminum boat. They are less subject to condensation and dampness than a fiberglass boat because wood is porous and absorbs moisture. While a wooden boat is long-lasting, it requires constant maintenance to prevent leakage caused by rotted wood and shrunken planks. If you don't mind spending more time working on your boat than cruising on it, a wooden boat may be for you. If you have always longed for a wooden boat, you may have to settle for a used one. Although it's possible to buy a new boat constructed of wood, it is a specialty item.

STEEL

Ocean-going craft may be constructed of steel, which can withstand collisions. However, its weight makes a steel-hulled boat harder to maneuver, and the metal is subject to rust and corrosion.

DECKS

On a fiberglass boat, the deck—the walk-around area of the boat—may be constructed of fiberglass imbued with a nonslip surface, or unvarnished teak. Unvarnished teak is considered nonslip. Teak decks are beautiful but require more upkeep than fiberglass decking.

RAILS

Protective rails surround the bow and walk areas of the outer deck to provide handholds and a degree of protection against man-overboards. Rails may be all or part stainless steel tubing. On sailboats, lightweight coated wire lifelines are attached to bow tubing. Port, starboard, and stern gates allow easy exit and entry.

WINDOWS

Windshields and side windows of the pilot house are usually made of tempered glass but may be made of Lexan, a sturdy form of plastic suitable for a marine environment. Certain model boats may require front windshield wipers. Hatches and portholes, usually made of Lexan, function as additional viewing as well as for air circulation. Built-in or removable screens, sunshades, and curtains may be standard or optional.

DECK STORAGE

Deck and cockpit lockers are used to store lines, fenders, sails, an extra anchor, deck chairs, cleaning gear, and any other items primarily used to dock, maintain, or enjoy the boat. If the boat is equipped with a stove, a propane or natural gas tank will take up a separate locker. An anchor locker holds the anchor rode, which may be a length of chain attached to a line or all chain.

ANCHOR SETUPS

Anchor setup usually includes a windlass, which is a rotating device used for hauling line or chain to raise and lower the anchor. For larger boats, a back-saving option is an electric or a hydraulic anchor winch for hauling. Anchor styles include Bruce (claw shaped), a CQR (plow), a Delta (wing), a Danforth (fluke), and a surge of new-generation anchors designed for superior holding. Bruce, CQR, and Delta anchors are good, all-purpose choices.

Cockpit Comforts

Cockpit cushions, if provided, should be of closed foam, so they will not absorb water, with a weather-resistant covering such as vinyl. These can also be custom made at a later time.

Dodgers, biminis, and cockpit enclosures offer protection against the elements. Many times these items are offered as options on a new boat. If this is the case, check out the styling to make certain you'll have enough headroom. You can also have such items custom made by a company specializing in boat canvas.

A hard dodger or bimini is a permanent part of the boat, whereas soft canvas versions can be taken down. Soft dodgers and biminis are typically constructed of weather-resistant Sunbrella canvas with treated plastic windows. With a bimini and dodger in place, it's possible to add removable panels to enclose the remainder of the cockpit—a godsend on a blustery or stormy day on the water.

Berths

On average, a cruising powerboat or sailboat has one or two cabins and an area in the saloon that converts to a berth. Larger boats have a midship, or captain's, cabin. On small to midsized boats, the forward berth is located under the bow and is usually V-shaped. Boats having a substantial deck locker in the bow area may have a queen-sized berth. Aft and midship berths may be single or double. Space-saving double bunks are also common. Upholstered mattresses are foam rubber. A coil mattress, like you have at home, may be offered as an option, or you can purchase one from a marine mattress dealer.

HEADS

The main toilet facility includes a head and a sink. Marine toilets range from a portable style to one similar to a home toilet. A portable unit is self-contained, operates on its own freshwater supply, and is totally removable. The traditional manual flush toilet uses raw or freshwater, depending on the model, and discharges to a holding tank located in the bowels of the boat. Upgradeable options include an electric toilet with push button flush, the popular vacuum flush toilet, and the newer automatic flush Tecma toilet. The vacuum flush and Tecma are water efficient, easy to operate, and, because they use freshwater, eliminate the odor issue typical of saltwater toilets.

With the exception of the portable toilet, freshwater is drawn from the boat's water supply, while raw water is taken in from the lake or sea water via a thru-hull. A toilet system with a holding tank requires a macerator pump to break up clogging. Depending on placement, it may function to pump into a holding tank or to empty overboard.

When a shower is included, it may be as simple as a retractable hose with a shower head set into the sink, much like your kitchen sink sprayer at home. Ask questions. If available, an enclosed shower is preferable.

WATER SYSTEMS

Water drawn from taps originates from the water tank on the boat. Smaller boats may have a manual foot or hand pump to access the water supply. There also may be a means of drawing in seawater, which can cut down on freshwater usage. Pressurized water may be standard or offered as an option. If you plan to shower aboard, make certain hot water is part of the deal. One option we enjoy is the ability to bring water directly into our sinks and showers using a hose connected to the dock water supply, thus conserving the water in our tanks.

Most times you will be close enough to a dock to refill your water tanks. However, if you are a saltwater cruiser who spends a great deal of time traveling (or your family members are water hogs), you might find a built-in watermaker, which converts salt water to fresh via osmosis, a great convenience.

GALLEY

Kitchen facilities include a sink, a stove of some sort, and a means of keeping food cold. Many powerboats have electric stoves, but on a sailboat a gimbaled, propane or natural gas stove is most common. Microwave ovens are popular for any style boat with enough space to accommodate one. The standard refrigeration unit may be an icebox which may or may not be battery powered or electrical. The later types will keep food consistently fresh. Styles include top loading, upright, or under counter. If a freezer is included, it may be a section within the refrigeration unit or it may be separate.

INTERIOR MATERIALS

A basic boat is fiberglass, inside and out. Walls and doors may be constructed of wood, which may be varnished or unvarnished teak—or another wood such as cherry, mahogany, oak, or bamboo. On a new boat, you may have the option to select from various woods. It's possible you might even find carpeted walls or walls with padded vinyl covering—very nice in the berth areas. Ceilings tend to be padded vinyl. The base flooring is usually teak planking. Carpeting may be standard or optional.

On a new boat you will be asked to select colors and counter materials. Corian is common. If you are thinking granite countertops, consider the added weight. Cushions are usually the same material as the mattresses on the berths, but you may prefer to upgrade the upholstery of your seating areas from cloth to Ultraleather or real leather.

HEATING AND COOLING SYSTEMS

Installing built-in heating and cooling systems requires air ducts. Putting in air ducts is most economical when the boat is being built. Three types of systems are available: reverse cycle heating/air-conditioning, diesel heat, and air-conditioning.

REVERSE CYCLE

The temperature-controlled reverse cycle heat/air conditioner, commonly known as a heat pump, is the most popular system for folks who live in a climate with many seasons, like we have in the Northeast. In cool weather, where water temperatures are below 45 degrees Fahrenheit, the heating portion of a reverse cycle system is inefficient.

DIESEL

Diesel heat is quiet and dry, much like your heat at home, and uses little of your precious fuel to operate. If you have a diesel engine and plan to cold-weather cruise, a diesel-fueled heating system is your best solution for warding off the chill. Reverse cycle and diesel heating systems can coexist on a boat.

Espar, a well-respected manufacturer of marine diesel heaters, maintains it is possible for a diesel heater to be used on a gasoline-fueled boat as long as a separate tank is installed to hold the small amount of diesel fuel needed to run the heater. As always, consult your dealer or boat manufacture about making changes of this nature.

AIR-CONDITIONING

Air-conditioning is the way to go if you normally cruise in a warm climate. Having an air conditioner will not only help control the temperature inside your boat, but it will also reduce mold-producing humidity.

AFFORDABLE BOAT OWNERSHIP

Let's face it. A boat is a luxury item unless you plan to make it your home and live aboard. I know folks who do, but it's a hard life. You can claim loan interest on your IRS tax returns if your boat has a galley, berth, and head; and you can deduct it each year as a second home (assuming you do not already own a vacation home elsewhere).

Depending on size, a boat can cost as much as a fancy car or house. Have no fear; unless you are truly flush and want to, there is no need to pay for a boat in a lump sum. That's what financing is for.

Take a hard look at your fixed family expenses.

THE ANNUAL COST OF OWNERSHIP

Once you have narrowed down your options, fill in the figures below and then add them together for a realistic estimate of what a specific boat will cost you on an annual basis:

Monthly payments multiplied by 12: $____

Registration fees: $____

Equipment: $____

Insurance: $____

Dockage: $____

Maintenance/repairs: $____

Taxes: $____

Fuel and oil: $_____

Off-season storage: $_____

CONSIDER OTHER OWNERSHIP OPTIONS

If you're feeling pressured about handling the total expense of boat ownership, consider sharing ownership with others. Needless to say, you all have to agree on a particular make, model, cruising location, and whatever expenditures come along with it. In such a deal, partners agree in advance on when and how long each will have access to the boat and set guidelines on personal storage, cleaning the boat, and leaving it in order for the next person's visit.

While it may seem okay to arrange to buy and maintain a boat with a group of pals on a handshake, this type of verbal deal may backfire on you one day. Have a lawyer you all trust draw up a partnership agreement you and your buddies can live with. In it, detail who pays for what and how, as well as what will happen if one partner wants to drop out of the deal or if the boat is sold.

Another option is to loan your boat for charters. Many charter companies offer yacht ownership programs, which pay boat owners a specified amount to use their boats for charter. Part of the deal is a guarantee that the boat will be maintained and ready to cruise at a prearranged time when the boat owner will use it.

CHAPTER 3

Make the Deal

Now that you've passed the glossy brochure stage and are in purchase mode, reality sets in. You climb aboard the boat you have selected and put on your buying glasses, checking out every feature and function, picturing yourself behind the helm, sprawled out on the queen-sized berth, or plugging waypoints into the fancy GPS. *This could be mine,* you think as you wonder what kind of deal you can make.

This chapter details how to evaluate a boat for quality, functionality, and performance, and how to negotiate the purchase with a reputable dealer. You will also gain an understanding of how to go about finding a boat loan and insurance coverage, and whether or not your boat can be documented.

GET SERIOUS ABOUT BUYING

Dealers, like realtors, stage boats with upscale decor to look appealing. When you're ready to do some serious shopping, look beyond a boat's stylish appearance to what's inside. Go aboard each boat you're considering, preferably with a dealer, and thoroughly check for quality, functionality, and practicality. Ask questions and keep a sharp eye out for issues that could become problems. When considering purchasing a new boat, look for workmanship; look for potential or preexisting problems when considering a used boat.

As you tour a boat, check out these features:

➢ Sit behind the helm and pretend you are headed out to sea. Are you comfortable? Is the instrument panel easily visible? Do you have a clear view of the area around the boat, especially the area in front of the boat?

➢ Walk the deck. Is it slippery? How many lines and fittings do you have to step over to reach the bow? Are all ladder, rails, and stanchions firmly fastened?

➢ Note the number and location of opening hatches and portholes on the boat you are considering to determine if ventilation will be adequate. Do they open, close, and lock easily? Is the caulking seal around them evenly applied?

➢ Where is the engine room? Can you get at it to work on system maintenance without being rubber-man? Does the door latch shut?

➢ Where is the electrical panel located? Is it easily accessible?

➢ Is the interior floor plan logical? Is the galley well appointed and convenient to the cockpit?

➢ Are storage compartments ample and fairly easy to access?

➢ Do interior doors open and close easily? Can they be locked in place when underway?

EVALUATE A USED BOAT

If you have come across a used boat that seems like a good deal, in addition to paying critical attention to layout and functionality, ask for details about the current state of the boat and for explanations for any signs that the boat has been in an accident or taken on water.

Gather the following information and make the following inspections:

- ➢ How old is the boat?
- ➢ How often has it been used?
- ➢ How long has it been parked without use?
- ➢ Examine the outside hull, deck, and cockpit areas for problems.
- ➢ Open every locker and cabinet inside and on deck to check for mold and deterioration.
- ➢ Test the operation of every system and moving part.
- ➢ Keep an eye out for corrosion, rust, and mold.
- ➢ Ask to see the maintenance records to review how well the boat has been kept in repair.
- ➢ Check the registration information against the hull identification number to assure they are in sync.
- ➢ Check the value for a particular make, model, and year boat against the market price according to the BUCValu site on line, or ask your dealer to do it for you.

Have the boat professionally evaluated by an accredited marine surveyor, which is a requirement for insurance. Locate surveyors in your area by contacting The Society of Accredited Marine Surveyors, www.marinesurvey.org/.

If you love the boat and are considering making an offer, find out from the dealer how long the boat has been on the market, the number of offers that have been turned down by the seller, and why that particular boat is being sold. Having this information in your back pocket will help you present a reasonable offer that is likely to be accepted.

GO FOR A RIDE

Never buy a boat without a shakedown cruise. It's customary for the boat dealer to manage the event. Usually, he or she will navigate to open water before turning over the helm to you—unless you request otherwise. Bring your whole family to make sure everyone enjoys the ride, too. No matter what people tell you or what the glossy brochure says about a particular boat, you will be the one using it. Wouldn't you rather find out before you commit if a certain boat provides a teeth-rattling ride instead of the smooth one you expect?

On your cruise, pay attention to these features:

> ➢ Before you depart, check every switch and lever for functionality. Look at the bilge, the area located underneath the floorboards. It should have no or very little water.

> ➢ Does the engine purr or is it making choking sounds? Does it start right up or does it need coaxing?

> ➢ Notice how well the boat handles when maneuvering in and out of its slip.

> ➢ Once you've taken the boat out on the water, open it up. How does it handle? Is the helm responsive when you change course?

> ➢ Does the boat take heavy seas without flexing or rattling as if it might fall apart?

CHARTER THE BOAT

If your primary reason for purchasing a boat is to use it for overnight cruising, ask to charter or borrow the boat you are considering buying (or one just like it) for a day or two. Likely, there will be a cost involved in doing so. Pay it. It will be worth whatever it costs to validate your decision. While you are aboard, be sure to sleep in the berths, prepare a meal in the galley, and test out the toilets and showers. During your stay, make notes on any issues you uncover, like a leaky hatch or an uncomfortable helm seat, and decide if the problem can be easily rectified.

As part of the buying process for our Freedom yacht, my husband and I chartered the boat for an overnight stay, and we tried out every function. With adding a bow thruster as a priority, we created a wish list of improvements we needed the manufacturer to implement as part of the sale. The changes we requested were incorporated into our boat loan, so we didn't have to deal with spending large hunks of cash and losing valuable cruising time once we took delivery.

DECIDE NEW OR USED

Ah, the smell of newly varnished teak, fabric finishes, and gear touched only by the crew assembling them. Who wouldn't want a brand-new boat over one that's been used hard? With luck, you won't need to worry about heavy-duty maintenance or repairs of a new boat for several years.

As wonderful as it may seem to be able to choose the exact boat built to your specs, a new boat can also have problems. When staff is rushed to finish building a boat on deadline, wires may be left unconnected causing systems to malfunction. On our Farr sailboat, we found a good bit of sawdust clogging our bilge and, on the torrid day we took delivery, the fan in our berth had to be connected.

Issues such as these are usually found and corrected during the commissioning process. A newly built boat is often shipped to the dealer for commissioning, although the company providing our Swedish-built sailboat performed the commissioning at the build site. After a sea trial in Swedish waters (which was very cool), we signed off on our new baby. They shipped her to Florida, where she was dropped into the water—masts up, fuel and water tanks full—ready for us to sail to Connecticut.

CHOSE A REPUTABLE DEALER OR MANUFACTURER

There's more to buying a boat than signing a contract. Go with a reputable dealer who will ease you though the process. One certified by the marine industry will ensure you will have top-of-the-line support both during and after the sale.

Here are some things to consider:

> ➢ Will this dealer coordinate necessities like the boat loan, insurance, and registration, or will you need to handle these critical items on your own?

> ➢ A company that has been in business for a good amount of time will be around to handle any warranty issues that may arise after the sale.

> ➢ Does the dealer have a good track record for keeping customers happy?

> ➢ If you are ordering a production boat (as opposed to a custom-made one), can you rely on your representative to communicate your requests effectively?

With a new boat there is typically only one dealer (or broker) involved. Used boat sales are handled much the same as real estate: both the buyer and seller have brokers and they split the commission.

Your broker, who might be your local boat dealer, knows the price and quality you are looking for and has a pulse on the market. Should you be interested in a boat offered halfway across the country, ask your broker to intercede for you by phoning his counterpart (who has the listing) to obtain the details you need to decide whether or not to pursue the boat further.

Boat sales is an up-and-down market. Boats are expensive to manufacture. When the economy slumps, it's not uncommon to have a manufacturer shut its doors. During the span of time my husband and I have been boating, we've had two manufacturers go out of business. What this means is boats like the one you have purchased will no longer be built.

While this is disconcerting, if the boat you bought is well respected in the industry, its resale value will hold steady. The Swedish company that manufactured our boat dissolved several years ago, but we have maintained contact with the former manager to order replacement parts only available abroad. And because by reputation Farr yachts are considered fast and seaworthy, its value has held.

GET FINANCING

As with any other sizeable expense, when you purchase a boat, you will apply for a loan, which is negotiated in much the same manner as a car loan or a mortgage. Start shopping around for a loan as soon as you've homed in on the kind of boat you want and have a feel for the amount of money it will cost you, including the optional accessories you need or want. If you find a loan organization offering good interest rates and terms, consider filling out an application so you will be prequalified to buy the boat you choose. Preparing for financing in advance of the sale will give you an edge when you make an offer. As a low-risk buyer, you stand a better chance of closing the deal your way.

In your personal financing budget, include the costs of interest, loan insurance, a title, closing, boat insurance, and taxes. Most lenders require a down payment, which might be as much as 20 percent of the selling price, and will depend on your credit history. Boats are financed much the same way as a car or a home and can be affordable under the right terms.

A loan for a new boat may be stretched over 10-, 15-, or 20-year terms, depending on the amount financed. Used boat loans have shorter terms and require a marine survey be conducted as part of the loan approval process. Use the cost estimate for needed repairs as a bargaining chip when you negotiate your offer.

FIND A BOAT LOAN

Opportunity is everywhere, it seems. While many organizations offer boat loans, you will want to pick one that will give you the most money at the lowest rates. An online search under the heading "boat loans" will uncover a variety of loan organizations; many sites offer loan calculators to help you estimate interest rates and possible payments. Boating websites usually have links to marine lenders.

Choose a company specializing in boat loans. Some will have booths at boat shows, enabling you to compare rates and terms for the boat you want to purchase. Ask about turnaround time to become approved for funding. Many marine boat loan financiers advertise in boating magazines and newspapers.

Find out how much a particular bank or loan organization is willing to lend you based on the boat's approximate value. Keep in mind that asking price and value are not the same figure. The value of the boat is what the Boating Blue Book says a particular make and model is worth on the open market plus whatever accessories you add.

Boat dealers can direct you to affordable financing and may even handle the arrangements for you, much like the closing on a home or car. They have established relationships with several finance sources and have access to extended warranty programs that can be included in your financing agreement. Because of their relationship with boat manufacturers, a dealer may be authorized to offer you special terms on particular makes and models, such as a delayed first payment, no interest for several months, or lower rates for a limited time.

Banks, finance service companies, and credit unions are other sources for obtaining financing. Many local, regional, and national banks are members of the National Marine Bankers Association. Some have boat-savvy representatives to handle boat loans. Finance service companies maintain relationships with local, regional, and national lenders, which give them broad access to financing programs.

Credit unions usually have competitive rates. If you are a member of one that has a marine lending specialist on staff, ask for a quote. A boat loan specialist will help you get the best interest rate, the necessary insurance needed for your boat loan, and a fast approval (assuming you have a good credit rating). He or she may be able to tailor the loan to accommodate your financial needs.

OBTAIN INSURANCE

Boat insurance is designed to provide funding to repair your boat if it's accidentally damaged or destroyed by a covered event such as fire, theft, windstorm, lightning, or vandalism.

It covers personal property as well as any other physical devices attached to the boat. Insurance rates vary according to boat length and type, cost of the boat, and level of coverage.

Insurers usually offer reduced rates to those who have completed a boater's education course. A good insurer will tailor your coverage to your exact needs, such as providing haul-out coverage for those in areas prone to hurricanes or extended cruising coverage should you want to sail to the Caribbean or cross the ocean.

While it may be tempting to include your boat in your homeowner's insurance policy, you may find coverage limited and end up paying out of pocket for major repairs or salvage and wreck removal.

Unlike policies for home or auto insurance, boat insurance policies vary from one company to the next. With boating insurance, as with any insurance, it's not merely a matter of finding a good rate. None of us expects trouble, but when it comes you need an agency that lives up to its promises. Your boat could be T-boned in a race and sink. A hurricane could send your boat off its mooring and crash it into the rocks, as happened to our brand-new Ericson 30 sailboat one fall. Thanks to a great insurance policy, some of our live-aboard boating friends were provided the funding to replace all of the electronics and systems that were damaged on their boat by a lightning hit.

Do an Internet search for A-rated companies in your area by checking sites for state insurance regulatory agencies at www.ambest.com/ratings.

CHOOSE THE BEST POLICY

Consider these types of policies. Both provide physical damage coverage:

Actual Cash: Actual cash value policies pay for replacement costs minus the depreciation of the boat's value at the time the loss occurred. The reimbursement for a total loss is based on the approximate market value of the boat in accordance with used boat pricing guides and other such resources. A partial loss is handled by paying the total cost of repair minus a percentage for depreciation.

Agreed Value: Agreed value policies allow you and your insurer to set a fair actual cash replacement value on your boat and any property associated with it, such as dinghies, sails, and canvas work. While such a policy may cost more up front, the value of a boat that is damaged beyond repair will not depreciate. In addition, the policy covers the replacement of old items for new in the event of a partial loss without a deduction for depreciation.

Physical damage coverage usually comes with a deductible, which is the amount you are willing to pay in case of a loss. The higher the deductible, the lower your insurance premium will be. Boat deductibles are usually calculated as a percentage of your coverage but may be an agreed-upon flat amount.

When reviewing a policy, pay attention to these terms:

> ➤ Personal effects coverage for such items as phones, computers, and clothing
>
> ➤ Boat liability coverage for protection against being sued for damages to property or injury to someone other than you or your family

> ➤ Medical payment coverage to pay reasonable expenses for hospital costs and ambulances for someone injured inside your boat or while boarding or departing it.

The uninsured boat owner section covers injuries you've received as a result of an accident when you cannot collect from the counter insurer, such as with hit-and-run accidents. Commercial towing and assistance may also be included in your policy. However, you can purchase this separately from companies like BoatUS.

REQUIRED DOCUMENTS

As part of the closing process on the sale of a boat, either the dealer or the mortgage holder will register your boat with the Department of Motor Vehicles (DMV) in your boat's home port state. Registration fee and sales tax are usually folded into the boat loan. You will be provided a bill of sale and either a Certificate of Number or Certificate of Documentation. These documents must be carried on the boat at all times, much as you would the registration for your car.

VESSEL NUMBERING VERSUS BOAT DOCUMENTATION

Federal law requires any motorized vessel, regardless of horsepower, to be numbered in the state in which it is to be used. States create their own numbering system, as long as it is in compliance with federal requirements. This applies to all of the United States except Alaska. There, vessel numbering is performed by the US Coast Guard (USCG). Most states also require numbering of sailboats and other nonpowered craft. Dinghies with less than 10 horsepower and used only as tenders may not need to have a separate number. The numbering fee varies from state to state.

If your boat weighs 5 tons or more and you are a US citizen, you have the choice of numbering your boat or documenting it. If you plan to cruise across the ocean or to foreign ports like Canada, Mexico, and the West Indies, having your boat documented will help you sail through customs clearance. Also, it will be easier to get that boat loan, as a documented vessel is regarded as a more secure form of collateral than a boat that is numbered.

There's a big difference between numbering and documenting your boat.

Certificate of number includes the vessel identification number, the registered owner's name and address, and the name of any lien holder.

Certificate of Documentation is a form of national registration that clearly identifies the nationality of the vessel.

A Certificate of Documentation is issued by the USCG. For updated fees, contact the USCG or view its national documentation page at www.uscg.mil/nvdc/. Documented vessels are not exempt from state or local taxes or other boating fees. Some individual states require a registration fee even if a boat is documented. The vessel identification number you are issued needs to be permanently affixed to the hull along with the boat's name and hailing port.

The USCG is the primary federal and lifesaving agency with maritime authority for the United States. It consists of ships, aircraft, boats, and shore stations and is responsible for law enforcement, maritime safety, marine environmental protection, and national security.

WHY BOATING EDUCATION?

Boating education helps you be a responsible boater, broadens your boating skills, and gets you a break on insurance costs. In some states, it is a requirement. Being a boat owner comes with the same responsibilities as being a car owner. At all times you are responsible for your vehicle and any damages or disruptions it may cause. While a "driver's" license isn't always required to operate a boat, it's a smart idea to understand how to cruise your boat without being a hazard to those around you.

Boating rules and regulations vary from state to state. Some states have a mandatory boating law that requires boating safety certification for operators of any motorized vessel (even small watercraft like dinghies and Jet Skis). An operator's license is usually awarded at the completion of a one-day class or online boating safety course.

Your boat dealer or insurer should be able to provide you the correct educational requirements, but you can check out the boating laws for your state online at www.americasboatingcourse.com/lawsbystate.cfm.

WHERE TO FIND BOATING CLASSES

The good news is boating education classes are available in most towns, as well as online. Classes range from basic boating safety to advanced navigation.

In my opinion, the best way to learn safe boat handling and advanced skills is through actual classroom attendance, where you interact with other boaters and seasoned instructors. If you can't squeeze classroom learning into your schedule, you can take the online highway. While the course content and testing may be the same, it's the equivalent of driving your boat by remote control.

Beyond the basic boating safety class, courses are offered on boat handling, reading the weather, and electronic navigation. There is even a class called Water 'N Kids. The most popular basic courses generally have from six to thirteen lessons and provide a good foundation for operating a vessel along with safety instruction.

Qualified volunteer organizations, such as the USCG Auxiliary and the US Power Squadrons sponsor boating courses at all levels throughout the country for recreational boaters of all ages either in classrooms or online for home study. Find a listing of these in the Appendix.

How to Obtain a Captain's License

The term *captain* is tossed loosely about to the point where a person with the actual credentials needs to clarify them. If you are in charge of the operation and well-being of a vessel, you are the captain. Unless you plan to take on passengers for hire or operate a commercial vessel such as a charter boat, ferry, cruise ship, or tanker, you do not need a captain's license. However, many seasoned boaters do go on to obtain an official license.

Obtaining a captain's license is a combination of taking a class (and passing the test), accumulating the required on-the-water experience, and meeting USCG physical requirements.

To qualify for a captain's license, you will need to perform these tasks:

➤ Document the equivalent of 360 days on open water, with one day counting as a minimum of four hours. Ninety days of your sea time must have been within the past three years of your license application. If you crew on a boat other than your own, you will need the owner's signature on the sea time form you submit.

➤ Contact the USCG Regional Exam Center (http://www.uscg.mil/nmc/recs/) to request an application. The government section of your phone book should have a listing as well. Complete all portions of the application, including the physical exam and drug test.

➤ Pass the written exam by taking a class locally or online. Study hard, because there is much content to remember.

➤ Present yourself at the nearest USCG facility for fingerprinting and review of your application. If all is well, you will receive your license.

Once you have earned the title Captain, you can go on to become a Master. The level you are awarded equates to the size vessel you are qualified to operate. For example, a 500-ton Master is qualified to operate a 500-ton commercial vessel.

PART TWO: GET SET TO GO

Okay, guys and gals, you've bought a boat. Now what? Why, you need to equip it for cruising. Primary to operating a boat is having aboard the required safety equipment. Of course, you'll need to find a place to keep the boat. Then, you'll spend some more money and outfit it with all the electronics and paraphernalia needed to travel in safety and comfort. The most important information you'll learn in this section is how to handle weather when on cruise.

CHAPTER 4

Outfit Your Boat

Safety is paramount on a boat. Carry aboard the wherewithal to protect the lives of your crew, prevent fire, and alert others to your distress situation. If your boat is not already equipped with any of these essential items, take a trip to the marine "candy store" to pick out navigation and docking essentials, as well as a tow-along dinghy. You can also obtain many of these items through a boat dealership.

USCG-REQUIRED SAFETY GEAR

If you already own a boat or have just purchased one, you likely have the essential safety gear. Standard equipment provided as part of a new boat sale is usually minimal. Check through what you have to be certain your existing equipment meets the current USCG regulations and is not outdated or expired.

You *must* carry aboard these types of safety equipment at all times:

- ➢ Flotation devices and rescue equipment
- ➢ Fire prevention equipment
- ➢ Alert and distress signals

MUST-HAVE FLOTATION DEVICES

Flotation devices are designated by type to indicate the amount of buoyancy each will provide. You will need one per person of a type I, II, or III, depending on your state's requirements for your type of vessel. The type and size (by weight range of designated user) will be printed on the inside of the jacket.

Descriptions of the four types of flotation devices follow:

Type I: Type I flotation devices are heavy-duty and designed for keeping one afloat in cruising areas where rescue may be slow to come, such as on the open ocean.

Types II & III: Type II and type III flotation devices are most common and are suited to boating in areas where there's a chance of fast rescue. Because many of these are bulky, some folks turn to inflatable vests. While these are easy to store and more comfortable, check to be sure any you buy are designated as a type II or III in order to meet USCG requirements.

Type IV: Type IV flotation devices are throwable devices such as ring and horseshoe buoys and floatable boat cushions. Because these are used for emergency man-overboards, all throwables need to be on deck and readily accessible. In some areas a throwable may no longer be substituted for a wearable vest in dinghies and other small boats.

OPTIONAL FLOTATION AND RESCUE DEVICES

Your cruising style will determine how in-depth you need to go when purchasing safety gear. If you are coastal cruising, for example, your dinghy can be a suitable life raft as long as you are not too far from shore or other cruising boats that may rescue you.

Important safety items to consider having on hand include the following:

Man Overboard Module: A self-deploying man overboard module (MOM) is typically attached to a railing at the stern of a boat. A MOM simplifies recovering a person overboard without endangering the crew or the person being recovered. The device is useful only if it's deployed very close to the victim, especially at night or in bad weather. Some models have an integral harness for recovering a victim from the water. If not, consider purchasing a winching device called a life sling.

Life Raft: Have aboard a life raft if you routinely travel out of sight of land and well away from common boating areas. A life raft self-inflates when kicked over the side. A floating line keeps it attached to the boat until you are ready to cut loose. Choose a raft large enough to accommodate the number of people you normally have aboard and that is equipped for either coastal or off-shore cruising. Basic survival gear such as a flashlight, fishing line, some water, and chalky nutrition in the form of hardtack is stowed inside.

Ditch Bag: A ditch bag is a duffel packed with survival supplies that will not already be present on your dinghy or life raft. Ditch bags are handy in situations where you need to jump ship and "live" in your dinghy or life raft for hours, even days, until help arrives. Purchase one already stocked and add to it, or make up your own. If you are straying very far from shore, ramp up on survival gear with portables: a watermaker, a Global Positioning System (GPS), an EPIRB, a VHS marine radio, and a few throwable flares. Comfort items like waterproof covers, dry sets of clothing, and candy bars are always a plus.

EPIRB = An Emergency Position Indicating Radio Beacon (EPIRB) is a device that transmits repeated signals from your location.

Sea anchor: A sea anchor is another helpful device to have aboard. It is a cone of heavy canvas with an attached line that acts much like a parachute. It creates drag by keeping the bow of the boat pointed into the wind and seas. A drogue is similar to a sea anchor, except it is towed astern to slow forward movement and to hold the stern steady.

FIRE EXTINGUISHERS

The best defense against fire is being prepared in advance to avert one. The movement of a boat causes all of its systems to vibrate, which leads to loose wire connections, chafing and wear, and propane gas or fuel leaks. Any one of these issues can cause a fire to erupt. On boats with an inboard engine, it pays to be particularly vigilant.

USCG-approved fire extinguishers are required on boats with enclosed engine compartments (outboards), enclosed living space, or with permanent fuel tanks. The size of your boat determines the number and type of extinguisher needed.

Fire extinguishers are designated by letters and numbers according to the class and size of the fire they can put out. The letter (A, B, C, or D) indicates the class of fire. The number is a measure of the capacity of the extinguisher. The larger the number, the greater the capacity of extinguishing material contained within the unit. Boats between 26 and 40 feet in length, for example, require one B-II or two B-I extinguishers.

While it is typical to mount a fire extinguisher in the engine compartment, releasing the contained CO_2 is a manual activity. Getting the extinguisher going by hand can be an issue if the fire occurs when you are shorthanded and underway. Be proactive by installing an automatic fire extinguishing system in your enclosed engine compartment. Activated by a rise in temperature, the unit can detect and douse a fire before you or your crew is aware one exists.

If you have a gasoline engine or are using a fuel with a flashpoint of 110 degrees Fahrenheit or less, you will need at least two ventilator ducts with cowls (or the equivalent) for the bilge of every closed compartment containing a gasoline tank (except if you have permanent tanks vented outside the boat and containing no unprotected electrical devices). Also, closed compartments housing a gasoline engine with a cranking motor must have a powered exhaust blower that is controllable from the instrument panel. This applies to boats built after August 1, 1980.

Must-Have Visual Warning and Distress Signals

None of us ever wants to be in a distress situation, but nasty stuff happens. For this reason the USCG requires you to carry approved signaling devices. Use these with discretion. Please don't send up a flare or radio an SOS to the coast guard if you go aground or run out of fuel. And if you see another boat in distress, the unwritten law of the sea deems you do your best to help it in whatever way you can.

The USCG requires you to carry three visual signaling devices, intended to summon help should the need arise. These can only be effective if potential assistance is in sight. Light-producing versions work best at night. Keep in mind that flares can only be used once and come with expiration dates. Before you leave port, make sure any flares or pyrotechnic devices you have aboard are fresh and stored where you can easily get at them.

Flares, or any fire-producing devices, emit a brilliant flash of attention-getting light. It's a no-no to toss one of these into a harbor full of boats on the Fourth of July because the ash can cause burns and start fires. In some states or countries, parachute or pistol-launched flares are considered firearms.

Choose from any of the combinations listed below:

> ➤ Three handheld red flares (day and night)
> ➤ One handheld red flare and two red meteors (day and night)
> ➤ One handheld orange smoke signal (day), two floating orange smoke signals (day), and one electric light (night only)

ADDITIONAL VISUAL WARNING SIGNALS

The USCG requirements are minimal. It pays to be prepared with additional warning aids for the (hopefully rare) occasion when a distress situation occurs while you are underway and far from shore. A lightning strike could zap your electronics, making it impossible for you to reach shore assistance; someone could go overboard and you need help retrieving him or her; or you could suffer a collision and be sinking fast.

As a backup plan, here are some ideas for items you can keep aboard and use to help attract the most immediate assistance:

➤ Use an electric distress light to flash the international SOS signal—and, no, a flashlight cannot be substituted.

➤ Wave a distress signal flag or anything that will attract attention. The SOS distress flag is a 3 × 3 foot orange square with a black square and a black ball, and it's available at marine stores.

➤ Throw a canister of bright-colored sea dye marker into the water (useful in an air search).

➤ Flash a mirror (this is not USCG approved, but if done correctly, it may do the trick).

MUST-HAVE AUDIBLE DEVICES

Bells, whistles, and air horns are audible devices used to let other boats know of your presence when visibility is restricted or poor. These work well at night, during torrential rain, and in fog conditions. To protect your boat from potential collision, sound your whistle, bell, or horn at regular intervals until all threats are past.

Be sure your boat meets these requirements:

Boats up to 40 feet in length: need a horn or a whistle. (This includes the dinghy.)

Boats over 40 feet in length: need a horn or whistle plus a ship's bell.

NAVIGATION GEAR

You can spend a ton of money on fancy electronics—and perhaps you already have. In reality, you can get by with very few basics. With a compass, depth sounder, chart of your cruising area, and the know-how from boating classes, you will be able to figure out where you are even when visibility is poor.

In our early boating years, my captain and I navigated in dense fog through some of the nastiest waters in New England by using a compass to direct us to markers, and then comparing the depth of the water underneath us with that marked on our boating chart. We used an air horn and our ship's bell to announce our presence to other boats.

GLOBAL POSITIONING SYSTEM (GPS)

GPS is a system of satellites, computers, and receivers that is able to determine the latitude and longitude of a receiver on Earth. It does so by calculating the time difference for signals from different satellites to reach the receiver. These days, most boaters own a GPS chart plotter. This technology is changing so quickly it is hard to keep up. A cockpit display works off a computer program to provide coordinates and directions for navigating coastal and inland waters.

If you are not ready to invest in one of the more complex built-in systems, begin by purchasing a portable GPS. You can use a GPS navigation application downloaded onto an iPad or other device. Bear in mind that you will require Internet access. As with the cell phone, no signal equals no data.

RADAR REFLECTOR

A basic reflector is made of metal or a material that will refract enough light so that your boat will show up as a radar target on neighboring boats. Its purpose is to avoid collision by visually alerting others to your presence. If you operate your boat in areas with shipping traffic or where fog and low visibility are common, the ability to be seen by radar-equipped ships can make the difference between cruising smoothly and being rammed. You can pick up a reflector for less than one hundred dollars. For optimum range, install the reflector as high on your boat as possible.

More elaborate and costly electronic radar units consist of a flattened globe installed atop a radar pole and wired into a display at the helm station. Data in the form of a "blip" on the radar screen indicates the location and directional movement of any (reflective) boats or obstacles surrounding you. Electronic radar units are often interfaced with built-in GPS systems. When dealing with commercial traffic, some serious sailors use an automatic tracking feature (AIS) that interfaces with their radar and allows them to identify the name of a particular vessel shown on the screen. AIS can be configured as uni- or bi-directional.

MARINE RADIOS (VHF)

Marine radios are often referred to as VHFs. VHF is a line-of-sight system, which means the radio waves won't bend to follow the curvature of the earth. The VHF antenna must "see" the antenna of a distant station, so be sure to install your antennas as high on your boat as possible. With a sailboat, put the antenna at the top of the main mast.

Very high frequency (VHF) = the ITU designation for the range of radio frequency electromagnetic waves (radio waves) from 30 MHz to 300 MHz, with corresponding wavelengths of ten to one meters.

The most basic and essential piece of equipment you need to have is a marine radio with a single sideband radio as an add-on option. Other supplementary devices are personal cell phones, Internet access, and if you plan international, deep-ocean travel, a satellite phone. Very high frequency (VHF) radios are the universal means of communicating while on the water. Use a VHF radio to call for help when needed, listen to weather reports, or hail shore facilities, bridge operators, or other boats.

Many VHF frequencies are designated for particular purposes. A frequency table should be included in the purchase of your radio, or you might have acquired this information in boating class. Marine radios are monitored twenty-four hours a day by the coast guard. When on cruise, turn on the radio and stand by on channel 16.

The radio unit consists of a microphone and a call unit from which you can access a variety of channels. Most radios come equipped with digital selective calling (DSC) capability (or "Mayday" button), which will ultimately coordinate with the USCG Rescue 21 system. When DSC is activated, your radio will broadcast an encoded distress call that can be picked up by nearby vessels equipped with similar capability. If your radio interfaces with a LORAN (long range navigation system) or a GPS, it will also broadcast your latitude and longitude.

BUILT-IN MARINE RADIO

A built-in marine radio, also called a fixed radio, is usually mounted in an accessible location inside the boat. All fixed-mount VHFs have a maximum output of 25 watts, the maximum allowed by the Federal Communication Commission (FCC). The range of a VHF radio is around 20 to 25 miles, depending on your location. For boats with outside helm stations, such as sailboats, having a VHF repeater unit at the helm station comes in handy.

PORTABLE MARINE RADIO

Handheld chargeable VHF units can be taken along in a dinghy for jaunts to shore to allow communication to your main boat, or to hail a launch if stranded. It can also act as an emergency backup to the main VHF radio. Handhelds have a maximum output of 6 watts. Due to their short antennas and low power, they have a limited range of 5 miles.

SINGLE SIDEBAND RADIO (SSB)

As a recreational boater, you do not need a license from the FCC to operate a single sideband radio unless you have a 65-foot or larger boat or plan to use your boat in a foreign country or waters, like the Bahamas or the Caribbean.

An SSB offers reliable voice communication over distances exceeding 25 miles from shore. Hailing range is affected by variables, such as the strength of the signal and weather conditions. Output power from an SSB is from 50 to 150 watts. SSB radios operate in the medium frequency (MF) and high frequency (HF) bands. In the MF band, the maximum range is fifty to one hundred fifty miles, whereas in the HF range you may be able to transmit thousands of miles. Installation of an SSB is more complex than it is for a VHF.

OUTFIT YOUR VESSEL FOR DOCKING

You can't cruise forever. When it's time to dock your boat, have on hand the necessary gear to anchor out or secure your boat to a wharf or mooring. You will also need to carry aboard a shore power cord to maintain your batteries when the boat is docked.

DOCK LINES

Having aboard lines in the kinds and quantities suggested below assures you will be able to tie up to any style slip or mooring or to reinforce holding power when a storm is imminent:

> - Two bow lines
> - Two stern lines
> - Two spring lines
> - One or more spare lines for mooring or other uses

At a marine store, it's easy to be overwhelmed when you stand before a wall of reels holding roping in a variety of materials, styles, diameters, and colors. Each type of marine cordage has its own use and characteristic.

When purchasing lines, you will need to know the answers to these questions:

> - What material is the line made of?
> - What thickness is best for your size boat?
> - How long should each section be?

According to marine expert Don Casey, the right material for dock lines is nylon. It is strong, flexible, weather- and sun-resistant, and inexpensive as compared to most other synthetics. Due to its ability to stretch, nylon absorbs shock and is less apt to damage cleats. Protect lines from chafing by wrapping prone areas with nylon (Cordura) tubing, leather, or urethane-dipped materials.

Lines come in various braids and colors. The braiding allows for flexibility and strength. Tensile strengths can vary by as much as fifteen percent. For example, 12-strand line is not as strong as double-braid line. Interestingly, colored line is not as strong as white line. A practical choice is 3-strand nylon because it doesn't snag, is easy to splice, and is cheaper and has more elasticity than braided line. However, braided line is stronger, more abrasion-resistant, and looks nicer.

As a rule, the larger the boat the heavier the line needed to support it. Here are some guidelines to help you choose the correct line thickness for your vessel:

Boats up to 25 feet in length require a 3/8-inch line.

Boats 26 to 35 feet in length require a 1/2-inch line.

Boats 36 to 45 feet in length require a 5/8-inch line.

Boats 46 to 55 feet in length require a 3/4-inch line.

Boats 56 to 65 feet in length require a 7/8-inch line.

Your dock lines will be cut to the length you request. As a rule, the length of bow and stern lines should equal two-thirds of your boat's overall length. Spring lines should be approximately the same length as your boat. Depending on the position of the cleats on your boat and at your marina slip, you may need longer lines.

The typical dock line has an eye splice at one end. You can have your lines spliced and wrapped professionally or do it yourself. In cases where you need an emergency dock line, it's all right to substitute a bowline knot for the eye splice loop as long as you are aware that it will not hold as long or as well.

FENDERS

Fenders, or bumpers as some folks call them, are padded or inflated items, usually made of pliable vinyl, rubber, or other soft material, used to keep a boat from bumping against the dock or other boats. Fenders come in a variety of shapes, sizes, materials, and colors. Talk to your marine salesperson about the best size for your boat or consult a chart in a catalog. A rule of thumb is 15 millimeters for every meter of boat length. Although you may be able to get by with three fenders, I suggest you carry at least five. Also helpful is a horizontal fender board to keep fenders in place in certain docking situations. Tie fenders to your boat with a piece of line that can be adjusted to accommodate tide changes and various docking situations.

BOAT HOOK

A boat hook is essential to snag a mooring and can be a godsend when trying to retrieve a hat or shoe that fell overboard. The typical hook is constructed of anodized aluminum tubing that telescopes quickly and securely locks with a twist. Choose a floating hook so you can snag it if it, too, goes in the drink. Boat hooks come in various lengths. Choose the size that will most easily store aboard your boat. Keep it handy by locating it within easy reach, preferably on deck.

SHORE POWER CORDS

Shore power systems work only when you are near an electrical source at dock. Generators and inverters are used underway to produce the same kind of electricity. The standard cord set consists of a 50-foot cord with two receptacles and a threaded ring, which has a hinged lid to allow for a locking waterproof connection. One end of the cord plugs into the boat's outlet, the other into a dockside electrical unit.

Depending on how your boat's power outlet is configured, you will need a cord set to accommodate either 30- or 50-amp service. All sorts of adapters and connectors are available to accommodate whatever the electrical outlet situation may be at your dock, as well as docks you will connect to in your travels.

If you plan to purchase a new cord set or upgrade your existing plugs, two new systems you should consider are the Easily Engaged Locking system (EEL) or the SmartPlug. These are designed to prevent overheating and water seepage issues common to traditional plugs and have a more relaxed cord length requirement.

ANCHORS AND TACKLE

What would you do to keep from drifting while you handle a boat issue, or when you just want to be sure the boat stays in place? Drop your anchor, of course. While having an anchor is not the law in every state, it can be one of the first pieces of emergency equipment you'll need. Often, an anchor assembly is included as part of a boat-buying package.

The primary anchor assembly includes the following parts:

Anchor: A stainless steel or aluminum anchor of the size and type best suited to your boat and the waters you plan to navigate.

Bow roller: A fixed bow roller to push the anchor rode or chain out beyond the bow.

Winch: A winch to drop or retrieve the anchor, if your boat is large enough to require one.

If you already have a primary anchor, don't stop there. Purchase a second anchor to use as backup should a passing boat cut your anchor line and send you adrift, or in situations where you need to reinforce or control the holding power of your main anchor. The second anchor is usually smaller than the primary anchor and of different style.

CHOOSE THE RIGHT ANCHOR FOR THE JOB

The type of anchor you need depends on the makeup of the bottom of the anchorage—whether it is sandy, muddy, or rocky, whereas the weight of the anchor relates to your boat size. Using the correct anchor for your boat and situation can save you a disruption in the wee hours to reset it.

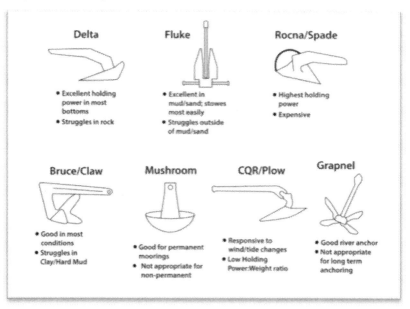

Scan through this listing of anchor types to understand which will work best for the majority of your boating situations. As discussed earlier, there are several styles of anchors, each normally referred to by its manufacturer's name.

PLOW (DELTA OR CQR)

Plow-style anchors are popular with boaters because they perform well on most bottoms and have good holding power.

When dropped in the water, a plow lands on its side and then buries itself when it's tugged to set. Its hinged shaft and shape allow it to reset to accommodate wind or tide shifts. Unless you have a bow pulpit and roller, a plow is heavy to manage, and it is difficult to stow. The Delta has a fixed shank, which makes it a better performer than a Coastal Quick Release (CQR), which has a pivoting shank.

FLUKE (DANFORTH OR FORTRESS)

Use a fluke for anchoring in sand or mud, but avoid rocky, clay, or kelp bottoms. When set correctly, the flukes, or arms, of this type of anchor dig into the bottom with a lot of force. Because this style of anchor tends to drag, it's not recommended for overnight stays. However, as a second anchor it stows flat and is perfect for harbor stops for lunch or swims.

KEDGE

Use a kedge anchor in heavy grass, weeds, or rocks where one arm can dig into a crevice. Avoid using a kedge in mud or loose sand. The weight of the anchor provides most of the holding power, so choose a heavy version. Another issue is that its fluke can tangle in the anchor line.

CLAW (BRUCE)

In most seabeds, except for those with weedy or grassy bottoms, claw anchors set quickly without playing out a lot of scope (or line). Because of its ability to turn in the bottom to align with a force, a claw anchor will hold tight with tide or wind changes. However, a claw is bulky to stow and not as efficient as some of the other styles of anchor.

MUSHROOM

The mushroom settles in, creating a hard-to-break suction. This style is commonly used to set permanent mooring buoys, especially in a sand or mud bottom. Most folks use small versions to anchor their dinghies.

GRAPNEL

The grapnel anchor works well for anchoring a dinghy, canoe, kayak, or other small craft because it has the same great holding power as the mushroom only it won't bury as deep.

NEW GENERATION ANCHORS

Some of the most common of the new surge of anchors on the market are the French SPADE, the New Zealand Rocna, and the Bulwagga. These are designed to set quickly with high holding power. Because they have not been time tested, they haven't acquired the status of reliability traditional anchors have—and they cost much more.

PICK THE RIGHT SIZE ANCHOR FOR YOUR BOAT

Anchor size is loosely based on the length and above-water profile of your boat, as well as its displacement and how and under what conditions you plan to use the anchor. Because so many factors affect the size anchor a boat needs, ask an expert at the marine store or dealership to help you choose the best size for your vessel.

Nevertheless, it is helpful to have general guidelines such as these:

> **Under 50 feet:** For boats less than 50 feet in length, the anchor should weigh 1 pound for every foot of boat length. A 25-foot boat might require a 25-pound anchor.

Over 50 feet: For boats longer than 50 feet, the anchor should weigh 1.5 times the length of the boat. A 50-foot boat might need a 75-pound anchor and an electronic means of operating it.

ANCHOR TACKLE

Ground Tackle refers to all the parts of an anchor package between the boat and the bottom of the sea. If you use only line, the ground tackle may be referred to as the anchor line.

As with dock lines, the best fiber to use for the anchor rode (or anchor line) is nylon, either three strand or braided. A rode made of a length of chain plus line is common in the United States.

In foreign countries you will see many boats with all-chain anchor rodes. Although a chain rode makes for secure anchoring, chain is very heavy and awkward to winch in. Stored in the anchor locker, it will weigh down the bow of your boat and create drag.

GO DINGHY HUNTING

Oops, sorry. You thought you were through buying boats, but you have one more purchase to make to complete your fleet. If your cruising plans include spending time in beautiful anchorages, you will need a means of carrying you and yours to shore.

Having a secondary way to travel makes a fine plan B for exploring intricate harbor areas or doing duty as a lifeboat in distress situations. As we discussed earlier, your dinghy can double as a fishing boat or be a tow for water sports.

Rowing a dinghy is great exercise, and a sailing dinghy is a lot of fun, but many prefer to tack an outboard engine to the stern of the boat and carry a set of oars as backup. The only restriction is that the dinghy you choose needs to be of a size, weight, and shape to be either towed or stored aboard your larger vessel.

DECIDE ON A DINGHY

Dinghies come in all styles, sizes, and materials. When deciding what type of dinghy to buy, match its features against your cruising waters, the number of people you normally would transport, and the kind of harbor activities you plan to use it for.

Choose from these basic types:

Hard: Hard dinghies may be constructed of plywood, fiberglass, or aluminum. These are rarely as stable as an inflatable dinghy. Because of the type of keel needed, sailing dinghies have a hard bottom.

Soft Inflatable: Soft inflatables are in the pontoon family. In addition to being stable, they are lightweight, can support heavy loads and easily accommodate an outboard engine. The downside is they are subject to punctures and difficult to row. Soft-bottomed inflatables often can be deflated, rolled up, and stowed in a bag. Inflatables are constructed of either Hypalon-reinforced fabric or one of the many PVC-based products on the market. Hypalon, a DuPont product, is resistant to abrasion, oils, and ultraviolet light. The Hypalon coating has either a nylon or a polyester core with two layers of neoprene to make it airtight. While a dinghy made of Hypalon is more costly than a PVC dinghy, Hypalon lasts longer and comes with an extended manufacturer's warranty.

Rigid Inflatables (RIBs): RIBs are pontoon-style dinghies with a hard fiberglass bottom, which makes them sturdier and heavier than soft inflatables. They are popular because they can accommodate larger loads and are the most stable in the dinghy family.

EQUIP YOUR DINGHY

Keep in mind that a dinghy is a boat, and as such it is required to have safety gear aboard in compliance with USCG safety regulations. At minimum, you must have these items aboard at all times to ensure the safety of your crew and to avoid being fined:

> ➢ A USGA-approved life jacket for each person aboard
>
> ➢ An air horn
>
> ➢ One or more lights, depending on the size of the boat, to be used for night transport and when visibility is poor

In addition to the required gear, you will need a means of propulsion and the wherewithal to tow, tie up, or secure your dinghy. So add these items to your shopping list:

> ➢ An outboard motor or oars. If your dinghy is motorized, be sure to keep aboard a set of oars for times when the engine poops out.
>
> ➢ A painter (tow line), preferably one that floats, made of polypropylene rope. A floating painter eliminates the risk of the line getting tangled in the propeller of the main ship. As a rule, a faster boat needs a longer tow line than a slower boat.
>
> ➢ An anchor to throw out when stopping to fish, swim, or beach your dinghy.

> ➢ An air pump and a patching kit for Rigid Bottom Inflatables (RIBs) or other inflatables.

HOIST AND STORE YOUR DINGHY AND OUTBOARD

When towing a dinghy in other than calm, nearby waters, most folks haul the engine on board and secure it on the stern. Doing so reduces drag for longer distances and protects the engine from bouncing about in heavy seas. If the engine you have chosen is too heavy to lift comfortably, check out the many hoisting devices available to help you manage the process without throwing out your back.

Some boaters lift the entire dinghy onto their vessel and store it on deck, sometimes in a cradle, or hoist it onto a davit astern. A davit is a crane-like apparatus used for supporting, raising, and lowering boats, dinghies, or other such devices. Using a davit is a convenient way to carry a dinghy. A davit may be installed as part of the sale of a new boat, or afterward, as long as the main vessel is large enough to accommodate it. Protect your dinghy from filling with sea spray or rainwater when it is on its davit by covering it with a tarp or ensuring its drain plug is out.

If you have ample space on the foredeck of your vessel, you may opt to hoist the dinghy and set it upside down on the deck or in a fixed cradle. If you do so, you will likely need to rig a mechanical means of lifting it aboard. Situate the dinghy where it will not obstruct the helmsman's view. Once you have done so, lash it in place to prevent it from slipping around as the boat powers over the water. Some folks choose to leave the outboard engine in place on the stern of the dinghy when they cradle it.

CHAPTER 5

Prepare for Launch

Good job on the outfitting. Let's move on. You've more decisions to make and there's work to do to get your "baby" ready for its seasonal launch. Although it sounds like you'll be toiling way, I guarantee you'll enjoy it. Sure, you'll be tired, but it's a good tired, a feeling of accomplishment, as you look ahead to those warm sunny days on the water. This chapter will help you evaluate a marina's facilities and to determine what items you should have on hand for repairing and cleaning your boat. Also included is information on naming and christening a new boat.

EVALUATE A POTENTIAL MARINA

The marina you choose will be your home base: the place where you hang out when you are not cruising, and where you repair and maintain your boat. For these reasons, you want to be comfortable there.

If you need a new home for your boat, the fastest way to precheck marinas that might accommodate you and your boat is to consult a cruising guide for information on water depth, types and numbers of slips or mooring available, harbor accessibility, and facilities.

Once you have narrowed down your selection, take a road trip to your cruising grounds to check out each possibility. If you are inclined, ask boat owners what they think of the place. Chat with the marina manager or dock master to find out what slips or moorings are available for your size boat. If a particular marina seems like a good possibility, obtain pricing info and review the contract. A contract protects you as well as the marina. Is there a discount for prepayment? What are your responsibilities and liabilities? Negotiate changes before you sign.

It's easy to get caught up in appearances. No matter how well appointed a marina's facilities are, it may not be the right spot for you to keep your boat. For example, one marina we called home for several summers had a skinny mile-long channel we needed to travel to reach open water. A sailboating friend there had to wait for high tide to enter or leave his slip to avoid going aground. As you stroll through each facility, envision it from a cruising perspective. Keep a sharp eye on the activity in progress, and be sure to ask a lot of questions.

Consider this laundry list of situations:

> What will it take for you to navigate from your slip or mooring to the nearest outlet to a waterway?

> Will you have to deal with bridge openings, tidal issues, or long, narrow channels?

> Is the water in the marina too shallow for your boat? Will you have to wait for high tide to depart or return to your slip or mooring?

> Is the lift used to launch and pull boats large enough to accommodate your boat?

> Are the lanes between docks roomy enough to allow boats to maneuver in and out of slips?

> Are the slips subject to wakes from passing boat traffic?

➢ Where is the closest fuel dock—on the premises, down the river? Will it be convenient to your future cruising?

➢ What facilities are available for pumping out marine discharge? Is there a roving pump-out boat for the area? Does your marina have its own pump-out facility?

➢ What's the neighborhood like? Will your boat be safe when you are not aboard? Is the marina entry guarded or kept locked from intruders?

➢ Is the marina kept clean and neat with few obstructions on the wharves and in the parking areas?

➢ Are water and electricity convenient to areas where boats are stored for the season? You will need access if you plan to bottom paint, wax, and clean your boat while it's on the hard.

➢ What is the marina's reputation for repair work? Will it allow outside contractors to work on your boat? Can you work on your own boat?

➢ Are the head and shower facilities clean and in good operating condition? Is there a laundry room?

➢ Are convenience items, like carts, provided for hauling gear to your boat? Does it have picnic tables and gas grills for Sunday night suppers?

➢ Is there a restaurant or takeout deli on the premises or within walking distance? A small convenience store for I-forgot groceries, newspapers, snacks?

➢ Does the marina offer any special services such as launch service or storage lockers?

➢ How accessible is the dinghy dock and what shape is it in?

➢ If you will be launching a second boat or are trailering your boat, where is the launch pad located? Is it out of the way of street traffic?

CHOOSE BETWEEN A SLIP AND A MOORING

The decision between renting a slip or a mooring for a season is cost based as well as convenience driven. Whether you opt for a slip or a mooring also depends on how you plan to use your boat and how much privacy you want. Of importance is the size and location of your slip or mooring. For a slip, you will consider roominess as it pertains to the length and beam of your vessel, as well as ease of entry and departure. A mooring needs to be of the correct size to support the weight of your boat in all sea conditions and should be located out of the way of boat traffic.

Consider these pros and cons when finalizing your decision:

➢ Seasonal rental of a slip at a dock is generally more costly than a mooring.

➢ At dock, water and electricity are easily accessed. With a mooring, you will need to go to a dock to refill your water tanks (unless you have a watermaker) and wash your boat. Although your boat's batteries can be charged by running the engine or generator, dockside power gives you a harder charge with fewer limitations.

- At a mooring, a boat is more exposed to weather and sea conditions and not as easy to protect.

- A mooring offers privacy and quiet, whereas dock life can be very social.

- At a mooring, a boat usually faces the wind and is free to move with the water. It is cooler and more comfortable than a boat restrained at a dock.

- It is easier to pick up the mooring pennant than to maneuver into a slip and secure the boat, especially in a congested area.

- With a slip, it is easy to transport and load supplies and get on or off the boat to access shore facilities. Getting to a mooring or going to shore requires a dinghy or marina launch ride.

- The water around a mooring is usually cleaner, with less chance of corrosion caused by stray currents from other boats, and may even be suitable for swimming.

PREP FOR LAUNCH

Your garage or basement is overflowing with the essential gear needed to cruise in safety. Your excitement mounts. Finally, it's here. Boating season. The date your boat is scheduled to be plopped into the water for the season looms as bright as sunshine. It's time to work on your boat and ready it for your first cruise of the season.

If this is a brand-new boat, you are off the hook for prepping the boat because most dealers will handle that for you. Once the boat is launched, you are free to move in. However, as a boat owner, the responsibility to see to the tasks involved in getting it ready to cruise is all yours.

INSPECT YOUR BOAT

Start the season right by giving your boat a good going over to eliminate as many potential problems as you can before taking it out on a cruise. Performing much of your own maintenance in a stable environment is a great way to learn how to take care of problems and may serve you well on cruise. If you are not comfortable performing the more complex tasks, make arrangements to have your boat checked over by trusted marina service personnel.

If end-of-season maintenance was performed on the engine and all other boat systems, you should be fueled up and ready to go. For other items, review the task list that follows and scratch off any chores you might have already performed:

> ➤ Tend to the hull. If it is constructed of fiberglass, remedy any scratches or problems with the gel coat. On an aluminum or metal hull, look for signs of corrosion. If you have a wooden boat, replace any rotted boards, seal leaks, and then give the hull a fresh coat of paint.

> ➤ Check the propeller for pitting, distortion, or dents. Secure cotter pins. If the propeller doesn't move easily when you try to turn it, a bearing may need to be replaced. Replace zincs on propeller shaft and hull.

> ➤ Inspect running lights, mast lights, and lights on the stern. If you have a sailboat, checking all wiring connected through the mast while it is unstepped will save you a trip up the bosun's chair later. Change bulbs if necessary.

➢ Disconnect the VHF radio, GPS antenna, and radar, and clean the fittings. Replace rusted or corroded fittings and damaged wires, then spray with a lubricant. Reconnect all wires and fittings, and then retest.

➢ Check for leaks by inspecting trim cylinders, hoses, and hydraulic steering pumps and rams. If leaking, replace the gasket or O-ring. Look for signs of leaks around the rudder and thru hulls. Inspect port lights, hatches, and deck fittings for areas that need to be recaulked. When the boat is in the water, check that the stuffing box stays completely dry. Inspect the interior of your boat for signs of water damage. Common signs of leaks are pools of water, dried water trails, rust, hairline cracks, displaced caulking, and dark spots at wood seams.

Zincs = pieces of sacrificial metal used to protect metallic parts that will be immersed in salt water from damaging electrolysis by attracting stray current. It normally needs to be replaced once every season, when it becomes pitted and ash-white.

RIG SAILS

If you have sent your sails out for cleaning, make arrangements to pick them up or have them delivered once your boat is in the water. If you are not comfortable rerigging the sails and hoisting them, hire a professional rigger to do the job.

SERVICE OUTDRIVES AND OUTBOARDS

At the beginning of the season, or at the end of the season to prepare for relaunching, drop off small outboards (dinghy engines) at a marine service center for annual maintenance and repair, or do the job yourself. Unless you are a whiz-bang mechanic, I suggest having an experienced marine mechanic perform heavy-duty maintenance and repairs on inboards, outdrives, and large outboards. (See Chapter 14 for engine maintenance.)

If you're handy, you may wish to perform these maintenance chores yourself:

> Replace anodes on the shaft, outdrive, and trim tabs, if necessary.

> Check to make sure the rudderstock isn't bent and the outdrive bellows don't have cracks or tears.

> Change the hydraulic trim fluid, if necessary.

> Check lower unit lube level for a bad seal. Creamy oil is a sign of water.

> Change the oil, if necessary.

> Service the fuel system by replacing any flexible gasoline lines that are not USCG approved. Check that fuel hoses are still flexible and free of cracks or soft spots and that cooling hoses fit snugly and are tightly clamped. Replace fuel filters and clean the air filter, if necessary.

> Check the batteries. Reinstall batteries if they have been removed for the season. Get help. These are mega heavy. Top up lead acid batteries with distilled water. Make certain batteries are fully charged. Clean and tighten all electrical connections and battery cable terminals. Apply a protective spray or grease to battery terminals.

> ➢ Inspect seacocks to ensure handles move freely when you open and close them, and check to be sure the hoses are double-clamped. Clamps should be made of stainless steel. Replace if rusted.

> ➢ Inspect the raw water intake strainer for cracks and corrosion. Check the top for a tight seal.

> ➢ Test the bilge pump. Does it go on automatically? Will it turn on using the manual switch? Are high-water switches and alarms working properly?

> ➢ Test alarm systems for smoke, carbon monoxide, and propane or LPG and change any batteries. Make sure sensors are not blocked or dirty.

BOTTOM PAINT YOUR BOAT

Whether you do the work yourself or hire someone, most areas require boats using their waters to have a solid coat of bottom paint to stave off any marine growth such as barnacles, algae, or general sea slime that may thrive on the underside of the hull. In addition to bottom painting your primary boat preseason, add a coat of paint to the underside of any dinghy that will be in the water all season.

The paint job can be performed by marina maintenance personnel, or you can do it yourself, as do many boat owners. The job requires sanding off the existing paint and applying a fresh coat or two. It's not healthy to inhale this toxic paint or allow it to soak into your pores, so be sure to wear coveralls, a hat, goggles, and a mask while performing the job. To capture the toxic dust, more and more marinas require tarps be laid on the ground and vacuum bags be attached to sanders.

The challenge is to select the least toxic paint that will effectively prevent fouling. While copper oxide is the dominant ingredient in most antifouling paints, what are now called slimicides keep a boat free of plant and animal growth. If you keep your boat in a lake or river, you may not have a barnacle problem. But a sitting boat will attract algae and slime, so chose paint with a heavy dose of slimicides. The effectiveness of a particular type of paint is determined by water temperature, salinity, and how long the boat will sit in the water. Marine growth adds weight and, therefore, drag, which impacts boat speed and maneuverability.

Selecting the right kind of bottom paint for your boat can be confusing. Don't be shy about asking for recommendations at your marine supply store. Be certain the type of antifouling paint you choose is compatible with the paint that is already on your boat.

Antifouling hard: Antifouling hard, or contact-leaching paints, create a porous film on the hull. These contain varying levels of biocides, which are released slowly when they contact water. Boats with planing hulls (speed boats) are generally painted with hard paints applied annually.

Antifouling Ablative: Antifouling ablative, or sloughing paints, are partially soluble, which means the active ingredient is continually leached out. This weakens the underlying film of growth as the boat moves through the water. Ablative paints contain lower levels of toxins than hard paints. But because these toxins are released steadily, the overall ecological impact is about the same. Ablative paint is most effective when a boat is used regularly. Some ablative paints are designed to last for more than one season. If you anticipate underwater hull cleaning, as you might do for racing, do not use ablative paint.

Nontoxic Coatings: Nontoxic coatings are the most environmentally friendly options. They contain Teflon or silicone and produce hard, slick surfaces that discourage fouling growth. At present, these coatings are not widely available.

CLEAN AND WAX THE HULL

While the boat is out of the water, it's easier to work on the hull. It's customary to wax the hull at the beginning of boating season. If you are not inclined to do the work yourself, have it done by a professional.

Hose down the boat or use a boat cleaner to prepare the surface (no sense waxing over dirt). For routine washing, use boat soap and a boat brush. For the most protection and longest lasting shine, use paste wax and buff by hand or with an electric buffer. If the hull is dull and chalky (oxidized), you may need to treat it with a restorative cleaner before waxing.

Speak with marine store personnel or the marina maintenance manager about the best procedure and products for your situation. Marine-grade fiberglass cleaners and wax intended for fiberglass boats also suffice for aluminum boats.

SPIFF THE DECK

Waxing the deck (please—not the nonskid walkways), polishing the stainless steel, and cleaning and varnishing the teak can be done at any time, but many boaters prefer getting the job done before launching. If you have fiberglass decking, apply cleaner and wax as you did for the hull. Shine up those stainless steel fittings using a marine-grade metal polish. Apply and buff by hand or electric buffer (depending on the size of the area). Work on rust spots and pitting with a nonscratch scouring pad.

If your deck is unvarnished teak, wash it with a cleaner containing chlorine to remove mold. Boat maintenance expert Georgia Schroer, former owner of B & G Yacht Services, uses Soft Scrub gel cleanser with bleach to remove mold from an unvarnished teak deck before layering on teak oil. While there are many fancier ways to care for unvarnished teak, my motto is to keep it simple.

If you have teak railings or other external areas that have been varnished, simply wash them. If the varnish shows signs of wear, you will need to strip it off and repaint. This is a tedious job, one that should be performed in dry weather with little wind. If you are not comfortable varnishing, save yourself some grief and hire a professional.

WASH THE WINDOWS

To wash glass or Lexan windows, use a traditional window cleaner. Products containing vinegar are gentler on the glass than those containing chemicals. I have found using a squeegee cuts back on the rubbing required to remove the cleaner and unveil the shine. Finish with a product designed to prevent water spotting, such as Rain-X, and your windows will not need to be washed that often. For the best shine, buff with a microfiber cloth.

While many commercial and marine-grade products are available to clean and condition vinyl windows, such as those found in canvas cockpit dodgers, on the advice of a marina maintenance fellow, I have always used lemon Pledge (wipes work particularly well). To avoid scratching the vinyl, remove dirt and salt residue with clear water beforehand.

Service the Water System

If your boat has been winterized, you will need to drain the water tanks to remove antifreeze, and then refill them with freshwater. This is usually done once the boat has been launched, when dock water is nearby.

Clean and Ventilate

A boat that has been sitting unused, even if covered, will accumulate a certain amount of dust. Cleaning the interior is akin to spring cleaning a home. If your boat has been exposed to weather changes, condensation may have left mold spores in lockers and areas that are not well ventilated. Open up everything and air out the boat. Mold creates that awful smell I call boat breath. Although there are many commercial products to fight mold, those containing chlorine will kill the spores and prevent reoccurrence.

Get started with this basic task list:

- ➤ Wipe down ceiling, walls, floors, cushions.
- ➤ Vacuum carpets or wash floors.
- ➤ Wipe out lockers.
- ➤ Scour the head and galley.
- ➤ Polish chrome or stainless sinks and fittings.

Stock Basic Cleaning Supplies

Marine stores and supermarkets are crowded with cleaning products. If you think it through, you can get by using simple household cleaners and polishes, many of which are environmentally friendly and have several uses aboard. See the Appendix for a suggested listing of general cleaning supplies. A spray bottle filled with water and a couple of tablespoons of chlorine bleach or a 50/50 mix of vinegar and water will handle most cleaning issues. Keep in mind that chlorine is bleach and may damage or discolor fabrics or leathers, so using white vinegar is the safer option for these surfaces.

ORGANIZE AND AMASS REPAIR SUPPLIES

In the process of preparing our boat for launch, we bought replacement parts and carted tools to and from the marina. Instead of toting the same cache to the boat for each visit just in case it's needed, decide which items you are most apt to use aboard and leave them there.

Organize the repair manuals for your boat systems so you can find what you need at a moment's notice. A loose-leaf notebook or a portable file box works well. Store the manuals in a dry place, near your toolbox if possible.

For routine repairs, collect tools in a kit. Leave that metal toolbox at home. It's not only cumbersome and weighty, but it can scratch surfaces and will ultimately rust. Use a nonmetal grab-and-go holder that will store easily. Waterproof canvas works well. Check the Appendix for a suggested listing of tools and repair supplies to keep aboard.

NAME AND CHRISTEN YOUR NEW BOAT

If you are satisfied with the name of your boat, you can skip over this part. Obviously, you will want to name a new boat, but what if you buy a used boat that is already named, or if the existing name is that of your ex-wife or ex-husband? A lot of superstition surrounds boating. Contrary to the popular belief, the seas won't swallow you if you change your boat's name. But why tempt fate when you can name/rename your boat in a manner that will make King Neptune smile?

Follow this procedure when renaming your boat:

> ➢ Remove all traces of the old name from the hull before replacing it with the new name.

> Update the boat's papers.

> Cart home any monogrammed glasses, towels, and the like.

> Perform a christening ceremony.

AVOID BOAT NAME PITFALLS

It's fun to pick out a name for your boat, but don't go crazy. Before you paint it on your vessel and fill in the boat name blanks on its documents, put your planned name to the sea test by considering these issues:

> How often will you want to explain what the name means?

> Is it too long? Repeat it fast three times, as others will do when hailing you. We thought *Joy for All Seasons* was an apt name for our boat until folks radioing us began abbreviating it to *Joy For*.

> Will others mispronounce it, as is common with foreign words or complex spelling? Is it a tongue twister?

> Is the name so common that your boat will be mistaken for another?

> Will your new name encourage bad juju? Avoid names like *Crash* and *Money Pit*.

NAME THE DINGHY

Avoid the temptation to name your dinghy after your primary boat, such as (Tender To) *T/T Spiker*. Whenever your dinghy is at dock, everyone will know you are off the boat. This sets you up for a robbery or worse.

How to Christen a Boat

Tradition deems that a good champagne be poured over the bow while dubbing a vessel with its name. This procedure requires a heavy hand delivering a smashing blow. You can purchase a bottle of the bubbly covered with net to prevent being injured by flying glass shards, or you can wrap the bottle in a towel.

When we christened our boat in Sweden, our dealer came up with a variation. We dribbled a little champagne over the bow, and then toasted each other with glasses filled with the rest. If conditions permit, take your boat out for a spin after the ceremony for a finishing touch.

CHAPTER 6

Make Your Boat Livable

The boat has been checked out and it's purring like a fat cat just waiting to go on its first overnight cruise with you and your family. But wait! If you are going for more than a day cruise, you'll need to have all your necessities aboard. Think of it as moving into a vacation home; once your boat is set up with the basics for living aboard, trips to and from the boat will be a matter of replenishing supplies.

This chapter will help you figure out what items you and your crew will need to keep aboard for eating, sleeping, being comfortable in a variety of weather conditions, and handling or preventing minor medical traumas. Also included is information on storage, packing gear, efficient stowing, and tips for staying stocked throughout the boating season.

The size, style, and facilities of your boat determine the types and kinds of items you need to make simple boat repairs and to equip your galley, berth, and head. I've omitted cleaning supplies in this chapter because you likely have left aboard much of what you used to wax and spring clean your boat. While not really a necessity, keep aboard the equipment you'll need for fishing, swimming, snorkeling, or whatever water activities you and your family enjoy.

For starters, let's get your galley set up.

Amass Galley Necessities

Your cooking style, availability of electrical power, storage capacity, and willingness to spend time preparing meals determine the type and count of galley-related items you choose to keep aboard for the season. The basic categories are serving utensils, dinnerware, storage containers, and a cache of nonperishable foods and beverages.

Cooking and Serving Utensils

After thirty-five years on the water managing the galley in boats ranging from 27 to 50 feet, I still keep aboard the same number and kinds of pans. Access to more reliable power, though, has allowed me to graduate from using a burner-top marine toaster and old-fashioned percolator to an electric toaster and drip coffeepot.

On a boat, less is more. Pots and pans are space hogs. You don't need a lot of fancy gadgets, utensils, or appliances to pull off a meal as long as you have a working stove. Bring to the boat a few spare pans of varying sizes from home, or purchase new ones. Look for heatproof handles and pans that will (somewhat) nest for storage. Before you haul that huge lobster pot to the boat, think about how often you will use it and where you will store it. See the Appendix for a listing of suggested galley gear.

Obtain Dinnerware

The elegance and style of the dinnerware you select depends on how much time you are willing to spend on cleanup, whether you have water to spare for dishwashing, where and how you will be traveling, your personal preferences, and how easy it is to get rid of trash.

If you have a spare set of dishes and silverware at home, start with that. Should you need to buy a set, don't limit your shopping to the marine store. Big-box and discount stores carry a large selection of pattern and styles of dinnerware and other kitchen goods and appliances at reasonable costs. In addition to a having a basic set of dishes, stock disposables.

Paper plates, bowls, and cups are usually a staple on any boat. No washing required, which means saving precious tank water. When they are dirty, they can be tossed in the trash. Using paper goods exclusively can become expensive, though, and if you are on the move, the issue of disposal surfaces. Not all harbors will take trash, and you will not be far enough offshore to toss used paper dishes overboard.

Most boaters keep a set of unbreakable dinnerware aboard. Invest in a set of marine plates and glasses, buy a set of melamine dishes, or pick up other plastic versions from a store selling outdoor dining supplies. Just keep in mind that these dishes are not recommended for the microwave.

If you decide to use breakable dishes and glasses, know that you will have to be careful about where and how you store them as well as under what conditions you will use them. Sailboaters shy away from anything breakable because of the amount of heeling and motion that occurs while the boat is underway. Broken china or glass is always a hazard. Powerboats are somewhat more stable.

A set of stainless steel dining utensils is a smart investment. To save space, choose a set with forks and spoons that will stack and lay flat in a drawer or bin and that has serrated knives. A serving spoon and fork are normally included.

You will need sharp knives for cutting meat. Find these in a set, often with a matching paring, carving, and bread knife. Avoid buying a bulky wooden knife holder. To keep knives sharp and protected without consuming an inordinate amount of space, either save the cardboard tip protectors, find more durable plastic holders, or look for a compact, stow-away holder for the set.

STOCK BASIC SUPPLIES

Don't be caught without basic food aboard. I learned my lesson about keeping emergency rations on board years ago. Our family of five set out to a remote anchorage with plans to join friends in a communal dinner aboard. I brought the coleslaw and they were bringing the steaks. Our friends never arrived, and guess what we ate for dinner? Had I a box of pasta and bottled sauce aboard, or some canned soups or stews, we might've had a warm meal and hardly missed those steaks.

Keep aboard the wherewithal to put together an emergency meal or two that will feed your crew in the event it takes longer than usual to reach port or your refrigerator goes bust, making consuming your fresh foods iffy.

NONPERISHABLE FOODS AND BEVERAGES

Any food items that don't require refrigeration to keep fresh and safe to eat are viable keep-aboard items. Look for items that are easy to heat and eat. In warm, humid climates, keeping cardboard aboard encourages infestation. Seal and store either the box or its contents in zippered plastic bags or vacuum-seal them before putting them aboard. Bottles and cans will keep a long time in nonfreezing conditions.

Having enough beverages on board is essential, because exposure to sun and wind can ramp up dehydration. Allow a minimum of 64 ounces of nonalcoholic beverages, preferably water, per day per person. Instead of hauling gallons and cases of freshwater aboard, install a water filter and you will be able to draw from your boat's water tanks.

While a Brita filter will work fine, for a long-term solution I suggest installing a Seagull IV purifying water filter, which requires no power to operate and is warrantied for many years. Powdered flavor packets can make bottled and filtered water tasty without usurping storage space.

ACQUIRE BEDDING & LINENS

Getting proper rest is almost as important as sustenance is for energy and good health. Beginning boaters often start out with sleeping bags, but ultimately upgrade to sheets and blankets for a more comfortable, climate-controlled sleep.

Traditional sleeping bags work fine, especially at the beginning and end of the season, when the weather is cool. An unzipped sleeping bag laid flat can double as an extra comforter. Compress sleeping bags into tight little rolls and store them in their sacks. Rolled up sleeping bags make good bolster pillows for the saloon or cockpit, and they are available when needed for extra warmth and for extra guests. Marine and camping stores carry washable liners. A sleep system, a berth-shaped bag with removable sheet and blanket inserts, is also popular, though a cost commitment. Like sleeping bags, sleep systems can be rolled away when not in use.

If you are frequently sleeping aboard, you deserve the same comforts you have at home. Have a set of sheets custom made to the contours of each berth or, do what I do, use traditional sheets. King, queen, full-size, or twin sheets and blankets fit most berths. Flat sheets will stay in place if knotted at any corners needing to be tucked under. Contour bottom sheets can anchor all three (v-berth) or four corners. Tuck under the extra yardage.

It's customary to leave a bed using sheets, blankets, and pillows made up during the day. However, you may not wish to do this, especially if you use a berth to store bulky odd items such as anchors, extra sails, and lines. If this is your situation, store sheets, blankets, and pillows in pillow shams, and use them as throw pillows on board during the day.

If you will be on a cruise long enough to require a change of bedding (or if someone left a hatch open and it got wet), keep a second set of bedding on hand, stored in waterproof storage bags.

When choosing pillows for sleeping or for decor, opt for those with synthetic stuffing that won't hold moisture. Avoid feather pillows and those stuffed with cotton batting or kapok. If you have a choice, opt for zippered covers that can be removed and cleaned.

While thick, luxurious towels are wonderful, thin beach towels are more practical because they stow and pack easily, can double as spare blankets, and dry more quickly. If you're in the market for new towels, invest in superabsorbent, quick-drying towels made of microfiber. Stock sets of hand towels and washcloths to be shared, or for each person aboard.

AMASS GROOMING AIDS

Keep a second set of your basic grooming aids on board and you will have one less thing to tote back and forth each week. I recommend duplicating your favorite shave cream, toothpaste, shampoo, and skin creams rather than settling for off brands or sample packets. If you are short on space, purchase these in travel sizes or transfer contents of larger containers into smaller ones. For women, invest in a fresh set of cosmetics in favorite colors and brands.

BE PREPARED WITH ALL-WEATHER GEAR

The sun may be shining when you leave port, but that's no guarantee you won't run into rain. It's always cooler on the water than it is on shore, especially if you are ocean cruising. Don't rely on everyone packing the correct clothing. Too often, I've had my kids or a guest show up in shorts and wish they had brought along a pair of jeans and a sweatshirt once we were on the water.

RAINWEAR

You and your basic crew members need to have sets of waterproof duds handy in the event of rain. A marine-quality set of foul-weather gear is costly, but super-protective in a downpour. Avoid blue or white outfits that will blend in with the water and make you difficult to find should you slip and fall overboard. The new fabrics aren't rubbery and are breathable. Waterproof alternatives are acceptable, as are any inexpensive rainwear set. In a pinch, plastic trash bags with an opening cut for a head will keep you somewhat dry.

At the minimum, everyone needs a waterproof jacket. Waterproof pants are nice to keep your bottom half dry on dinghy rides into shore. If you wear rainwear into shore or home, be sure it makes a return trip to the boat so it will be there whenever you need it. A sou'wester hat keeps water from dripping into collars, and rubber sea boots keep feet dry while offering traction—and they are good to wear for shoveling snow at home during the winter.

COOL-WEATHER WEAR

Be prepared for chilly or windy weather by keeping aboard lightweight hooded windbreakers, sweatshirts, sweaters. The popular fleece jackets are warm and will wick water, but will not protect against the wind. Foul weather jackets can do double duty to keep you warm and wind protected.

SUN-PROTECTIVE PRODUCTS

Why risk skin cancer? While the sun feels wonderful, too much of it can create health problems. With so many reflective surfaces on the water, it's easy to absorb more sun than you realize, even when it's overcast. In addition to lots of sun block, you will need sunglasses, hats, and sun-protective cover-ups.

FOOTWEAR

Many sneaker-style shoes have come on the market since the traditional loafer-style boat shoe. To prevent slipping on a slick deck, choose a shoe specific to boating. The rubberized sole is designed to grab and squeegee out water. Avoid having to try to remove black streaks from a fiberglass deck by sticking with white or light-colored soles. Although going barefoot or wearing flip flops is tempting, a shoe with toe protection prevents injury when you are active on deck.

FULFILL MEDICAL NEEDS

The first aid kit on your boat is the foundation of medical care for you and your crew. The longer you plan to be on the water, the more extensive the kit should be. Purchase a ready-made kit that suits your cruising needs or make up your own.

The typical kit contains packets filled with whatever you will need for a variety of minor emergencies, such as stings and slivers. Be sure it contains cold and hot compresses.

Review your kit at the start of each boating season and replace expired, rusty, or incomplete supplies. As you use items, it's important to replenish them so your kit remains complete. A handy item to add to your kit is a first aid booklet. Keep everything together.

In addition to your primary first aid kit, you will likely want to keep common items like aspirin and bandage strips handy. If you or any of your crew requires daily prescription drugs, I suggest keeping a small backup supply aboard in the event someone forgets to bring enough meds along to last the trip. See the Appendix for a listing of basic over-the-counter medical supplies.

If you have limited space or if the storage area you've chosen is prone to moisture, store medical supplies in a waterproof zippered bag that can be easily moved about, or buy pills in sealed packets.

KEEP CHILDREN AND PETS SAFE

If you will be traveling with small children or pets, avoid extra hauling on each visit by leaving aboard the items you will need to travel with them, and to contain, care for, and amuse them. If your dog, cat, bird, or pig is part of your family, leave aboard a cache of their things, as well as yours.

Enclose the perimeter of your boat with lifeline netting to prevent children and small animals from slipping overboard. Marine-grade netting is weather resistant and constructed of high-strength nylon meant to buffer a lot of weight. Check the netting's strength by pushing hard against it all around to be sure it can sustain the weight of small children flinging themselves against it.

Underway or at dock, use a harness with a tether to control an active child or pet's range of motion, and to keep him or her from falling into the water or moving to a perilous area of the boat.

This gear is common to a moving boat:

Jackline: a line or strap used to help keep a crew member on deck. Having one continuous jackline from stern to bow makes it easy and safe to stay clipped on when moving forward to the bow from the cockpit. Most often, jacklines are associated with deep ocean boating, but there no reason they can't be used to control the movements of a child.

Lee cloth: a canvas hammock or set of straps designed to prevent a person from falling out of his or her bunk on a boat when the boat is heeled over or bouncing about with the waves.

Lifeline: a wire or cable supported by stanchions that runs along the perimeter of the deck and is used to help restrain passengers.

Safety harness with tether: an assembly worn by a person to enable him or her to hook securely onto a lifeline or jackline when moving about the deck of a boat.

Not all boats will accommodate a portable crib. An alternative is to enclose a section of a berth using sturdy netting or canvas. Fasten it in place with snaps or ties, as you might a lee cloth. For pets, leave aboard a duplicate crate or soft carrier equipped with the animal's bed to give your pet a safe place to stay while the boat is in motion or while you are ashore.

You may need these items:

➢ A portable high chair with straps to hold a child in place

➢ Extra formula, canned baby or toddler food, pet food, and treats

➢ Diapers for children, litter box for cats, and doggie pee mats

➢ Life preservers sized and styled for small children and animals

➢ Special feeding apparatuses: bottles, baby spoons, pet feeding and water bowls. Choose nonspill styles

➢ Soft toys and amusements

GET READY TO HAUL

If you have had a boat for a while, I don't need to tell you that in addition to keeping it repaired and maintained, much of your time is spent hauling goods to and from the boat. The most hauling you will do is at the beginning and end of boat season. Once the boat is set with the basics, your loads will be less ponderous and will be limited to items needed to accommodate your activities aboard.

By the time you have finished gathering everything for your first real visit to the boat, it's common to think, "Crap, all this will never fit." This is why it's important to think through every single item you plan to stow aboard.

When preparing to pack an item, ask yourself these questions:

➢ Can we do without this item for the amount of time we will be on cruise?

➢ Does it have more than one use? Can that hard cooler do double duty as a seat?

> ➢ Is it practical? Do you really need that tuxedo or ball gown?

> ➢ Is it too large to fit anywhere? Avoid buying gargantuan sizes of anything, unless you plan to repack it into smaller containers.

PLAN STORAGE

Before you haul carloads of gear to the boat, survey its storage areas. Locate useable space by opening and investigating each locker, drawer, and cabinet on deck, in the cockpit, and inside the boat.

Determine the following:

> ➢ How accessible is each locker?

> ➢ Do you have to remove boards or cushions to get at it?

> ➢ How are you using each locker now?

> ➢ Will relocating items to different spaces make the area more useable?

> ➢ Is there a dry place to store tools so they will be accessible without unloading the locker to get to them? How about boat brushes and cleaning supplies?

Decide on the best place to store each kind of item. As a rule, items should be stored as close as possible to their place of use. Needless to say, food prep supplies should be in the galley or near it. Of course, bedding and personal duds should be stored in berths.

Use outdoor lockers for storing lines, fenders, boat brushes, buckets, snorkel gear, and the like. If you are storing a boat hook in a locker, can you relocate it outdoors where it will be handier? Will you string up fenders for docking on the stern or hide them in a locker?

FIND STORAGE

During your storage search, analyze each locker and any open or hidden areas to determine if it can be made more useable.

Here are some questions to consider:

> Is there any dead space that can be converted for use?

> Can you add a floor to support gear in oddly shaped lower lockers or in a dry bilge?

> Will ventilating a storage area that is prone to moisture make it dry enough to use?

> Can you add shelves to increase storage in upper cabinets?

> Can you make open shelving more practical by adding support bars to prevent items from flopping out?

STORE SMART

In addition to structural means of increasing storage, you can purchase household storage devices to help you increase the efficiency of open space, such as walls and cavernous lockers.

Try these suggestions:

> Use kitchen and bath organizers to divide and contain items within cabinets and drawers.

> String up mesh hammocks in berths and in the saloon to contain breads, paper goods, clothing, and other lightweight supplies.

> ➤ Folding plastic milk crates or flexible plastic boxes can be squished to fit the curves of lower lockers, as well as to keep items contained and off the bottom of storage areas.

> ➤ Mount hanging shoe organizers on walls or inside cupboards to stash small items.

> ➤ Use suction-backed holders, which adhere to odd spots and are easy to remove or relocate, to stabilize and hold supplies, like soap, toothpaste, and dish detergent.

> ➤ Find marine-grade Velcro fasteners sturdy enough to keep small appliances in place on a countertop or to mount items on walls.

> ➤ Squish plastic storage bags containing bulky items like extra blankets into under-the-berth lockers, which tend to be deep.

> ➤ Store large chart books under or behind cushions.

Once you get thinking, I'm sure you can come up with more storage ideas.

ORGANIZE GEAR

Sift through your past season's gear. If you dumped gear into bags and boxes when removing it from the boat, brought it home, and left the lot of it in your basement, don't bring that same load back to the boat without reorganizing it. Toss out rusty and nearly empty cans, check through tools for rust, and clean them up. Make a list of items needing to be replaced or added.

Once you have done this, survey the mountain of boat gear you surely have purchased in anticipation of boating season. Segregate items according to where they might be stored on the boat. The extra anchor, for example, goes with front deck supplies. For convenience, keep items of the same type, such as fenders, together. To reduce volume, remove and discard shipping boxes and extra wrappings, being sure to save packing slips and receipts.

PACKING TIPS

When we began boating, we kept our boat on a mooring. This meant all our gear needed to be transported to the boat by dinghy or, if we were lucky, by launch ride. Some days were clear and beautiful, but many times the dinghy was damp with water from a previous rainfall and needed to be pumped out. Sometimes we traveled in the rain. I learned then to pack in ways that would keep our gear dry and secure, and make it easy to manage.

Here are a few helpful hints:

> ➤ Hard, rectangular suitcases, especially with wheels, and hard-bodied coolers are unwieldy to store and may damage indoor flooring. Pack clothing and toiletries in soft, foldable duffel bags. Once the bags are empty, they can be hung and used to hold laundry or folded away.

> ➤ Instead of using plastic or paper grocery bags, pack boat supplies and nonperishable food and drinks in canvas totes. These totes are meant to hold weight, and the good ones are waterproof. (Originally these were used as ice bags.)

> ➤ Use coolers to transport perishable foods and drinks (like milk) to the boat. Traditional hard coolers will do the job, but I have found marine-grade soft-sided coolers are just as effective in keeping items cold and are much easier to handle and store aboard.

> ➤ Use plastic containers (sized and intended to be placed right into their storage space on the boat) to prepack supplies, such as boat maintenance materials, that need to go into a deck locker.

> ➤ Use plastic bags to pack and possibly store and protect spare sets of clothing, bedding, or unboxed boat gear. Trash bags work fine. I also save the zippered plastic bags from blanket purchases. They are sturdy, reusable, and will sit square when stored.

TRANSPORT GEAR

Once you are at the marina with all your gear, the problem of transporting everything from your car to your boat surfaces. If your boat is on a mooring, you have an extra step because these same items need to be first loaded into your dinghy or the marina launch.

Many marinas provide two-wheeled carts for customers to use to carry gear to a dinghy or boat slip. If you constantly find these carts are in use and not one is around when you need it, you might want to collaborate with a few boating friends to purchase a cart. Secure it for your collective use by chaining it to a fixed spot with a combo lock.

STOW GEAR

Once aboard, surrounded with piles of bags, boxes, and whatever, getting everything stowed can seem like a nightmare. If you planned ahead, you either packed sandwiches or picked up lunch on the way into the marina. In my experience everyone will be hungry at this point. If it is late in the day, before you get going unpacking I suggest getting the berths made up so you can flop into them once you are finished.

Assign designated places for everyone to store their clothing and gear or you may be tripping over it. If you must hang clothes in your lockers, use plastic hangers. Metal hangers, unless they're stainless steel, will eventually rust and ruin your clothes.

Divide and conquer. Don't let the family sneak away without being given an assignment. Many hands make light work. Each person can take personal gear to his or her assigned berth and stow it while you and your spouse tackle the community goods.

When unpacking food, take care of time- and heat-sensitive items first. If you've brought ice for the ice box, set that inside before unpacking the milk, cold cuts, and cheeses inside it. If you have refrigeration, has it been turned on? If not, keep spoilable foods tucked away in the cooler until the fridge is cold enough to accommodate them.

KEEP STOCKED

Once your boat is set up with the essentials for overnight cruising, it's easy to enhance and fine-tune your inventory of provisions and gear on each subsequent visit.

As the season progresses, take home unnecessary items to make room for those you really need. For example, in the spring and fall you'll need extra jackets, warm fleece sweats, cozy wool blankets, and quilts. As the summer heats up, you'll work up a sweat just looking at these things. Free that space for snorkel gear, swimsuits, and beach towels.

Make lists to manage your supplies. Each time you leave your boat to head for home, jot down a list of things you'll need to buy or bring for the next time. If you are the really organized type, create on your computer a master checklist of commonly used items and make several copies to keep on board. Fill one out each time you leave so your return list will be complete. List the necessities you already have on the boat so you won't duplicate them.

Create your shopping list from your inventory—be sure to include sizes and quantities—and replenish items that are low or depleted. By the end of the season, you will have established a packing pattern. Your boat will be perfectly equipped, and you will have figured out exactly what you need. This information will come in handy for the next season.

Part Three: Go Cruising

Congratulations! You have reached the exciting part of your journey into Marinaland. Consider this section as a supplement to all those boating classes you sat through, as well as a step-by-step guide to handling many of the conditions you may encounter while on cruise or at your destination. Now, get on that boat and let's go cruising!

CHAPTER 7

Navigation Smarts

One of the happiest days of the season is when the boat goes into the water (and the saddest is when it comes out). Now that you've done all the work and all the waiting, you can finally drive down to the dock, climb aboard, and get ready for your first cruise.

This chapter covers important information about how navigational markers and charts can help you reach your destination, how a shakedown cruise can prevent problems later, how to deal with other boats, and the safest way to navigate rivers, inlets, guts, constructed waterways, and bridges.

KNOW THE AIDS TO NAVIGATION

At one time the waters were open. Ships navigated by trial and error using sightings to determine landfall and the stars to determine direction and course. In the shipping era, it was common for island folks to wave torches and lure ships onto the rocks so they could steal their cargo. Once lighthouses began to go up, some of these scavengers were pretty angry.

The United States Aids to Navigation System, as we know it today, is designed to provide safe travel for all boaters by pointing out hazards and designating the best ways to navigate around them. If you haven't obtained a copy of *Navigation Rules (Rules of the Road)* from your boating class, buy a hard copy or download the booklet online (www.navcen.uscg.gov/?pageName=navRulesContent). By all means, read it, keep it handy, and obey the rules. Those you will encounter most frequently are covered in this section.

HEED MARKERS

It has been said that if you can navigate Long Island Sound, you can cruise anywhere because this strip of water has a sampling of almost any kind of marker and hazard you may encounter. In fact, the Long Island Sound chart is often used as a training aid for new boaters.

Buoys and beacons act as markers, which coordinate locations with area navigation charts. These markers include nuns, cans, lighthouses, bell buoys, gongs, whistles, channel markers, and radio beacons. Markers assist boaters in making a safe landfall, enable them to follow a channel, and provide a continuous chain of charted marks for plotting a course in coastal waters.

If you are new to boating, you will want to keep a chart handy of the various types of buoys and beacons and their purposes until you learn to recognize them by their color, shape, sound, and light pattern.

One of the more repeated, and important, rules of navigation has to do with knowing how best to approach a channel. As part of a boating course, the phrase *red right return* is drilled into our heads as a good way to remember on which side to pass red and green buoys when entering or leaving a harbor. So when entering a harbor or inlet, red is to starboard and green is to port. When departing a harbor or inlet, green is to starboard and red is to port.

Here's the catch. Keeping the red nun buoy to starboard when returning, or entering a channel or waterway, only works if you are truly *entering*. Confused signals can leave your boat on the rocks or aground. To avoid this, check your navigation chart to be sure what you perceive as an entrance isn't really a departure from one waterway to another.

FOLLOW THE RULES OF THE ROAD

Yes, I know you probably studied all this to receive your license to operate your boat, but now you have to actually put these rules into action. The rules of the road apply to everyone and are strictly enforced by the water cops, aka the USCG. These rules are meant to help commercial and recreational boaters travel the waters safely and comfortably. So, it's all good, right?

OBSERVE GOVERNMENT SECURITY AREAS

United States government-mandated security measures were put in place in conjunction with Homeland Security to protect our waters after the 9/11 attacks. If you notice any suspicious activities, report them to the coast guard. By all means, stay clear of mandated restricted areas.

If encountering the naval protection zone, operate at minimum speed within 500 yards of these vessels. If absolutely necessary, request permission to pass within zone limits by hailing the ship on channel 16 on your marine radio.

You also need to steer clear of military or United States commercial vessels, including cruise ships. These folks are serious. Venturing within the naval protection zone will earn you a loud bark over their radio loudspeaker. If you fail to depart immediately, your boat will be boarded and you may be fined for a felony, punishable by up to six years in prison and/or up to $250,000 in fines.

Heed warning signs regarding land-based military and petroleum facilities, as well as cruise line ports. You may also see restricted signs posted near dams, power plants, and the like. Getting too close is perceived as a threat and will earn you an immediate and severe warning.

USE YOUR MARINE RADIO

It's common for folks to feel uncomfortable when broadcasting over a marine radio for the first time. Don't let this keep you from relaying important information, such as spotting an abandoned boat or conveying a problem to the coast guard or nearby boats.

Boating classes teach you the importance of a marine radio and how and when to use it. In review, you should monitor VHF 16 at all times. Think of channel 16 as the 911 of boating.

These are commonly used VHF frequencies and their purposes:

> **Channel 16:** the primary hailing channel for emergencies, distress calls, safety alerts, and USCG Notice to Mariners, as well as the channel used to contact other boaters or shore facilities (before switching to another channel for conversation).
>
> **Channel 13:** the commercial channel used to reach bridge tenders and commercial ships.
>
> **Channel 9:** the supplementary calling channel for recreational boaters.
>
> **Open channels:** secondary contact points to reach marinas and other groups as well as being available for chitchat.
>
> **WX1 thru WX7:** used by the National Oceanic and Atmospheric Administration (NOAA) to report sea conditions for various areas.

When you are tuned into VHF 16, you will notice many of the hailing and response patterns are like those used with ham and CB radios. You may hear these expressions over the radio:

"Sniper, Sniper, come in please"

"Switch and answer channel x"

"Grey Goose standing by one six"

"Over" (when completing a statement or request)

"Out" (when ending a broadcast)

Beware of using your radio improperly. This means that the kids shouldn't be singing sea ditties over it, and you and yours should avoid tying up commercial channels with lengthy personal conversations.

These suggestions may save you a reprimand or fine from the coast guard, or a nasty call out from other boaters monitoring the primary channels:

➢ Call out MAYDAY only when lives are endangered. False maydays will earn you a reprimand and a fine from the coast guard.

➢ Save the words PAN-PAN for situations requiring coast guard attention, such as a man overboard, that cannot be resolved by those on board.

➢ Be prepared to communicate on VHF 13 whenever you are near a bridge or a large vessel, such as a barge, tanker, or dredger.

➢ Chat with your pals on an open noncommercial channel. When trying to reach other boats or shore points, after hailing them on channel 16, announce your switch to another channel for conversation.

➤ Radio checks are commonly heard on channel 16, but they are prohibited by the coast guard because the channel is reserved for a quick hail to another boat or shore point or for distress. Perform your radio check on channel 9 (or another working channel), or sign up for an automated radio service.

When you have finished using your radio, check to be sure you have not left your mike open. Its static will permeate the network and drive other boaters nuts until you realize your error.

KEEP CRUISING MATERIALS ABOARD

Whether you are cruising on a lake or an ocean, keep abreast of what to expect by having aboard a cache of necessary guides and books for reference.

CHARTS

Navigation charts are the road maps of the waters. Unless you are traveling with local knowledge, have on hand some sort of chart for every area you plan to cruise. Original paper charts have become outmoded and mostly taken over by digital versions designed to work with a GPS chart-plotting system. If you have this system, make arrangements to receive updated chips (or ones to cover new cruising areas) from your GPS provider—companies like C-MAP, Garmin, or Navionics.

As we all know, electronics have the potential to fail. In addition to digital devices, you should have paper charts handy. Many boaters find chart books more convenient to use than a large folding or rolled area chart, although large charts are great for plotting an extended cruise because you can view an entire area at a glance. If you have a choice, opt for water-resistant paper.

Electronic or paper charts are necessary to plotting courses from one destination to another. The information provided will help you locate and interpret navigation aids and determine the water depth at any given location. You can also reference your chart to find the best route around hazards. If using a paper chart, know when you begin finding markers missing or encounter uncharted buoys, it's time to buy a new chart. Stay up-to-date on changes to your sailing area by checking the USCG website. If you will be referencing or storing your paper chart in an area prone to moisture, use plastic protective covers.

CRUISING GUIDES

Cruising guides are available for almost every navigable harbor in the world and are provided by many sources. Use such guides to obtain general information about a given area as well as specific information about each harbor or waterway.

It's possible to find downloadable information online, but I suggest buying hard copy versions of these guides to keep aboard, and then referencing the Internet for updates on a particular destination. Find charts at any marine store or buy online. If you already own a guide, check the publication date to be sure you have reasonably current information. Nothing stays the same in the world of boats. Facilities rates change, radio call channels change, and marinas go in and out of business.

Reference a cruising guide to find the following information:

> Geographic and atmospheric detail about an area

> ➢ Suggested navigational approaches to an area or harbor

> ➢ Blowup charts and insets of harbors and photos of an area

> ➢ Information on bridges, canals, and other special circumstances

> ➢ Anchorage locations, holding ground descriptions, and comfort for overnight stays

> ➢ Marina locations with charts detailing slip and mooring availability, water depth, utilities, and amenities

> ➢ Contact numbers for dockmasters, towing and repair services, and shore facilities

> ➢ Shore attractions, dining and recreational activities, and historical information

TIDE AND CURRENT TABLES

The farther north your cruising area, the higher the tides and the greater the difference between high and low tide. High and low tides are caused by the gravitational forces between the earth and the moon. In most places, the tide rises and falls twice a day at six-hour intervals, reaching a maximum height called high tide on each rise and a minimum level called low tide on each fall. In the spring and fall and during a full moon, tidal differential is even greater. For example, Maine experiences a tidal span of 10 to 12 feet, whereas Florida and the Bahamas may see a 1 to 2 foot difference.

We boaters who cruise the Atlantic coastal waters reference the *Eldridge Tide and Pilot Book*. Updated annually, Eldridge tables give the time and height of high and low tides and the time and strength of the current for the entire East Coast.

I'll admit I am not familiar with an Eldridge equivalent for other areas, but I'm certain there are many. If you cannot locate one for your cruising area—and you feel you need one—simply doing an Internet search of tide tables will provide you updated information on almost any body of water worldwide.

KEEP A SHIP'S LOG

Buy a log book at any marine store or ask for one as a gift. You may also find a digital version you can keep updated via computer or tablet. Keeping a log of your travels will help you remember the cruising conditions, weather, and good or bad experiences you've had during your cruises to various destinations.

In this log, record mileage, time to destination, and return information such as the name and cell number of the dockmaster, the channel to use when calling pump-out service, and notes about restaurants and sights.

The value of such a log is retrieving the information. The next time you plan to return to a place, a glance at your log will refresh your memory about cruising conditions on the previous trip and provide a valuable first step in planning where and when to cruise.

PREPARE TO GO

Why risk being stranded mid-trip when the engine sputters, the gears stick in reverse or a through hull lets loose? Boats don't like to be dormant, even brand-new ones. Parts corrode, bolts loosen, and hoses crack. Before you load the family and gear into the boat and set off for a weekend on a beautiful island, take a short cruise to make certain all systems are working as they should.

For your cruise, be sure to let someone ashore know your cruising plan, follow the rules of the road, and practice safe and courteous boating.

Loved ones who are not traveling with you worry and emergencies may occur at home. Keep people informed about your whereabouts whenever you leave dock by telling someone where you are headed, when you will return, and how to reach you. If you will be traveling out of cell phone range, monitoring the VHF radio for a hail is particularly important.

Before departing, be sure to tend to these issues:

> ➢ Check the weather forecast to assure fair weather. Tune into NOAA weather service on your VHF radio and listen to the forecast for your cruising area, or consult online marine weather sites. If the seas are up, the wind is howling, or a storm is imminent, use common sense. Plan your cruise for a nicer day.

> ➢ Perform precruise testing. It's easiest to test your engine, inverter, generator, pressurized water, refrigeration, air-conditioning and heating, toilet facilities, and other systems at dock to be sure they are in good working order.

> ➢ Train your crew. People forget what they know about boating or need time to learn. Take the time to train or retrain your crew and to refresh your own knowledge of your boat's operation.

> ➢ Practice plotting by charting a course on paper or setting waypoints in your GPS.

➤ Test all your navigational equipment to be sure it is working as it should—we all know about software issues. Does your software need an upgrade? If you have autohelm, use it to be sure it doesn't require adjustment to maintain the correct course. A traditional dial-face compass can be off a few degrees. If your compass is off, check for an item made of metal that may be near its workings. If that is not the case, you will need to deviate your compass. This can be done by a professional, but we have been successful by simply motoring to an open area and making slow circles until our compass righted itself.

➤ Perform a radio check on your VHF marine radio to verify the range and be certain your hail can be heard.

Most likely, everything will work perfectly and you can begin planning a longer cruise without arranging for repairs. If issues should surface during the shakedown period, make note of them and then decide what you need to do to correct them.

AVOID COLLISIONS AND FINES

You are not alone. Yes, that's right. On the water you are no more alone and able to do as you please than if you were a car on a highway. As we discussed earlier, hard-and-fast rules are in place for commercial and military vessels. As a pleasure boater, much of your behavior when approaching and passing fellow boaters comes down to using good sense and common courtesy.

As you cruise, keep this information in the forefront of your mind in order to avoid collisions or fines.

➤ **Regulate your boat's speed.** You are responsible for your wake—and any damage it may cause. Operate your boat at a safe speed for your boating situation. Use caution when entering a harbor, channel, or any narrow waterway.

➤ **Pay attention to no-wake zones,** usually in channels and protected waterways. Typically, posted signs will designate a speed of 5 knots. If caught or reported, the USCG will find you and fine you.

➤ **Stay away from any boat larger than yours,** especially commercial vessels such as a tug with a tow, a barge, or a tanker. Hail commercial vessels on channel 13—or other boats on channel 16—to alert them to your presence and learn their intended course. It's always reassuring to know they see you. The larger a boat, the longer it takes for it to slow down or change course. You may have right-of-way because you are under sail, but even if the vessel spots you, there's no guarantee it can change course or slow down quickly enough to avoid colliding with you.

> **In foggy, rainy, or stormy conditions**, use radar (if you have it) to monitor the progress of other boats and obstacles, and sound your horn at regular intervals to maintain awareness of your presence. Boats with installed radar may be aware of you via your boat's radar reflector, but small fishing boats and the like may not spot you until you are close enough to shout at them.

> **Don't mix alcohol and drugs with boating.** Save your cocktails and other delights for times when you are at dock and not in charge of a moving vessel. On the water, mistakes in reaction time and clarity can cause collisions and even death. Keep your head clear and your mind sharp.

RESPECT RIGHT-OF-WAY

All boats are not created equal. On the water a pecking order exists defining which vessels and under what conditions you need to give leeway. These are listed by priority below:

1. Vessels under command such as tankers

2. Vessels having restricted maneuverability such as a boat under tow or a tug hauling a barge

3. Deep draft boats (sailboats) when they are navigating shallow waters

4. Boats under sail

5. Boats under power

CROSS PATHS WITH OTHER BOATS

As mentioned earlier, give any sizeable vessel wide berth, especially those under tow or with restricted maneuverability. Watch for fishing boats that move about erratically as they drop or pull anchor to circle about for a new location. Small boats may not show up on radar or even respond to a hail. At night or when visibility is limited, encountering small boats could be your worst nightmare.

Avoid a potential collision by following these steps:

1. Track the movement of surrounding boats on radar or by sight using binoculars if needed to determine if you will cross them by continuing course. If a boat continues to remain in the same position relative to yours, you are headed for a collision.

2. Altering your course by 5 degrees to port or starboard should take you out of harm's way.

3. If you are uncertain as to a boat's course in relation to yours, hail it on your radio. State your position and course—and slow down.

An example of what you could say if you have to hail a boat to determine its position in relation to yours, is, "This is the sailing vessel *Stinger* latitude 41 minutes 2 seconds, longitude 71.3 minutes 4 seconds traveling a course of 275 degrees calling the powerboat in Block Island Sound. I have you in sight. What are your intentions?"

If you receive no reply, and it is a commercial vessel—a barge, tanker—repeat the hail on channel 13. If you still get no reply, remain at slow speed, continuing to watch the boat's movements until you can figure out its direction. Whatever you do, steer clear.

HOW TO PASS A BOAT

If you feel there is enough room for you to pass a slower boat, crank back your speed so as not to cause a wake. In shallow or narrow passages, a wake will stir up the waters, making them shallower. This can cause a boat with any sort of keel to go aground.

Issue a warning by hailing the boat over your VHF radio or sounding your horn. Next, communicate that you plan to pass on its port or starboard side. Be aware that commercial boats and some recreational boats use horn signals to indicate how they plan to overtake a vessel. One whistle means the approaching boat will pass on the port side; two whistles mean the approaching boat will pass to starboard of your boat.

If a boat makes it clear it wishes to pass you, resist the temptation to speed up. Instead, throttle back your engine to idle so the approaching boat can pass you without having to speed up and create a wake that could impact you as well as other boats in that area of the water.

BEWARE OF BOATS UNDER SAIL

Boats under sail are considered to have restricted maneuverability because steering ability is limited by the wind strength and direction as well as by the current. The law of the sea says sailboats have the right-of-way—and they do unless they are running their engine.

Keep in mind these cautions:

> ➤ Sailboats rely on the wind for steerage. In a crossing situation, pass well behind them or to their lee side so as not to block their wind.

> ➤ Don't speed past and throw a wake. This can send a sailboat off course or aground.

> ➤ Can the sailboat crew see you? Understand that a heeled-over sailboat has limited visibility. Passing within the helmsman's blind spot can cause a collision.

> ➤ In a highly trafficked area or narrow passage, if you absolutely can't get out of a sailing vessel's path, sound your horn or hail the helmsman and pray.

NEGOTIATE NARROW PASSAGES

Traffic in a narrow passage can get rush-hour nasty as all manner of boats vie to pass through rivers, inlets, guts, and other channeled waterways. In such places, high tides flood the area with additional water, increasing the speed at which the water flows through, creating current. Wave height and wind velocity and direction also affect the height and strength of the waves.

When the seas are up, expect any narrow strip of water to become a maelstrom of steep chop as extra water fights to pass through. The smart boater plans to pass through any narrow or current-driven waterway with the tide or at slack tide to avoid beating against opposing current and seas.

Heed these cautions when navigating any narrow passage:

> ➤ Watch for swimmers, canoes, kayaks, dinghies, and small sailing boats apt to be meandering about and unaware of your approach.

> ➤ Space is tight. Some boats require more room than others to pass through. Whenever possible, give wide berth to boats larger than yours or those with limited maneuverability.

➢ If sailing is permitted, please don't take this opportunity to tack through the passage and become a nemesis to other boaters who just want to power through.

NEGOTIATE A CANAL

Canals are man-made waterways that connect two bodies of water—lakes, rivers, oceans—in much the same way a bridge might connect two shore points. These shortcuts were originally built as shipping channels to simplify travel and reduce the amount of time at sea.

You are apt to find canals anywhere, even within city networks. You've heard of the Suez, Erie, and Panama Canals. These are the most famous. In the northeast United States, we have the Cape Cod Canal, which connects Buzzards Bay to Cape Cod Bay and was built in the late 1600s to simplify travel between New York and Boston.

Follow these suggestions when negotiating a canal:

Heed the tide. If negotiating a canal is on your boating agenda, read up on it in your cruising guide and consult tide tables in *Eldridge* or your go-to tide reference to determine the optimum time to negotiate it. This is particularly important if your hull speed does not exceed the speed of the current. For example, if your maximum hull speed is 5 knots and the opposing current is 5 knots you are apt to be in that canal until the tide changes.

Monitor VHF 13. Traffic through the canal is monitored by the marine control station at the entrance. Canals are open to commercial as well as recreational boats, so you could find yourself trying to overtake a barge or slammed with wake by a speeding powerboat. Stay tuned to channel 13 on your VHF for alerts and to report problems.

DEAL WITH A CANAL LOCK

As you plot the course to your destination on your navigation chart or GPS, you may come across a notation about a lock, which should include the dimensions of its holding chamber. If you will encounter a lock, research further. Check for larger scale insets. Read about it in your cruising guide. Information in your guide should familiarize you with details about the size and approach required for a particular lock.

Locks can be simple or complex, depending on where they are located. You may encounter a lock on a lake, as we did on Lake Mendoza in Wisconsin, or need to negotiate through a more complex one, such as the lock at the Panama Canal.

When passing through a lock, follow these steps:

1. Watch for the posted arrival sign about .25 miles before the lock.

2. Contact the lock operator or channel 13 (or whatever channel is indicated in your guide) and state your wish to pass through. If you get no response, sound two long and two short blasts with your horn and wait for acknowledgement.

3. Prepare lines and fenders for docking or mooring as instructed by the lock operator.

4. Listen or watch for a horn or light indication that the lock is ready to receive vessels.

5. Enter the lock slowly but with enough power to maintain steerageway and with your crew in position to manage docking.

6. Select a docking point, pull in, and then tie off with enough slack to afford time to move about and reset the lines as the water level changes.

7. Wait for the operator's signal to exit the chamber. Keep to the marked channel.

Your lock passage is complete once you pass the arrival point marker for incoming traffic.

TIPS FOR NAVIGATING BRIDGES

Bridges serve land transportation by providing cars and trucks a means of traveling across the water. Be prepared to encounter fixed bridges or drawbridges wherever there is a body of water.

Keep the following information in mind as you proceed:

➢ There is always current around bridges, so don't crowd other boats passing through.

➢ Boats traveling with the current have the right-of-way, as does any boat much larger than yours.

➢ If you've a low-riding boat, lower nonstructural items such as antennas to avoid clinking and losing them as you pass through.

➢ The tallest part of the bridge, barring a construction defect, is at the very center. Aim your bow toward the dangling line that marks this spot.

> Check overhead clearance, especially if yours is a tall-masted boat. Watch for a set of tide boards marked with numbers—65, 64, 63, 62, and down—flanking the bridge entry. These numbers denote the distance between the water and the underside of the bridge, given the current tide conditions. Binoculars may come in handy. Numbers rub off or gather sea crud so they are not always legible.

> As you near the entry, don't freak out when it appears you are going to scrape along the underside of the bridge. If you have predetermined your boat has sufficient clearance, you'll be fine.

> Never cut your engine under a bridge or drop your anchor there, no matter how foul the weather. This is a dangerous practice. If caught, you will be boarded by officials and fined.

DRAWBRIDGES

Some drawbridges open on demand; others at scheduled times. Contact the bridge tender on channel 13 to advise him or her of your approach and to request an opening or verify the next opening time.

Once you are inside the half-mile mark, the tender should acknowledge you and hold the bridge. Keep communications flowing so he or she knows you are doing your best to get there in time.

A bridge tender may decide to delay or extend a scheduled opening in order to balance car and boat traffic, or to accommodate a convoy of approaching boats. If a bridge has an unscheduled opening, you may be able to sneak though.

Should you miss a bridge, there's little to do except pirouette outside it until the next opening. This means paying constant attention to the current flow, the shallow surrounding areas, and the other waiting boats that pile up around you.

TRAVEL CHALLENGING WATERS

If you are a daredevil looking for bragging rights and own or want to crew on a boat that doesn't require constant refueling (like a powerboat), feisty waters await you. Mother Nature is hard to beat. Those who win the man-against-sea battle surely have earned their stripes.

Throughout the United States and its contiguous waters, there are known bodies of water containing areas that require respect and due diligence to travel. The ones with which I am most familiar are on the east coast of the Atlantic Ocean.

THE GULF STREAM

The Gulf Stream is a huge, constantly moving and changing "river" of warm water that runs along the Atlantic Coast on its eastern side. It originates in the Gulf of Mexico (thus the name Gulf Stream), exits through the Straits of Florida, and follows the eastern coastline of the United States and Newfoundland. The area between the Northeast United States and Bermuda is the widest part of the stream and a challenge for many sailors. If you are traveling in East Coast Florida waters, you will not be far outside one of its inlets before you encounter the Gulf Stream.

BAY OF FUNDY

Another challenging cruising area, also on the Atlantic Coast, is The Bay of Fundy in Nova Scotia. This unique body of water is infamous for having some of the highest tides in the world. We're talking at least a 50-foot differential between high and low tide, so you might imagine the issues that can occur when the water "disappears." These tides, combined with an irregular sea floor, result in whirlpools, turbulence, and large swells.

AVOID POTS

Now we go from he-man challenges to avoiding the lowly fish or lobster trap, known by boaters as pots. Anglers and lobstermen lay these out in chains, often in and around channels and the mouths of inlets, rivers, and other traveled waterways. Be especially wary of pots toggled together or in a grouping attached to a net in a fish trap area, which may be marked on your navigation chart.

While these bobbers poking out of the water attached to fish, crab, or lobster traps are hardly dangerous, snagging one in your propeller can stop your boat cold until you manage to untangle it. This could mean diving in with a knife to cut the line, doing some fancy gear work to release it, or having your boat hauled and in the hands of professionals. Stealing a catch from the pots is a criminal offense.

CHAPTER 8

Weather Watch

Your boat is in great operating condition, and now you have a good sense about how to navigate safely and courteously in most situations. All this will ensure travel, but let's not neglect the major element that could turn your trip from a pleasant cruise to a disaster—the weather. When boating on any sizeable body of water, it's important to keep abreast of weather changes, know how to use barometric pressure and radar to avoid bad weather, learn what signs in nature you should heed, and understand how to deal with fog, squalls, and hurricanes.

CHECK THE WEATHER

Don't judge the weather by your surroundings. You may have already noticed that weather varies from place to place. It could be pouring rain at your home, yet ten miles down the road it's just overcast. And by the time you reach the marina, the sun is trying to peek through, making you glad you didn't cancel your plans after all. Likewise, if you are on the water tucked into a sheltered cove or marina, there's no guarantee you won't emerge from the area and find yourselves bucking heavy seas and winds.

To avoid surprises, tap into as many forecasting resources as you can before departing your safe haven, then go with your best guess. As we all know, even when using the latest technology, meteorologists don't always get it right. Mother Nature is fickle and conditions can change in a flash, often with minimal advance warning.

For normal lake cruising, weather reports from your local radio station should be sufficient. However, if you plan to cruise one of the Great Lakes or the coastal waters of the ocean, it's important to consult marine forecasts. The best overall source is the National Oceanic and Atmospheric Administration (NOAA). Tune into the local weather channel on your VHF radio for its latest predictions. Online, in additional to the NOAA website, Buoy Weather at http://www.buoyweather.com provides forecasting for any marine waters worldwide. Reference any weather applications you have downloaded to your smartphone or computer. Get any of the NOAA apps.

For an extended trip, find out in advance what weather conditions you can expect at any given point by hiring a weather routing service. For a reasonable cost, you can have the weather for your trip faxed to you in advance, which allows you to change routes or reschedule to avoid problems, and to receive updates en route—either by fax, phone, or online log-in.

If your ocean voyage includes navigating the Gulf Stream, be sure to consult Jennifer Clark's Gulfstream website (http://users.erols.com/gulfstrm/) for the most reliable weather and sea predictions. Jennifer Clark is a highly respected Gulf Stream guru who has spent the past forty years studying, analyzing, and forecasting the world's ocean currents. Her site includes links to other stream-related sites.

IS IT WISE TO LEAVE?

Once you have accumulated weather information, as captain it's up to you to decide whether to set off. Understand that you are responsible for the safety of your crew. Too many times I have seen captains depart the dock in fog, rain, heavy winds, and when a storm is forecasted. This is especially true when they are anxious to get home to meet scheduled responsibilities on shore or at work, or are working around the schedules of crew members. Whether you are a small craft or not, know that when NOAA issues an advisory, it's a sure thing you will endure heavy winds and seas.

Set aside your macho and use common sense. Mother Nature is stronger than you are. She will beat down on you with all her might and threaten your safety— and your crew will say never again. If all signs point to weather problems, settle in at dock, go sightseeing, or drive home with plans to go cruising another time.

WATCH BAROMETRIC PRESSURE

Common knowledge is high pressure systems mean blue skies and sunshine, whereas low pressure systems predict rain or worse. Barometers have been a weather-predicting resource for centuries, and for the most part they are accurate. By tracking changes in barometric pressure you can be your own weather forecaster.

Chances are you already own a barometer. (If not, get thee to the marine store and buy one.) It makes no difference if a barometer is a showpiece, brass-plated model with a dial, or a modern style with digital readout. Both provide the same information to help you predict changes in weather patterns that are apt to affect your travels.

Learn these important facts to decipher your barometer readout and predict the type of weather you may encounter while you are on cruise:

> Decreasing barometric pressure indicates storms, rain, and windy weather.

➢ Rising barometric pressure indicates good, dry, and colder weather.

➢ A slow, regular, and moderate fall in pressure indicates a low-pressure area is passing in a nearby region. Marked changes in the weather where you are located are unlikely.

➢ A small, rapid decrease in pressure indicates a change in weather near you, usually followed by a brief spell of wind and showers.

➢ A quick drop in pressure over a short time means you can expect a storm in five to six hours.

➢ A large, slow, and sustained decrease in pressure is a precursor to a long period of poor weather. This weather will be more severe if the pressure had been rising before it began to drop.

➢ A rapid rise in pressure during fair weather and average or above-average pressure means a low-pressure cell is approaching. The pressure will soon decrease, forecasting poorer weather.

➢ When low pressure quickly rises, a short period of fair weather is likely.

➢ A large, slow, and sustained rise in pressure means a long period of good weather is on its way.

CONSULT RADAR

I realize every one of you may not have installed a radar system, but if you have radar, use it. While a radar system's main function is to spot obstacles and report their position relative to a fixed object (your boat) via a blip on the radar screen, a side benefit is you can use it to spot masses of precipitation and track their progress.

Radar (radio detecting and ranging) transmits microwaves in a focused beam. Some of this microwave energy bounces off objects and returns to the radar to be measured. The radar sends pulses of energy, rather than a continuous signal, and it measures how far away an object was when the microwaves reflected off it. Combined with the radar's ability to scan up, down, and in a circle in all directions, modern radars can measure the three-dimensional distribution of precipitation within 100 miles of the radar.

Precipitation shows up as a blob, which is colored differently (ours is blue) than land masses and the like. Once you notice precipitation headed your way, you can evade it by delaying departure or changing course, or you can prepare to deal with it.

READ NATURE

It's common for us to sense changes in the weather. You may look at the clouds, the color of the sky, feel a change in the wind or humidity, and intuitively know what to expect. But sometimes, nature gives us tangible clues.

UNDERSTAND THE SKIES

Clouds are formed from water that evaporates from oceans, lakes, and rivers. When warm, moist air rises, it expands and cools, creating humidity. The presence of high, puffy clouds usually means the air is dry and air pressure is high. Horizontal, flat clouds are a sign of rain. Lowering clouds means moisture is collecting and it may rain, whereas rising clouds signify clearing. The darker the cloud, the greater the chance of rain. Clouds that appear clumpy and wispy, like fish scales (mackerel sky) or a horse's tail (mare's tail) often precede a storm.

The adage is true: Red sky at night, sailors' delight. Red sky in morning, sailors take warning. The red color is caused by light refracting off dust particles in the air, which indicates a lack of moisture. When the sun goes down in the west, turning the sky red, dry weather is approaching. A red sky at sunrise means dry weather has moved away and moisture is in the air. If the sky is gray to the west, it means rain is coming; to the east, it has likely passed.

Is there a rainbow? If the wind is coming from the direction of the rainbow, the rain is heading toward you. Conversely, if the rainbow is in the opposite direction, it has passed you. When the sun is in the east in the morning, and the shower and associated rainbow are in the west, it's going to rain.

A halo around the moon or sun is caused by high cirrostratus (ice crystal) clouds that signal the approach of a warm front and is a sign that rain will fall within twenty to twenty-four hours. The US Weather Service confirms that rain follows about 75 percent of sun halos and about 65 percent of moon halos.

NOTE WIND SHIFTS

Change in wind strength and direction is easy to determine because you can actually feel it. Your hair will blow wildly about or lay flat, and your skin may sting from it. Anything that flaps, such as the flag on the stern of your boat or the telltales (strips of yarn or ribbon) on a sail, will give you clues about the direction and strength of the wind. If you have one installed, a wind gauge or a wind direction finder will verify what you may already know.

When you tune into the weather channel on your VHF radio or other such device, you may hear mention of the Beaufort scale. Devised back in the 1800s, this scale was originally used to gauge the effects of wind on ships at sea. The Beaufort scale classifies wind from Force 0 (calm, at less than 1 mph) to Force 12 (hurricane, at 74 mph or greater). Categories 1 through 11 include light air, five levels of breeze, four levels of gale, and storm-force winds.

Wind is air in motion moving horizontally at any velocity along the earth's surface. It is created when warm air expands, becoming less dense (thus lighter), and rises, and then is replaced by colder, denser (heavier) air. These differences in temperature create local breezes and global winds. The larger the area, the more heat or cold air it will hold and sustain. Coastal cities near the ocean are warmer or cooler than those inland, depending on the season and time of day.

CHECK THE WATER

Choppy white water indicates a rapid shift or increase in the prevailing wind conditions. An increasing swell plus advancing storm clouds mean an approaching low with a large area of strong winds.

UNDERSTAND FOG

While heavy rain can certainly deteriorate visibility, nearly anywhere there is a temperature difference between the air and the water, rain is often combined with fog, often referred to as pea soup. If you live in the northeast United States, like I do, you know what fog is. Fog can occur almost any time of year on lakes and rivers, as well as on oceans. Due to great differences in water and air temperatures, you won't see much of it in the south or the tropics, but you will be plagued with it in northernmost areas. It also occurs in places where humidity in the air is high enough to form condensation.

When you listen to the weather channel on your VHF radio, NOAA will state the visibility in certain areas. For example, 100-foot visibility means if another boat is 100 feet from you, you will not see it. You will hear descriptions like "dense fog" or "patchy fog." They may predict the fog will burn off or remain for a certain period of time (as when accompanied by a low-pressure system), as well as the areas fog is located. Use this information to rethink your destination or the course to your destination, plan your departure time, or reschedule your cruise.

If you are in port and can't see past the end of the dock, I highly recommend delaying or canceling departure until the fog lifts. Fog can vary from a light haze due to humidity in the air, to a total whiteout-type situation. Not only will fog impact visibility, but it will muffle sound and magnify obstacles.

The denser the fog, the lower your chances of detecting the presence of another boat, a buoy, or a land mass. It's as if the sky dropped a white sheet over everything, except the small circle of water surrounding you and your boat. Although you may feel alone, you're probably not. When a buoy or another boat looms up in front of you, seemingly out of nowhere, it's scary.

NAVIGATE IN FOG

No one wants to encounter fog, but there are situations where it can't be avoided. Navigating in fog requires sharp eyes and quick reflexes.

If you are underway and fog rolls in or you run into an area of fog, follow these ten steps:

1. Reduce your speed.

2. Turn on your navigation lights to increase your boat's visibility to other boats.

3. If you have radar, monitor it for the presence of other boats or obstacles, and track any movement that could result in a collision.

4. Assign a crew member with sharp eyesight to keep watch.

5. Stay at the helm. Steer manually and be prepared to switch direction if an unexpected boat or object looms up out of the fog.

6. Keep to a course using each marker to verify your exact position relative to your destination.

7. Compare the designated water depth on your navigation chart with your actual depth as shown on your instruments to verify your location as you move along. If you are in 12 feet of water when the chart states you should be in 50 feet, you are way off course.

8. Sound an air horn or the horn on your boat at regular intervals to alert others to your presence.

9. Pray the fog lifts soon.

HOW WEATHER FRONTS CAUSE CHANGE

Weather changes begin with what we call a front, which is the boundary between a cold and a warm air mass. The air masses do not mix but move with respect to each other, resulting in a change of weather conditions at a particular location.

Fronts can be warm or cold, but in either case they mean a weather change is on the way. As a rule, warm fronts bring good weather, whereas cold fronts signal rain. Some parts of the country, like the northeast United States, can experience several weather changes in a single day.

You may encounter one of these types of fronts:

Cold front: An oncoming cold air mass pushes under a warm air mass and forces it upward. This causes a drop in barometric pressure and signals a line of approaching rain. Cold fronts generally move from northwest to southeast. The air behind a cold front is colder and drier than the air ahead of it.

Warm front: A warm air mass approaches and overrides a cold air mass. Light rain, snow, or sleet (depending on the climate) may occur before and as the front passes. Behind the front, expect clearing skies and warmer temperatures.

Stationary front: This occurs when a front slows down with little or no forward movement. Once it resumes motion as a warm or cold front, expect a temperature change or a wind shift as it crosses from one side of a stationary front to the other.

Occluded front: This kind of front may be warm or cold. In either case, the front has defined vertical boundaries between the coldest air, the cool air, and the warm air, which results in air pressure changes and winds typical of storms. In most cases, storms begin to weaken after a frontal occlusion occurs.

COPE WITH STORMS

There are various types of storms, and none of them are fun to be caught in while on cruise. Sure, a passing rain shower may be uncomfortable, and you may get wet, but it isn't threatening until the winds pipe up, thunder rolls, and bolts of lightning streak from the sky.

Thunderstorms are common in tropical areas or during summertime, when the air is warm and humid. The radiant heat from the land absorbs moisture from nearby water and rises to produce thunderheads. A cold front may be preceded by squall lines, or a row of black storm clouds. Wind shifts unpredictably and accelerates. Lightning can occur for miles in front of a storm and after the storm appears to have passed.

When a storm is brewing, barometric pressure drops. Clouds drop lower, and fair-weather clouds (cumulus) develop vertically and become thunderheads. The temperature drops and winds and seas will surge.

PROTECT AGAINST LIGHTNING

Lightning is a brilliant electric spark discharge in the atmosphere, occurring within or between clouds or between clouds and the ground. A lightning strike can blow out your electronics, blast a hole through your hull, or electrocute anyone in its way. Water is a natural conductor of electricity.

Since water is all around us when we are on cruise, it's easy to panic when it storms. If it's any consolation, marine insurance statistics have shown that the odds of a boat being struck by lightning in a year are 1.2 to 1,000. Of the boats struck, what we don't know is how many had no lightning protection.

Lightning protection equipment may have been included when you purchased your boat. If you aren't sure, have your boat checked out by a marine service person and, if need be, get an estimate on having it installed. Really. It's important. I've had boats of two friends struck by lightning. Fortunately, they were not aboard and had insurance coverage for such an event. In both cases, all electronics, and most of the boat systems needed to be replaced.

To lightning protect a mast, a grounded, low-conductivity cable equipped with lightning arresters (usually made of copper) is installed to divert the lightning away by providing a cone of protection twice the radius of the height of the mast, thus diffusing the lightning. Proportionately, the mast needs to be high enough to protect the entire surface of your boat. All metal on the boat should be interconnected (bonded) and grounded by a professional.

> *lightning arrester = a device used in preventing damage to radio, telephone, or other electrical equipment.*
>
> *lightning rod = a rodlike metal conductor installed to divert lightning away from a structure by providing a direct path to the ground.*
>
> *surge protector = a small device to protect a computer, telephone, or other electrical device from damage by high-voltage electrical surges.*

WHAT TO DO IN A LIGHTNING STORM

If the sky is alight with jagged bolts, protect yourselves and your boat as best you can until the storm is over. Keep within a protected area in the center of the cabin or low in the boat, depending on the design of your boat. If your hair stands on end and your body tingles, lie flat on the floor. This is the first warning of a strike or flash. Don't dangle arms and legs in the water.

Disconnect and then do not touch or use major electronic equipment, including the radio, throughout the storm. Avoid making simultaneous contact with any two components of any portion of the boat that are connected to the lightning protection system.

If your boat has been hit by lightning, or you suspect it has, the extent of any damage caused may not be obvious. Once you have checked the electrical system and compasses, consider having the boat hauled to have the hull inspected to be sure the point at which the lightning exited is not cracked or damaged in any way. Even a tiny crack can create a leak that could ultimately sink your boat.

If a crewmember is struck and disabled, call for assistance using your VHF radio. Know that there is no danger in touching a person who has been struck by lightning. Increase his or her chances of survival with immediate medical care, artificial respiration, or CPR.

HOW TO HANDLE A RAINSTORM

It's Sunday and you need to cruise home because you have to work tomorrow, the kids have school, and your spouse has a dentist appointment. It's raining and the sky looks black; NOAA predicts the weather will deteriorate as the day progresses. You make a decision to leave early to miss the worst of it. Heck, in two hours, you could be in the car driving home.

So you head out. The seas are rougher than you expected, but you push on anyway. As you progress, the weather worsens, but you are an hour from home and it's too late to turn back.

The first thing you should do is reduce speed and proceed with caution to the nearest safe harbor, where you will be in the lee of the storm.

In the interim, take these steps to secure boat and crew:

1. Point your bow to the wind.
2. Take waves at a 40- to 45-degree angle.
3. Don personal flotation devices (PFDs).
4. Close all hatches and ports.
5. Secure any loose items that could be tossed about.
6. If lightning is expected, lower or remove and tie down the radio antennas and any protruding devices not part of the lightning protection system of your boat.

AVOID SQUALLS

A squall is a burst of violent weather accompanied by intense winds. Many kinds of squalls occur over various places on Earth. Some are the result of unique local conditions and do not occur elsewhere; others emerge from normal weather processes. You may encounter these basic types of squalls:

Rain squall: This is usually part of a line of thunderstorms forming along or in advance of a cold front. The winds increase quickly, churning up the waters and usually bringing heavy rain. A squall may last ten minutes or half an hour but should be taken as a warning sign that more such weather is on the way.

White squall: You may have heard the term *white squall* or read about one in an old sea story. The name refers to the color of the waves caused by a sudden increase in wind velocity in tropical and subtropical waters. White squalls are common on the Great Lakes of North America. This kind of storm sneaks up on you because there are no black clouds, typical of rain squalls, to warn you of its approach. Some say a white squall and a microburst are the same.

Microburst: This is a sudden and intense downdraft within a severe thunderstorm that produces powerful winds. Unlike a tornado, the winds in a microburst travel downward and outward and do not rotate. It lasts between five and fifteen minutes with winds of more than 100 mph causing significant damage.

WHAT TO DO IN A SQUALL

When the wind shifts 180 degrees and wind speed builds from a pleasant breeze to chilling proportions, you are likely going to be slammed with a squall. This happens so quickly that there often isn't time to get to safety.

If you are under sail, drop and secure all sails and close all hatches. If possible, turn on the engine. Proceed at slow speed, steering bow to the wind and at a 45 degree angle to the waves. Use autohelm if you have it. Have anyone who is not essential to the operation of the boat hunker down in the central, most protected area of the boat until the storm has passed.

PROTECT AGAINST DANGEROUS STORMS

Everyone wants to run for cover when a hurricane is on the way. If your boat is in the water at such time as a hurricane, cyclone, or tropical storm is predicted, take all precautions to protect it (and you) from damage.

Hurricanes and cyclones are cut from the same cloth. Both are circular storms carrying great winds. A hurricane travels counterclockwise; a cyclone, clockwise. On the North Atlantic coast, hurricane season begins in June and ends in November. Storms brew in the Caribbean and head north, hopefully losing intensity and veering away from land.

A serious storm is named and its progress is monitored closely by weather experts. These storms may pick up strength or lose it, head for land or out to sea. As always, predictions are anyone's best guess.

force = the strength of a particular hurricane to do damage.

hurricane = a storm having 74 mph winds or greater.

tropical depression = a storm with less than 35 mph winds.

tropical storm = 35 to 73 mph winds.

PAY ATTENTION TO WIND STRENGTH

Once winds for an approaching storm are predicted to be greater than 74 mph, the storm is classified by the National Hurricane Center using the Saffir-Simpson Hurricane Wind Scale. Do not confuse this with the Beaufort scale, which deals with winds less than 74 mph. The categories on the Saffir-Simpson Hurricane Wind Scale are specific to hurricanes and factor in the degree of damage expected by the wind forces indicated. A Category Five Hurricane will inflict the most damage, for example.

> **Category 1 hurricane:** sustained winds of 74 to 95 mph (64 to 82 knots or 119 to 153 kilometers per hour).

> **Category 2 hurricane:** sustained winds of 96 to 110 mph (83 to 95 knots or 154 to 177 kilometers per hour).

> **Category 3 hurricane:** sustained winds of 111 to 129 mph (96 to 112 knots or 178 to 208 kilometers per hour).

> **Category 4 hurricane:** sustained winds of 130 to 156 mph (113 to 136 knots or 209 to 251 kilometers per hour).

> **Category 5 hurricane:** sustained winds greater than 156 mph (136 knots or 251 kilometers per hour).

WHAT IF A HURRICANE IS PREDICTED?

Regardless of what you have heard or may think, a boat is safest from harm on land. A boat, battened down and securely tied to a dock slip can be pushed up and over the dock in a storm surge. On a mooring or at anchor, lines can chafe and break and the mooring ball or anchor may lift with underwater surges affecting the seabed and send a boat careening with the wind into the nearest obstacles.

If you're thinking of riding out a storm in your boat, I suggest you get your head examined. The boat can be replaced; you cannot. Be smart: do your best to protect your boat, then go home.

Understand the difference between a watch and a warning:

Hurricane watch: You could experience hurricane conditions within thirty-six hours.

Hurricane warning: Expect sustained winds of at least 74 mph within twenty-four hours.

In the event of an approaching hurricane, here are some measures you should take:

> ➢ Check your insurance coverage. Some policies cover the cost of having the boat hauled in case of a watch, whereas others will pay only if there is a warning. Be aware, too, that if a hurricane is downgraded to a tropical depression, it is no longer a category storm. Insurance coverage for haul-out based on hurricane warnings or watches may no longer apply.

> ➢ Relocate the boat. Have it hauled or move it to a protected harbor.

> ➢ At dock, point the bow of the boat toward the direction of the storm. Set spring lines in a weblike pattern, allowing enough slack for the boat to move vertically.

> ➢ Guard against flooding. Empty and clear the bilge of debris to ensure the bilge pump works. Close all seacocks.

- ➤ Seal hatches, ports, windows, lockers, and vents with duct tape, and cover glass windows to prevent shattering.

- ➤ Reinforce dock and mooring lines; double up lines, add chafing gear in spots where lines may fray.

- ➤ Remove or tie down anything that can rip, act as a sail, or shake loose, including canvas and frames for biminis and dodgers, exposed electronics, radar antennas, dinghy engines, barbecue grills, and beach chairs.

- ➤ Take home portable electronics, boat documents, and yourselves.

STAY CLEAR OF WATERSPOUTS

A waterspout is the marine counterpart of a tornado and is most frequent in the tropics. A funnel-shaped tail forms under a cloud and grows downward toward the sea. If it fails to dissipate before it hits the water, expect major turbulence and sea spray as it strikes. Needless to say, if you spot one in the distance, stay clear.

Fair-weather waterspouts: These typically form when cold air moves over a warm body of water. Although they connect to the cloud base, like a tornado, they are usually weak but can still cause damage.

Tornadic waterspouts: These form from supercell thunderstorms, another fine reason not to be on the water in a storm.

PART FOUR: GO CRUISING

This is the good part: the time when you and your family (or pals) can get out on that water and enjoy using your boat. In this section we'll cover everything from planning your cruise to arriving at your destination and having fun.

We're off!

CHAPTER 9

Plan Your Cruise

The boat is in perfect shape, and the weather is looking good. Where will you go? What will you do? Why, plan your cruise, of course. Opt for the kind that you and your crew will enjoy without breaking your budget, then learn how to figure out the cruising time to a destination, and how to decide if a particular harbor or marina is right for you.

CONFIGURE YOUR TRIP

If you are planning a simple overnighter, cruise planning is pretty much a no-brainer. Pack up your provisions and your crew and go when there is a good two-day weather forecast. Weekend cruises take a bit more planning, but likely you'll head for no more than two destinations. The real planning occurs when you decide to take a longer, multistop cruise. Most folks schedule this around their annual summer vacation, which may be one week or even two or more.

When putting together your itinerary, consider these suggestions:

> ➤ Divide your trip into manageable legs. Don't overextend. If you travel for eight hours one day, make the next day's cruise a short one.

> ➤ Allow a blend of quiet and natural with the bustle of more commercial harbors.

> Plan to be at your farthest destination halfway through the trip so your return leg can be just as enjoyable.

> Factor in layover time to avoid battling bad weather to get home.

INVOLVE THE FAMILY

If you will be traveling solo, you only have to consider your personal needs and wishes. Perhaps you need time away from it all or have plans to visit friends who live near various boating destinations. This doesn't let you off the hook for planning, mind you. The procedure is the same. Most likely, though, your cruise includes others such as your family or a group of friends. This complicates matters. To set departure and return dates for the cruise and to make the trip enjoyable for all aboard, have a talk with each of your crew members.

DETERMINE TIME CONSTRAINTS

What will your crew members need to give up to go on this cruise, and how willing are they to do so? Say you have a week off from work, and it happens to coincide with your spouse's work schedule, what about the kids—or your friends? Will your son miss playing the final baseball game in his team's tournament? Will your daughter miss her best friend's birthday party? Will your wife miss her sister's wedding? You get the drift.

Think compromise. How important is that particular activity to that person? If you carry these individuals off so they miss a special event, will they hate you forever? Likely not, but know if you can't agree on a middle-of-the-road solution, sulky kids and an upset spouse can make that vacation of yours pretty unpleasant.

What Do They Want to Do?

This should be an easy question, but sometimes answers can surprise you. You may plan to veg out and enjoy being parked in what I call a cook-aboard harbor reading the latest Baldacci thriller, but what about your wife? This is her vacation, too. Is she looking forward to dining out, shopping, and sightseeing in new places? Is your son into fishing and water sports? Is your daughter whining because she wants to bring a friend?

Again, compromise. You can likely please everyone, including yourself. There's no reason why you can't hang out on the boat while your husband or wife takes the kids into shore or to the beach or vice versa. Maybe you don't want to be responsible for taking along another child, but if you think hard, you might find a way to have your daughter in contact with other girls her age while on cruise. Talk to your boating friends. Maybe you can travel together or meet up with them so the kids can get together.

Set Departure and Return Dates

Once you have settled on a schedule, pencil in the dates on your calendar with an eye to the long-term weather forecast. The beauty of boating is nothing is cast in stone. The various ports of call are not going to go anywhere. If you don't get there on this trip, there's always the next one to look forward to.

If you plan to depart Friday night and the weather is miserable, why not enjoy the night on board in comfort rather than subject yourselves to a nasty trip? By the next morning, when the sun is shining, it will be a much more pleasant day—and what have you really lost? You've enjoyed your boat and your family.

To relieve the stress of having to return in foggy or stormy weather, factor in one or two layover days. Plan to arrive home a day in advance if the weather looks iffy for your drop-dead return day.

If your cruise includes several stops, take the time to figure out how long it will take, given the average hull speed of your boat, to reach each location, then add an extra hour or so for unexpected sea conditions. A sailboat beating into the wind and traveling against current travels at a slower than normal speed; and a powerboat experiences drag and requires more speed, thus more fuel, to power through such conditions.

PLAN EXPENSES

The budget never goes away, even on vacation when you wish you had Monopoly money to spend. Anchoring in a pretty cove and barbecuing dinner is less costly than staying at a slip in a touristy area. But don't be a cheapskate. The best trips are a mix of both.

Take a poll of your crew members and do your best to make it fun for everyone (you want them to like the boat and being on it). Don't make Mom cook every night; it's her vacation, too. And no matter how you try to avoid it, there will always be a place to shop, whether it's to buy a T-shirt or an expensive piece of jewelry.

Cruising is so much more than plugging into a dock slip and exploring the shore. There's no need to break the bank trying to show your crew a great time. On a boat, you can pick and choose how you want to spend your money. Consider your primary expenses, and if you freak out at the number, look for places to cut back without sacrificing pleasure. Needless to say, once your boat is equipped with fishing gear, kayaks, and fun water toys, you can easily keep your family entertained without spending an additional dime.

Your primary costs will be for fuel, dockage, provisions, shore transportation, restaurant meals, and shore activities. Try these suggestions for controlling costs without sacrificing fun:

> ➢ Save on fuel. While a sailboat may get by with a few fill-ups a season, a powerboat may require refueling at each destination. If your boat is a fuel hog, limit the distance you travel. Save fuel by motoring at a slower speed, traveling with the tide or currents, and by setting a course where you will not need to deal with wind resistance. And don't forget fuel for the dinghy. While it may cost a pittance compared to a tankful on your primary boat, if you've children who are dinghy crazy, you could easily be filling up that tank a lot—unless you've taught them to row.

> ➢ Don't skimp on provisions. Keep aboard plenty of beverages. If you keep your boat stocked with nonperishables such as boxed and canned goods, you'll only need to replenish fresh foods for each trip—meats, vegetables, milk, cheeses. As we all know, crap happens. Your refrigerator could go bust or you may not make it to your destination for that restaurant meal and you'll be darn glad you had a can of chili aboard.

➤ Anchoring is free in most places. With a properly set hook, your boat will be as secure as if it were on a mooring. Obtaining a slip or a mooring will have its price. In a fancy harbor like Newport, Rhode Island, slips are pricy, and even a mooring will cost you plenty. There may be restrictions on how long you must stay, and usually a reservation is needed in advance of your trip.

➤ Save on shore transportation. If you are on anchor or on a mooring, your dinghy will be your primary means of reaching shore. Some marinas offer launch service, which can save you a dinghy ride in foggy or stormy weather. This service may be included with a mooring or charged on a per-trip/per-passenger basis. If you have chosen a location with not much on shore, you may need to hire a cab or rent a car to get groceries, reach a restaurant, or attend a local event. Some marinas loan out courtesy cars for short jaunts, which is very nice, or offer shuttle service into town.

➤ Balance the dine-in/dine-out situation. No one wants to be on vacation and have to worry about providing three meals a day for the entire trip. It's always nice not only to be served, but to pick choices from a menu—someone else's—and to have the dirty dishes whisked away, never to be seen again. Give the cook a break—order pizza or Chinese food. If you have lunch in town, you won't mind dining aboard that night. During your trip, try to hit at least one nice restaurant so your cook will feel appreciated.

> ➤ Find free shore activities. Depending on where you go and the activities available, you could be paying for tickets to an amusement park, a movie, or a tour. If you have four people, this could add up. Before you depart, check out websites for the local tourist bureau or visitors' center for a wealth of information about special events, activities, and sightseeing in the area.

CHART YOUR COURSE

Suppose you are making three stops in the course of a week's vacation. First stop, a quiet cove; next stop, a charming seaside village; last stop, a busy shore town. Instead of guessing the amount of time it will take to reach each stop, be exact. That trip your boating buddy says takes three hours, in reality may take six hours. You need to know this information, and so does your crew, for planning provisions and making dockage reservations.

Chart a course to each stop. This may mean adding waypoints into your GPS or drawing lines on a paper chart. Either way, your goal is to determine the distance you must travel to reach a particular harbor, and if you can make it in a single day without angst.

A GPS should give you mileage and time to the destination based on a conservative estimate of your boat speed. On a paper chart, the distance in nautical miles for many of the legs of your journey may already be marked. If it's not, measure and record the distance from marker to marker using the scale on the chart and a protractor. Add all the measurements to arrive at total distance. Don't forget to include the mileage from the harbor entrance to the marina, especially if it is a long channel.

Next, do this mathematical calculation:

travel hours = nautical miles per hour /average boat speed

Take the number of miles you have arrived at and divide by your average boat speed. For example, if a sailboat's average speed is 5 knots and it needs to travel 20 miles, it will take about 4 hours to get there.

Once you have arrived at an average travel time, pad it. For a day trip, factor in an extra hour or two to compensate for delays caused by sea and wind conditions. If you calculate four hours, plan for five. If you come up with twelve hours or more, decide if you want to travel after dark or tuck in overnight elsewhere and reach your final destination the next day.

STUDY YOUR CRUISING GUIDE

Once you have determined a general float plan, get specific. Using the cruising guide for the area, look up details about each location. If you are lake cruising and no hard copy or web information is available, ask fellow boaters and take notes about the various harbors you plan to visit. Various publishers present their guides differently, but there is common information you should find within.

DETERMINE THE HARBOR LAYOUT

The maps and insets contained within a cruising guide aren't supposed to be used for navigation, but they are a great help in providing an overview of an area as well as a view of harbor entry, which shows depths, markers, and anchoring areas.

A harbor may have no marinas or it may have a collection of them. Some cruising guides might indicate the locations of marinas by numbering them and marking anchorages with an anchor symbol. Each numbered marina could then correspond to a chart of facilities and services. Photographs of the harbor are often included.

EXPLORE APPROACHES

Read the entire section on navigation and mark it with a sticky note to review again once you are approaching a particular harbor. This section tells you exactly how to approach and enter the harbor using course coordinates, markers, and landmarks. The information could save you from overrunning an underwater hazard or going aground. Here, you will also find information on any bridges or locks associated with a harbor.

FIND OUT IF A HARBOR SUPPORTS ANCHORING

Anchoring detail may be separate or included in the navigation section for that harbor. Not all anchorages are comfortable for overnight stays or have good holding ground. Depending on its location, an anchorage may be protected or exposed to seas and prevailing winds. Moorings are often located within an anchorage. It follows that whether you are on anchor or on a mooring, you will experience the same wind and sea conditions.

DETERMINE IF A MARINA CAN ACCOMMODATE YOUR BOAT

The listing corresponding to the marina numbered on the chart provides valuable information about the number of slips and moorings available for rent to transient boaters, and whether the facilities are available year-round or just seasonally.

Review the sections on the largest vessel a marina can accommodate and the dockside depth at mean low water

(MLW), which is the average height of all low waters recorded at a given place over a nineteen-year period.

If a marina doesn't have a slip large enough for a boat greater than 40 feet, and your baby is 45 feet, you can cross that one off as a no. The same goes for deep-keeled boats. With a 6-foot keel, 3 feet of water at dock will not work.

If you belong to a yacht club that has exchange privileges with other clubs, your membership will allow you to reserve or secure a slip or mooring at participating clubs. Yacht club facilities won't be listed in your guide, but their locations and phone numbers will be. Call for availability of a slip or mooring for your size boat.

LEARN ABOUT SERVICES AND AMENITIES

Services vary among marinas; larger marinas usually have the most offerings. Your guide will tell you which marinas have fuel docks, the brand of fuel, and whether they have gas, diesel, or both. Note also which marinas have a service center for repair and a lift capable of handling your boat in case you have boat problems that can't wait until you return home.

Whether a marina has a dockside pump-out station will be listed as well. But you can also ask the dockmaster if there is a traveling pump-out boat servicing the area.

Dockside power is listed by voltage accepted and maximum amps. If you plan to plug in, be sure the marina can accommodate your boat's electrical requirements and that you have the correct size power cord and connectors aboard. Water is usually available dockside or at the fuel dock, except in harbors with no facilities at all.

Does the marina have shower facilities, a launch service, a marine store, an on-premises restaurant? Is it close to a grocery store? Your cruising guide will tell you about favorite restaurants, seasonal events, historical sites, and more. Read through the see and do section for a preview of activities.

NOTE EMERGENCY INFO

Many guides contain a listing of shoreside and emergency services with call numbers for medical help, fire, and police, as well as for taxis, trains, and buses. When traveling away from home, it's always smart to know where to call if you need assistance in a flash. Marinas should provide you this kind of information at check-in. In deserted harbors, though, it pays to have a number on hand to call if you need help. Find information online or call the visitor or tourist center for the nearest town to that area.

GET RESERVATION DATA

The marina guide provides contact information for each numbered marina and yacht club, and the hailing channel for the VHF radio, which may be different from the usual channel 16.

Be sure to make a reservation for a slip if you want one. The dockmaster will want to know the length and beam of your boat as well as the depth of your keel in order to place you in a sufficient slip. Some places have minimum stay limits of two or more nights. If you don't show up, you will be charged for the slip or mooring. If plans change, call as soon as you know and adjust your stay accordingly. You will hold the slip or mooring with a charge card number.

WRITE A FLOAT PLAN

By this time, you should have a good idea of when and where you will go, how long you will stay at a particular harbor, what you can expect when you get there, and what day you will return.

Write up a float plan detailing your planned itinerary and reach numbers. As a safety net, add in the telephone numbers of the marinas where you plan to stay in case your cell phone signal is weak, so you can be contacted in case of a home emergency. Keep a copy for yourself, and give one to someone at home.

Before you depart, let your home port marina know how long you will be away and your expected return date. It's common to rent out empty slips and moorings to transient boaters. It's no fun to return home to find another boat occupying your spot.

PACK FOR YOUR CRUISE

Begin by counting the days you will be gone and then checking to be sure you and your crew have enough changes of clothes (especially underwear) to accommodate everyone for any and all potential conditions.

Will it be warm enough for swimming? Is it supposed to rain? Do you have enough warm or weather-tough clothes for you and your crew? By checking the weather at your marina, at the area where you will be sailing, and at your destination in advance of your trip, and knowing what items are already on your boat, you'll have a good sense of what to pack. Prepare for the unexpected.

What are your plans? Do you need grungy clothes for cleaning and fixing up the boat? Are you cooking aboard, or will you be dining at a local restaurant? If you are planning to go into shore, know the dress code. In New England, upscale ports such as Newport, Edgartown on Martha's Vineyard, or Nantucket require nicer attire than beachy Block Island.

PERSONAL PACKING

Everyone's packing style is unique. If possible, allot each person his or her own bag. A large or extra-large duffel bag will normally suffice for a weekend. If there are laundry facilities at your stopover ports and you don't mind giving up sightseeing time to babysit a load of wash, you may be able to bring fewer clothes and pack lighter.

Stick to knits or fabrics that dry quickly, pack without undue wrinkling, and can be rolled or folded easily into a duffel. Don't forget hats, sunglasses, sun-protective shirts and pants, and swimwear.

Bring along personal gear for staying connected online and for amusement—books, iPads, laptops, cell phones, and games.

PLAN FLEXI MENUS

With the variety of stops and potential for change, it can be a challenge to figure out how much and what kinds of food to bring along. Unless you have a reliable freezer or refrigeration system, perishable foods like milk and meats can easily go bad sooner than you may imagine.

Here are a few tips:

➢ Begin a trip by stocking a minimum of enough fresh food to last until you reach the first harbor, where you can restock provisions.

➢ Keep it simple. Plan meals requiring little preparation and using as few ingredients (and cooking pots) as possible. Choose versatile foods that can be cooked and served several ways. If it's pouring rain or too blustery to dare grill off the stern, can that piece of chicken, fish, or steak be prepared in your galley? If plans change and you decide to dine off the boat, can those shrimp keep another day?

➤ Have ice on hand. Blocks will keep longer than cubes and can save your food if your refrigeration goes kaput. Extend the refrigerator lives of meats and fish you will not use immediately by bringing them to the boat in a frozen state.

CHAPTER 10

Anchors Aweigh

Finally, it's vacation time. You've planned your cruise, checked the weather, and the boat is good to go. Let's get you off the dock and moving. This chapter covers the procedure for departing port, how to keep your crew safe from harm, how to avoid and treat seasickness and sunstroke, tips on managing laundry and trash, and what to do if you go aground or are sinking.

PREPARE TO DEPART

When preparing to leave port, pay attention to boat and crew to ensure you will be safe and comfortable while underway. Stow loose items that are apt to go flying. If you will be cruising for four hours or more, prepack lunch and healthy snacks to avoid having to dig out supplies and prepare food while bouncing about. Make certain that children under twelve and roving pets are wearing their PFDs. If you have not done so already, enter waypoints into your GPS. Now, slather on the sun block and don your hat and sunglasses.

While underway, it's a good idea to keep these items nearby:

- ➢ Charts
- ➢ Cruising guide bookmarked for your destination(s)
- ➢ Binoculars

➢ Air horn (if you don't have a built-in horn on your boat)

➢ Bottled water and soft drinks

➢ Seasickness preventive medications

➢ Cell phone (as backup to the VHF radio to reach a dockmaster when heading into port)

ASSIGN TASKS

You do not have to do everything yourself. Involve as many of your crew members who are willing and able to perform tasks associated with departing and entering port. Older children will feel useful if you give them a job to do. Young children like to watch and be part of the action.

Crew members always enjoy learning how to participate. Teach one or more crewmembers, depending on age and ability, how to control the helm, coil and throw lines, and how and where to set up fenders. Show everyone where everything needs to be stowed, how to pick up or drop a mooring, and the best way to assist with anchoring. On a sailboat, it's always nice to have help adjusting the sails and controlling the winches.

PREARRANGE HAND SIGNALS

Trying to communicate between the helm and other deck areas of the boat is always a problem, especially if the wind is blowing the wrong way. While walkie-talkies can solve this problem, people tend to forget to take them along. In my experience, establishing simple hand signals are the easiest method of bow-to-helm communication when steering through a dicey area, docking, mooring, and anchoring.

These are common hand signals:

Stop: Hold one hand palm out or cross your arms.

172

Slow down: Move one hand up and down in a vertical wave pattern.

Steer to port: Point one finger to the left.

Steer to starboard: Point one finger to the right.

Everything's okay: Thumbs up.

It didn't work: Thumbs down.

We're screwed, or #$%@#&*: Middle finger up.

SET OFF

It's time to head out. If you will be steering into a busy channel from a slip's fairway (the open water between opposing docks at a marina) or an anchorage, be sure to toot your horn to warn other boats of your approach. The ease of your departure will vary. Read over the necessary processes I've detailed in the sections below.

DROP A MOORING

One of the advantages of being on a mooring is that freeing your boat is very simple. Have a crew member go forward and drop the mooring line from the bow cleat. If you have attached your own line, remove it, coil it, and stow it. Steer out into the channel.

PULL ANCHOR

When it's time to depart, the anchor needs to be pulled from its ground onto the deck, where it will be stowed until needed once more. For a smooth departure, follow these steps:

1. You or a crew member goes forward and determines the location of the anchor by pulling up on the rode.

2. The person at the bow indicates the direction of the anchor, while the person steering slowly motors toward it.

3. The person at the bow takes up the slack line as the boat nears the anchor. The rode can be hauled aboard manually, hand over hand, or by coiling it onto a winch. Winches may be manual or electric.

4. Once the anchor is free and dangling off the bow, the helmsman steers the boat into the channel while the person on the bow locks the anchor in position and performs deck cleanup and stowing tasks.

DEPART A SLIP

Departing a slip is more complicated than simply dropping a mooring line or pulling tackle. The experienced boater performs these tasks:

1. Tend to the dinghy. The dinghy should be in the water, snubbed up to the stern with its two painters (or bow lines) tied bridle-style onto the port and starboard stern cleats. If you have docked stern in, tie the dinghy to a bow cleat (leaving some slack) until you make the turn out of the slip.

2. Disconnect shore power. On your boat's electrical panel, turn off shore power. Next, flip the power switch to *off* at your dock connection. Unplug the cord at both ends. Coil and stow aboard.

3. Disconnect your water hose. Coil and stow aboard.

4. Turn on all instruments, including GPS. Start the engine in neutral.

5. Remove lines from dock cleats. One person should remain at the helm, while another tends to the lines. Remove the slackest lines first, leaving a final taut line to hold the boat in place. Once the final line is dropped, the crew member needs to make a quick leap onto the boat, unless there is someone on the dock assisting. Remove all loose lines from deck. Coil and stow.

6. Pull out of the slip, checking for traffic.

7. Have a crew member tend to the dinghy. Play out each painter so that it extends far enough behind your stern to be clear of any engines and is less apt to bounce high and flip over when your boat hits its highest speed. Retie painters to stern cleats. If the dinghy is forward, have a crew member untie the lines and "walk" it to the stern, where it will be retied in the manner described above.

8. Coil and stow loose dock lines. Remove and stow fenders.

SAFETY UNDERWAY

Safety is always of utmost importance. Once you are on the water, sailing or motoring along, keep in mind that you are in control of a moving vehicle. Listen to and watch the area surrounding you for unexpected or uncharted obstacles such as a fish pot that could tangle in your propeller, a tug towing a barge, or an oncoming or crossing boat hidden by your sails.

When someone is moving about belowdecks, in the galley preparing food or using the head, don't decide to tack your sailboat, shift to high speed, or make sharp turns. If you can't avoid making such changes, be sure to call out a warning.

SET RULES

Lay down a few laws to keep crew members safe from injury or from falling overboard. Accidents happen all too fast. It's much easier to prevent them than to deal with the results. No matter what style boat you own, at any given moment you are apt to encounter erratic movement—the jolt from a passing boat's wake, a wind gust, or bouncing waves. The noise from the engine or the surf could block the splash of a person slipping or being thrown overboard.

My husband and I insist crew and guests follow these cautions when they are aboard, especially when we are underway:

> - Should an adult want to go on the upper deck to lie out or just sit, send him or her with a floatable boat cushion.

> - Don't allow children to go out of the cockpit to the upper deck without an adult accompanying them.

> - No running on deck or belowdecks.

> - Wear boat shoes on deck to prevent stubbed toes or slipping.

> - Wear sailing gloves when handling lines on a sailboat to prevent painful rope burn.

> - Proceed on the upper deck using one hand to hold onto the boat to prevent going overboard, in case the boat lurches.

> - When belowdecks, while the boat is in motion, move about as little as possible using handholds to prevent falling or injury.

> - No dangling legs over the side. This dangerous action could send someone overboard and in harm's way of the propeller.

> - Discourage men from urinating off the back of the boat while the boat is moving. While convenient, statistics shows this practice is a major cause of deaths on the water.

PREPARE FOR SEASICKNESS

Seasickness, also called motion sickness, is a condition in which a difference exists between visual perception and the body system's sense of motion. For many, seasickness is a side effect of cruising. In my experience, anyone can become seasick under the wrong conditions. Seasickness can be brought on or escalated by movement, fuel or food odors, sun and heat exposure, lack of air, or eating spicy or rich foods.

People exhibit seasickness in ways other than nausea. Watch for pale skin, glazed eyes, and unusual quietness. Does the person refuse food or turn up his or her nose at a smell? If the person is yawning, appears lethargic, or complains of a headache, he or she could be seasick.

PREVENTIVE MEDICATIONS

Over-the-counter and prescription medications, such as Dramamine, Bonine, or the scopolamine patch, take several hours to work. Most will stay effective for twelve to twenty-four hours; the patch keeps its effectiveness until it is removed. If a person expects to be affected by motion, he or she should take seasickness medication at bedtime in preparation for an early morning departure, or upon waking when preparing for a later departure.

In addition to medications, have aboard a selection of these noninvasive products to prevent and ease seasickness symptoms. You can find these at a marine store, boat show, pharmacy, or online:

>**Acupressure bands**: Also called sea cuffs or sea bands, these are adjustable wrist bands with a small plastic bubble that puts pressure on a certain spot on the inside of the wrist and often inhibit or ease nausea. The bands are inexpensive and can be purchased at a marine store or in a pharmacy (found with the stomach treatment medications). Many people find slipping on a pair of cuffs eases or prevents seasickness. When our grandchildren cruise with us, I offer them these colorful "bracelets" to wear before we depart. Believe me; doing so has saved many a mess.

>**Relief Band**: A more costly and intrusive version of the sea band, this wristlet is worn like a watch. It works by providing tiny electrical pulses to the wrist.

>**Motioneaze**: This product is a blend of natural oils meant to be dabbed behind the ear to quell seasickness symptoms.

Quease Ease: This is an inhaler imbued with essential oils said to alleviate the effects of seasickness.

Ginger: About 1/4 teaspoon of ginger in any form will alleviate nausea. Keep ginger ale, ginger cookies, candied ginger, ginger candies, ginger tea, or ginger tablets on hand.

Soft drinks: Carbonated drinks such as Coke and Sprite can prevent feelings of queasiness and mild seasickness.

WAYS TO HELP

If you notice one or more of your crew exhibiting signs of seasickness, such as actively vomiting or appearing pale and listless, here are some ways you or another crew member can help the person feel better:

> ➤ Offer plain crackers to absorb stomach acid.

> ➤ Have the person stare at a fixed spot on land or at the horizon.

> ➤ Hand over the helm to take the person's focus away from his or her symptoms. I don't suggest this if the person is actively vomiting, listless, or sleepy.

> ➤ Suggest the person lie down, eyes closed and in an airy environment to stabilize his or her body and to shut off the visual portion of the motion.

> ➤ Keep the person on deck, if possible, and exposed to the breeze. Often, the worst possible place for someone who is seasick is belowdecks, where the brain can't reconcile the motion of the inner ear with what is happening visually.

> ➤ Find the person a spot amidships, where the boat's movement is calmest.

> ➤ If you expect someone is going to vomit, position him or her near the rail on the leeward (downwind) side of the boat, or provide a plastic bag. Be kind. Offer damp washcloths, water, or whatever the person seems to need.

> ➤ Do not under any circumstances describe personal bouts of seasickness or wave smelly foods under a seasick person's nose.

AVOID SUNSTROKE

On the water, it's easy to forget the power of the sun. You are surrounded by reflective surfaces—the shiny white fiberglass, plastic or glass windows, and water. Cloud cover magnifies the intensity of the sun's rays and can result in a bad sunburn or worse. Not to be confused with sunburn, sunstroke is a form of heat exhaustion resulting from overexposure to the sun, especially when the heat is accompanied by high humidity. The body relies on the production of sweat to stay cool in warm temperatures. When sweating under a hot sun fails to cool the body, its temperature can rise rapidly, and sunstroke symptoms quickly develop.

Keep life-threatening sunstroke at bay by protecting yourselves:

Stay hydrated: To avoid going belowdecks to reach the head, people often refuse to take in enough liquids. This can lead to dehydration, a main cause of sunstroke. Insist all aboard drink a lot of fluids, even if they claim they aren't thirsty. Understand that caffeinated and alcoholic beverages are diuretics and can exacerbate dehydration.

Avoid overexertion: I don't expect you and your crew will be running about the boat while underway, unless you are involved in a high-tension sailboat race. Nevertheless, overexercising in hot, humid weather can lead to fast dehydration.

Embrace sun protection: It's common to want to enjoy the sunshine, but too much of a good thing spells trouble. Protect yourselves by putting up a bimini in an open cockpit and wearing sun-protective clothing. This is especially important for anyone taking a medication that causes sun sensitivity.

RECOGNIZE AND TREAT SUNSTROKE

While sunstroke is not common, it does occur—and it shouldn't be ignored. When the body overheats, the brain and internal organs can literally fry, causing death or permanent injury. Treat this as a medical emergency and get professional medical help immediately by contacting the coast guard on VHF channel 16. Possibly, a doctor cruising nearby will hear your hail for assistance and swing over to help. While waiting for help, offer hydrating fluids with electrolytes and do whatever you can to cool down the person's body.

A person exhibiting these symptoms may be experiencing sunstroke:

> ➤ Headache
>
> ➤ Muscle cramps
>
> ➤ Dizziness
>
> ➤ Hot, dry, or flushed skin
>
> ➤ High body temperature
>
> ➤ Lack of sweating
>
> ➤ Rapid pulse

> ➤ Rapid breathing
> ➤ Disorientation

DEAL WITH TRASH

During your cruise, you'll be discarding items like used paper plates, cans, and bottles. The longer you are on the water, the more garbage you will accumulate. Contain trash in plastic bags, separated for recycling once you reach shore facilities. If you will be traveling several days before you can get rid of your garbage, stuff bags in a deck locker or put them in the dinghy—but never throw them overboard.

Never toss anything overboard that is made of plastic or its derivatives, such as Styrofoam. Paper, glass, and metal will ultimately disintegrate, but plastic will never break down. Before tossing anything overboard, check the USCG chart for mileage-from-shore restrictions for each kind of item.

While it's okay to toss most food garbage overboard, beware of doing so when you are within sight of land or in an anchorage or mooring field. Food attracts large fish, which could present a danger for swimmers and snorkelers.

Never pump the contents of your head overboard unless you are offshore and past the 3-mile limit.

HEED THE USCG DUMPING LAWS

It is illegal for any vessel to dump plastic trash anywhere in the US oceans' navigable waters. Annex V of the MARPOL Treaty is an international law for a cleaner, safer marine environment. Violations of this law may result in a penalty up to $25,000, a fine, and imprisonment.

Coast guard regulations require boaters to visibly mount a plaque that cites these dumping rules:

Within 3 miles of shore: it is illegal to dump plastic, garbage, paper, metal, rags, crockery, glass, dunnage, and food. This applies to all US lakes, rivers, bays, and sounds.

3 to 12 miles from shore: it is illegal to dump plastic, dunnage, and packing materials that float. Paper, crockery, rags, metal, glass, and food may be dumped if ground to 1 inch or less.

12 to 25 miles from shore: it is illegal to dump plastic, dunnage, and lining and packing materials that float.

Beyond 25 miles from shore: it is illegal to dump plastic.

State and local regulations may further restrict the disposal of garbage.

HANDLE LAUNDRY

Reduce the amount of laundry by drying wet shower towels and reusing them. Whenever possible opt for donning a swimsuit to cut down on dirty underwear, shorts, and shirts. Swim suits can be rinsed and hung to dry overnight.

Keep once-worn or laundry-ready clothing separated from clean clothes. This is especially important if you are cruising on salt water. The salt in the air sticks to clothing, leaving it gummy and damp feeling to the touch, and it will taint surrounding items. To prevent the formation of mold, allow damp or wet clothes, towels, and such to dry completely before putting them in an enclosed laundry bag or locker.

GET FUEL

Fuel docks offer gasoline and diesel fuel, and are also equipped with a watering hose to rinse fuel off boats or for water tank fill-ups. If you are at your home port, it's easy enough to pick up fuel at the nearest dock. If you are cruising, check the area waterway information for locations of fuel stations.

You may find these tips on obtaining fuel helpful:

> ➤ When approaching the fuel dock, having a person at the bow with docking lines ready is a signal to the attendant that you will be coming in for fuel. If there appears to be no one at the fuel dock, toot your horn, hail the attendant on the VHF radio, or call on the cell phone to alert the attendant to your presence.

> ➤ If the fuel dock is full, you will have to circle outside and wait your turn. If several boats are waiting, it's smart to communicate your wish to fuel to the attendant via a hail on the radio to be put in order the list.

> ➤ Once you have secured a spot at the fuel dock, take care of business and depart right away to leave the space open for other boats needing to refuel.

> ➤ When fueling, keep paper toweling or absorbent pads handy to catch spills from going overboard and leaving a gas slick on the water.

> ➤ If you are on cruise and need to run a few errands or even wash down your boat, instead of usurping valuable space at the fuel dock, ask to be assigned a temporary slip for a few hours.

YOUR BOAT IS STUCK!

You know you are in trouble when the boat stops with a sudden jerk. Every boater runs aground at least once. Sometimes it's due to inattention, but often it can't be helped. Not all shallow areas or submerged hazards are marked by a danger buoy.

If you are aground, stop the boat immediately. If motoring, put the engine in neutral. With an inboard/outboard vessel, lift the outdrive and shift the weight away from the impact point. If under sail, drop the sails.

Find out if anyone is hurt, and then assess your surroundings. Are you close to shore and near assistance, in a desolate area, or in the path of heavy boat traffic? Check your chart to determine the depth of the water around you. If you are not in immediate danger, set the anchor using the dinghy.

Anchoring will help keep the boat from being driven further aground.

Will you need help? If it seems you are on your own, and you have determined setting the boat free will cause no further damage, hail a towing service or contact the harbor master for assistance.

SOFT AGROUND

If you're stuck in sand or mud, you have hit soft. You are not in danger, and you likely can free your own boat. If the tide is dead low, you will be able to float off as it rises. This could take several hours. If you are in a highly trafficked area, your boat could become a hazard. Check the depth of the water around you to determine where deeper water lies. Look at your chart, or test the depth around your boat with a boat hook, a drop line, or by dinghy.

Try these moves to get free:

> ➤ If you are stuck on a small shoal in otherwise deeper water, try to motor off. Turn the helm sharply toward deeper water. If this doesn't do the trick, put the engine in idle to avoid digging your keel in further. If you are under sail, you probably can't sail off unless you barely touched bottom.

> ➤ If you were moving slowly when you grounded and hull damage is minimal, try backing off by shifting the weight farthest from the point of impact and using an oar or boat hook to push off. Do this carefully to avoid digging in further, sucking muck into the engine intake, or damaging your propellers or hull.

> ➤ Hail a passing powerboat and ask the captain to zip past throwing off a wake. The wave action may be enough to loosen your boat and set it free.

> ➤ Use your set anchor to kedge off by pulling or winching in on the anchor line attached to the anchor (or kedge) you have set. This action may jerk your boat free.

> ➤ Heel the boat by putting as much weight as possible on one side and causing the boat to rock from side to side. This action may break the boat free.

> ➤ Get towed off by a commercial service or a captain who knows what he or she is doing.

HARD AGROUND

If you hit hard or struck something and no one needs immediate medical attention, stay calm. You are not in danger of sinking if you are on a rocky shoal, where you and your crew can step off the boat.

Check for hull damage. The rocks you are on might be the only thing keeping your boat afloat. If the damage is serious, set out an anchor or two to keep from drifting and call the coast guard or harbor master to advise them of your situation. If you are in a remote area, you can also issue a pan-pan on the VHF.

While you are waiting for help, do what you can to plug leaks and pump or bail water from the boat. If you have T-boned a rock or object and water is pouring in so fast that the boat may sink and you all may drown, follow the steps in the next section and issue a mayday on the VHF.

YIKES! THE BOAT'S SINKING!

I hate to end your cruise on a negative note, but let's be truthful. Crap happens—my mantra in this book, it seems. Your boat could be sinking for many reasons, but what really matters is do you know what to do?

Follow this general procedure to save yourselves, and, hopefully, your boat:

1. Don life jackets.

2. Hail mayday on VHF 16.

3. Find the leak. Plug it with a bung plug, wadded clothing, or anything available.

4. Use a water pump to bail.

5. Unless you are already aground, steer for shore and try to ground the boat on a sandy beach where you and your crew can step off the boat.

6. Stay with the boat if it remains afloat, even if it has capsized. You will remain safe while being more visible to nearby boats and from the air.

CHAPTER 11

Coming Into Port

You're almost there. You can see it: the entrance channel to your destination. If you are familiar with this harbor, or have read about it in a guide and know entering the harbor will be relatively easy, just follow the channel on in. In this chapter, you will learn the best way to enter a harbor, and how to go into a slip, pick up a mooring, set anchor, and raft with other boats. We'll also cover the unwritten rules of etiquette at dock, in an anchorage, or when rafting.

ENTER THE HARBOR

If you are unsure of your approach, or just can't remember everything you have read about a particular harbor, take a hard look at your chart and fix the configuration of the entry channel in your mind. It also helps to get out your cruising guide and ask someone to read aloud the navigation instructions.

Next, locate the marina, mooring field, or anchorage you are heading for on the navigation chart or reference the inset on your chart or in the cruising guide. If yours is a deep-keeled sailboat, note the water depth of the channel leading into the harbor as well as the area where you plan to dock.

CHECK IN AT A MARINA

If you have reserved a slip or need a mooring, contact the dock or harbor master. Your cruising guide will tell you which VHF radio channels the marina monitors. Have the marina's cell phone number on hand in the event marina personnel are not responding to your hail.

For a reserved slip, you will be provided a dock location. For example, Dock A, slip #23. Let the dockmaster know if you will come into the slip bow in or stern in. Ask if this will be a port or starboard side tie-up, then pass on the information to your crew. In the case of a reserved mooring, you will either be provided a mooring number to locate on your own, or the harbor master will motor over to lead you to it.

If you failed to make an advance reservation, ask if a transient slip or mooring suitable for your size boat is available for the number of nights you plan to stay.

ENTER A SLIP

When steering into a slip, plan your approach keeping in mind the wind direction and current. Wind gusts can blow your boat onto or off the dock. A strong current can veer you off course. If you have not done so already, I recommend practicing docking at your home marina until you learn the best way to position your boat for entry.

If you are cruising solo and plan to go into a slip, your timing and preparations must be meticulous. You will need to stay in control of the helm, move about the deck to set up lines and fenders, and, if no assistance is available, hop off the boat to tie up.

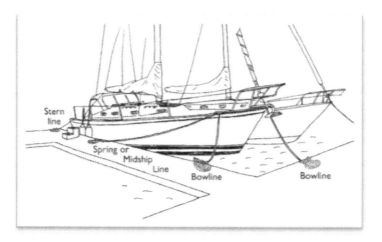

Have ready one or more bow lines, stern lines, and spring lines. A floating dock typically needs only a bow, a spring, and a stern. A fixed dock requires double this amount. In some situations, extra fore and aft lines will be needed.

> *fixed dock = a slip where lines are attached to heavy wooden or steel pilings driven vertically into the harbor bottom. A finger pier may or may not be available for ease in getting off or on the boat.*

> *floating dock = a slip supported by metal pipes on which it can move up and down with the rise and fall of the water level.*

The number and size of fenders you will need depends on the kind of slip you're taking as well as the length, weight, and overall shape of your boat. Have these available and prepared for use.

MANAGE CREW

As you approach your slip, have a crew member toss (to waiting hands) the spring line or bow line, depending on the wind and current conditions. Securing the spring line first stops the forward motion of the boat. Once that is done, it's easy enough to get the bow and stern lines out. If the stern line goes out last, the helmsman can usually handle it because the engine is in neutral and the boat is under control.

Your crew members will rely on you (or the helmsperson) to tell them where you need control most. Give your crew enough time to set up fenders and lines. Circle outside the marina if necessary. Communicate accurately how and where lines and fenders need to be set up to avoid a last minute switcheroo that could result in injury. Decide the order in which each type of line needs to be thrown.

The following are responsibilities of whoever is assigned to perform deck duties:

> Set up fenders.

> Cleat lines to the boat in appropriate spots, per captain's orders. Once cleated, pull the remainder of the line out and over the lifelines so it won't get caught as it's tossed.

> Have all lines untangled, coiled, and ready to heave.

> Get in position. With the full line, or the first few coils from the end, position yourself between amidships and the bow and hope that someone spots your approaching boat and offers to help you dock.

> Toss lines and call out if it's the bow line, spring line, or stern line so the person assisting dockside will know which cleat to secure it to.

Note to crew: A hefty length of line may be heavy when fully coiled. You do not have to throw the entire coil. Instead, take off a few coils from the end to toss, holding the remainder of the coil in your other hand. Keep the remainder of the coil free to unfurl, being careful not to ensnare your feet. Now, toss the end coils up and out with a slight twist, aiming as close to the waiting hands as you can. If you miss, quickly pull the line back to you. It will be wet and heavier now, so give it some extra oomph when you retoss it.

GET DOCK ASSISTANCE

It's great when the marina sends someone to help you dock your boat, but it isn't always possible. Don't panic. If you think you need help, wave, shout, toot a horn, or find another way to attract attention as you approach. Sailboats, especially, are so quiet that fellow mariners often aren't aware that one is slipping in until it's too late to help.

Boats under 32 feet in length usually don't require assistance under normal sea and wind conditions, unless the dock is too high or too low for disembarking. The larger your boat, the less frequently you'll be called upon to bring it in unassisted.

Once you are settled in your designated slip, head for the marina office to check in and set up payment. Often, you will be provided a packet of information about marina facilities, entry codes to the toilet and laundry facilities, and information about local restaurants, events, and sights.

PRACTICE DOCK COURTESY

Boaters help each other. If you are at dock and see a boat headed into a nearby slip and no marina personnel seem to be around to help, offer to catch lines and assist with docking.

Keep your neighbors smiling by practicing good dock etiquette:

> ➢ Keep the area around your slip clear to avoid accidents. Roll up and stow hoses, buckets, mops, tackle, dock lines, and other items. If dock lines, power cords, or hoses must be strung across the dock, make sure they lie flat.

> ➤ If your bow anchor protrudes into the walk area, drop an orange life jacket, or some sort of noticeable item, over it as a warning.

> ➤ When finished with carts or other marina-provided equipment intended for common use, put them back where they belong so others can use them.

> ➤ Always request permission before boarding another person's boat. Think of it this way, the dock is your "yard" and the boat is your "house." Would you enter someone's home without ringing the doorbell or knocking?

> ➤ Use designated areas to dispose of trash. Separate it as the marina requests. If you have paid for a slip, there should be no disposal charge.

> ➤ If you are having a party aboard, or are just having fun, be considerate of your neighbors. Don't blast tunes until late into the night or make undue noise early in the morning.

OPT FOR THE ANCHORAGE

While being on a slip is convenient, it comes with a price. In addition to costing more than staying on a mooring or setting anchor, it can be noisy and intrusive—especially during holiday weekends when blender wars hold court.

Should you opt to stay in the harbor, rather than a slip, understand that you will lose the advantage of having an external source of electricity to keep your boat's batteries charged. You will need to run your engine or a generator twice a day, morning and night, for as long as it takes to restore your batteries.

If you have an inverter, turn it on in between charging to enable use of an electric stove, microwave, hair dryer, or other appliance. If you notice that when you're using the inverter electrical power is draining the batteries, give it a boost by also turning on your engine.

For the active person who deals with people all week, a mooring or anchorage can be a restorative haven. You can choose to be alone or socialize, with shore activities a mere dinghy ride away—although traveling to shore can be messy in rainy, blustery, or foggy weather. In such situations, remaining aboard or taking advantage of launch service may be your safest and most comfortable option.

On a mooring or on anchor, you will be cooler on those scorching hot days. Your bow will always point to the wind, bringing a cool breeze through open hatches and into the cockpit.

Interestingly, in turbulent conditions a boat on a mooring or at anchor is often more comfortable because there is no dock to bang up against or restraining dock lines to fight. However, when high winds and heavy seas are forecast, you may want to hightail to shore and try to secure a slip in a protected area. Otherwise, the smartest action is to seek a more protected harbor or a spot within the anchorage in the lee of the wind.

ADVANTAGES OF MOORING OVER ANCHORING

Staying on a mooring will offer you more stability than being on anchor. A mooring block, the part of the mooring that's buried on the ocean's floor, isn't going to go anywhere under most conditions. Even a well-set anchor can pull loose with tidal changes, so it must be checked frequently.

On the other hand, moorings can come with restrictive policies and be pricey, especially in fancy harbors like Newport, Rhode Island, or Nantucket. Anchoring is usually free, although of late a few foreign harbors, such as Marigot Bay in St. Martin, are charging.

At a marina, paying customers often are provided free launch service or use of the marina's heads, showers, and laundry facilities. If you are anchoring or on a free mooring, a marina launch may pick up your group, but it isn't likely you'll ride free.

PICK UP A MOORING

When you're a beginner at picking up a mooring, you'll do so when you're bone tired, at the end of a long, hard sail, and at cocktail hour in waters crowded with already moored or anchored boats.

Don't be embarrassed if you are having trouble anchoring or have made several swipes at picking up that dang-blasted, elusive mooring. While you are likely entertaining surrounding boats, know that they are silently cheering you on. It's common for someone to hop into a dinghy and come over to assist.

While a selection of mooring balls may look the same, don't grab the first free mooring you come across until you've checked it is substantial enough to hold your boat. If the number of pounds a mooring will support is not marked on the ball, hail the harbor master to find out which moorings you should use.

Transient moorings are offered by many marinas and may be available through the town dock. While some marinas or yacht clubs will take a reservation for a mooring, often these are available on a first come basis. If you are not certain which moorings are available for pickup, contact the harbor master or the associated marina to find out what their moorings look like, and where in the anchorage they are located.

If no transient moorings are available, you may be able to take advantage of a vacant private mooring. Contact the harbor master to ask permission to use the mooring. It may be reserved for the owner or for another boat arriving late—or it may not support a boat your size. Policies vary from harbor to harbor. If you cannot reach a harbor master, other moored boat owners may be able to provide the information you need.

If you have risked picking up a private mooring without permission, be prepared to find another spot if the owner shows up or the harbor master kicks you off it.

Cruising solo? The process of picking up a mooring is very doable, as long as the waters are calm enough to allow you to leave the helm to go forward and grab the mooring. However, it's always nice to have help.

TIPS ON THE APPROACH

Once you have spotted the mooring you want, slow down. Once in the mooring field, you shouldn't be traveling any faster than 5 or 6 knots. By the time you reach the mooring ball, your helm should be in neutral, with the boat speed reduced to 1 knot using the forward momentum of the boat. If you are going too fast, the person at the bow will not have time to grab the mooring; or may get it and find the pull so great that he or she needs to drop the mooring line—boat, hook, and all.

Take a look at the direction in which the bows of other moored boats are pointed. Approach your designated mooring ball from the same angle, which will be directly into the wind. As the boat nears the mooring, visibility is greatly reduced. You (or the helmsperson) will need to rely on hand signals from the deck person to indicate the location of the mooring, its distance from the boat, and whether or not it's been captured.

PICKUP PROCEDURES

Every mooring is different. Most often you'll grab the mooring by means of a loop that's attached to it called a pennant, or by a handy pickup stick called a mast. You will almost always need a boat hook, which acts as an extension of your arm and allows you to reach farther down to hook the mooring line. Keep an extra line ready just in case the loop won't go around the cleat on your boat or the pennant is too short. If you see the line is frayed or damaged, select another mooring. If this is not possible, strengthen the line by looping the end of your own line through the eye of the mooring ball. Understand how to deal with these kinds of moorings:

MOORING MAST

A mooring mast, or a pickup pennant, enables you to grab hold of a mooring without using a boat hook. It floats high enough so you can snag it by hand, arm extended. To pick up a mooring mast, lie down flat as close to the bow of the boat as you can, or bend over the lifeline—whichever position works best. As the helmsman approaches the mark, reach out for the pennant. Haul the pennant up. Drag it under the lowest lifeline until you see the loop of the mooring line. Quickly drape the loop around the bow cleat while the line is slack or the boat will begin pulling away once the wind catches the bow.

TRADITIONAL MOORING

Unfortunately, not all moorings are equipped with mooring masts, so you do have to learn the traditional method of snagging a mooring. If you miss, the helmsman will have to circle around for another swipe at it.

As the helmsman rounds up to the mooring, poke an extended boat hook under the lowest lifeline (on some boats you will be able to reach by simply leaning over at the bow) and hook the line just behind the float on the mooring. Try for any part of the line you can hook. Quickly draw the line up onto your boat. Find the loop. If it is long enough and will fit, loop it around the bow cleat. If the line is short, be ready with an extra line tied to the bow cleat. Thread the end of the line through the loop on the mooring and bring it back to the cleat, and then tie it off.

EXTENSION MOORING

Oops, no line on the mooring? You'll find extension moorings in some harbors. In our cruising area, we've run into them at Cuttyhunk in Cape Cod. The mooring ball has an attached fiberglass pipe with a short pennant topped by a loop. The idea is to grab the pennant and thread your own line through the loop. Cleat one end of your line to the bow. Grab the rod using your hand. Thread the bitter end through the loop, then bring it back onto your boat and secure it to the bow cleat.

Use your hand rather than the boat hook. A boat hook will get stuck in the metal loop and you're apt to drop the hook (as I have on many occasions). Don't be discouraged if it takes several go-rounds before you succeed. Sometimes, a kind person will come by in a dinghy and assist you.

There are a couple of schools of thought on whether or not to form a bridle or just do a double tie on one side of the bow cleat. In my experience, a bridle can become tangled with the anchor if the wind is up or changes direction.

Now that you're moored, turn off the engine and have a cold drink. That's all there is to it. Once you are settled, someone may come along to collect the night's fee (always get a receipt), or you may need to dinghy into shore to pay at the office.

ANCHORING

You can read all the articles in the world about how to anchor, but the best way to feel comfortable with it is to practice, practice, practice. Setting an anchor is trickier than picking up a mooring because if it is not done correctly, your boat will sashay through the anchorage, headed for trouble. Your first job is to choose a good place to anchor within the harbor.

Here are a few tips:

➢ To avoid kissing bows or clinking dinghies with your neighbors, look for a spot with swinging room in all directions. Should the wind change, your boat will swing bow to the wind or with the current, whichever is stronger.

➢ If moorings are mixed into the anchorage, consider the swing room needed by the boat already on nearby moorings. If the mooring is vacant, be particularly careful of leaving enough space around it, lest its owner shows up and has your boat relocated by the harbor master while you are ashore.

➢ Boats using all-chain anchor rodes won't swing as widely as those with a combo chain-and-line rode. Anchor between boats displaying the same kind of anchor rode as you will be using.

➢ Anchor using the same method used by nearby boats. Those using both a bow and a stern anchor will swing less than a boat with a bow-only anchor.

➢ A raft swings less due to its size and weight, but it requires more space.

SET ANCHOR

As with any docking procedure, it's easiest if at least two people are involved in the anchoring process: a helmsman and a crew member. Single-handed anchoring can be done; but, like pulling into a slip alone, it requires skill and practice. A word to the wise: never anchor from the stern alone because the boat could swamp or capsize.

Since most of the work of anchoring is performed on the forward deck, it may make sense to have your first mate or other capable crew member handle the helm while you see to the anchor. If you do not have any form of windlass, the back-breaking chore of tossing out the anchor (and hauling it in) should belong to the most muscular person aboard. Is that you?

If your boat is not equipped with a windlass or any electronic means of dropping or picking up your anchor, the person on deck needs to rig the anchor and rode and to check that the shackles are secured with wire to prevent the screw shaft from opening. Lay out the amount of rode needed on deck so that it will follow the anchor into the water without tangling, then cleat off the anchor line at the point you want it to stop.

Successful anchoring relies on the cooperation between the helmsman and the deck person, or anchor manager.

The helmsman should follow this procedure:

1. Approach the anchoring location at slow speed going directly into the wind, as you would for a mooring. Once there, put the boat in neutral.

2. Call out the depth of the water to the person on the bow.

3. Watch and follow hand signals from the person on the bow.

4. Keep the helm into the wind and pointed at the chosen location.

5. Once the anchor is down, the boat will drift back as the scope is played out by the person on the bow. Do not try to motor forward. Switch gear to reverse, and then back to neutral when requested. Remain at the helm with the engine in idle until the person on the bow gives the all clear sign.

6. Once your boat settles into its swing radius, make sure it remains in the same position relative to your surroundings. If it doesn't, you're probably dragging anchor. Repeat the procedure and reset the anchor. Delay heading to shore until you are certain the anchor is holding.

The person on deck is in charge of anchor setup. His or her responsibilities are to get the anchor and its tackle positioned to drop, to determine depth and bottom conditions, and to calculate the amount of rode needed. The deeper the water, the more anchor rode needs to be laid out. Because of its weight, an all-chain rode requires less scope than a rope-and-chain rode.

This is the general procedure for the deck person to follow when dropping the anchor:

1. Release the anchor clip when the boat is in position. Lower the anchor until it lies on the bottom. Check the depth. If necessary, recalculate the amount of scope you will need. When day anchoring in pleasant conditions, allow 5 feet of rode for every foot of water. If overnight anchoring, allow 6 to 8 feet of rode to every foot of water.

2. Check to be sure the anchor is set. When enough scope has been let out, have the helmsman back down on the anchor in reverse gear. This is a quick burst of speed to create enough pull on the anchor for it to dig into the bottom and "set." When set, the rode will rise out of the water and go tight. You will feel the boat jerk and stop. Signal "stop" to the helmsman when this occurs.

3. While reversing on a set anchor, keep a hand on the anchor line. A dragging anchor will bump along the bottom and shake the line.

YOUR ANCHOR RODE IS CUT!

If you are on board—hopefully you will be—when another boat overruns your anchor rode, you will know it at once. The movement of your boat will suddenly change, and you will feel a slight jerk and possibly a thump, which will be the sound of your boat colliding with another.

Here's what you need to do:

1. Dash to the helm and get the engine going.

2. Take control of your boat.

3. Reset using your backup anchor. (You do carry a second anchor, don't you?)

4. Once the boat is secure, make arrangements to have someone dive for your anchor. If you can find the culprit, demand a replacement rode.

Bring this and any other issues to the attention of the harbor master.

ANCHORAGE NO-NO'S

When you chug into a beautiful harbor with plans to moor or anchor for the night, be aware of others who may be sharing the space with you. Slow down when entering an anchorage so as not to jostle existing boats. Choose a spot with plenty of swing room between boats. If yours is a noisy crowd or you like loud music, choose a spot to the lee of the wind to avoid disturbing your neighbors.

If you notice another boat positioning to pick up the mooring you intended to get, back off and choose another. Witnessing a fight over a mooring is not pretty. If the mooring you have reserved is occupied and the "illegal" boat is unattended (or its captain refuses to give up the spot), settle the situation with a call to the harbor master.

Once, settled, be a good neighbor by following these suggestions:

> ➤ Respect quiet times. Don't run your generator or engine very early in the morning or late at night when people are apt to be sleeping. At night, if you need to use a spotlight or flashlight, try not to inadvertently blind your neighbor.

> ➤ Don't pump out. If your head's holding tank is about to burst and you neglected to pump overboard when you were within legal discharge limits, resist the temptation to pump out and foul the waters. In most cases, a pump-out service will be available to relieve the problem for you.

> ➤ When in an anchorage, don't throw garbage overboard, even if it's legal according to the dumping laws. Food will attract large fish and may endanger swimmers. As it floats away or leaves an oily slick, it spoils the beauty of the waters.

> ➤ Avoid being known as the laundry boat by limiting the amount of clothes, towels, etc., that you hang to dry on your lifelines or elsewhere on the exterior of your boat.

> ➤ Be friendly but not intrusive. If you are riding around in your dinghy and want to say hello to another boater, approach to starboard and stay 6 to 10 feet away—unless you are invited to come closer or to come aboard.

> ➤ Don't sleep naked. On anchor, be ready to react to any and all situations. Crap happens fast. If your boat is drifting or collides with another boat or obstacle, you will lose precious time by having to pull on your pants—not to mention that you will be exposing your privates to oglers.

RAFT WITH OTHER BOATS

On occasion, you may need or want to raft your boat to one or more boats. Rafting is sharing a slip, mooring, or anchor situation by tying up to one or more existing boats. The best kinds of rafts are those with friends. Rafting with other boaters can last for hours or days. Some rafts are organized in various formations as part of boating events.

You may have to settle for rafting at a marina when docks are overloaded on a busy weekend, even if you have reserved a slip. Once in a while, you will run into a marina that expects mooring customers to raft to strangers.

If on anchor, the largest boats anchor first, with smaller boats tying up from one side to the other. If this is a large raft, every third boat drops an anchor. Once you have the general rafting procedure down pat, you'll be comfortable rafting in almost any situation.

Get started with these tips:

> ➤ If possible, tie up to a boat of similar size. When rafting two sailboats, consider the spreaders on the masts and note if they will tangle when the boats rock from side to side.

> ➤ On a two- to three-boat raft, the anchor or mooring ball connected to the centermost boat holds the raft.

> ➤ In stormy or high wind situations, rafted boats need to be prepared to break from the raft and find a new place to moor or set anchor.

> ➤ When breaking up a raft of same-sized boats, the boats on the ends leave first. (See the departure procedures for all rafting situations below.)

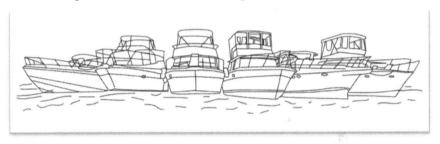

JOIN A RAFT

Prepare to raft as if you were heading into a slip. You will need two to four fenders and one or two sets of lines—bow, spring(s), and stern. If you are part of a large raft, you may also need an anchor and its rode and a boat hook. Unless you are Magic Man or Woman, you will need deck assistance.

Follow this ten-step process:

1. Get out fenders and lines and have them ready to set up.

2. When you are within 50 feet of the boat you intend to raft to, hail the captain on the VHF (or phone) to ask what side he or she wants your boat on. If you have a choice, opt to tie up on the leeward side rather than windward, where the wind can push you into the raft.

3. Have your crew set up fenders and lines on the correct side, much the same as if they were going into dock. Snub fender high enough to buffer the coaming (the raised section of the deck surrounding the cockpit) of the boat you will be rafting to.

4. Have your crew in position to toss lines when you give the word. If yours is a powerboat, trim the engine full in and lift up the trim tabs to achieve maximum maneuverability.

5. Note the direction and speed of the wind. The rafted boat will be facing the wind. Approach the raft from astern (or into the wind). Watch for swimmers, kayaks, and small boats under sail.

6. Motor toward the raft at dead-slow speed so as not to jostle the raft with a wake. Powerboats use bump throttle to maintain momentum without speeding up.

7. Come alongside the raft, and then put the helm in neutral. Leave the engine in idle.

8. Have your crew toss lines to the rafted boat. Usually, someone will be aboard to catch the lines. If not, a crew member will need to leap onto the boat you will raft to in order to catch and cleat your lines.

9. Use fore and aft spring lines to keep your boat from moving forward or rearward due to wind direction, current, or waves.

10. Secure attached lines loosely until you have adjusted the position of the boat so it is stern to stern or gate to gate. Adjust fenders as necessary.

DEPART A RAFT

At some point, you or another boat will want to leave the raft. To avoid a major scramble and last minute leaps between boats, choose a time when the owners or crew of your neighboring boats will be on board to assist. If your boat is attached to the mooring or holds the primary anchor, you will need to transfer the mooring or anchor to another boat before setting up to depart.

Departing from the end of a raft is pretty simple. Ask the crew of the boat to which you are rafted to toss off your lines, slackest lines first. Motor forward slowly so as not to create a wake until you are clear of the raft.

Departing from inside a raft is more complex and requires coordination and the cooperation of crew from boats on both sides of yours. If your boat is holding the anchor, reset the anchor to one of the boats on either side of yours. This can be done by dinghy so as not to disturb the position of any remaining boats on the raft.

Now, tie a long line to the bows of the boats on either side of you. The crew should be in position on neighboring boats. Tie a second long line on the sterns of the boats on either side. Have the crew hold, but not cleat, the line.

From the boats on either side of you, take in your spring lines first, and then release both of your bow lines. (Your bow is being held in place by the extra line on the opposing boats.) When you are ready, release your stern lines.

Posted crew on one side of the raft will control the connected stern line to allow you to back out. Slowly back out of the raft until you are well clear of it.

The two boats remaining in the raft need to tie up quickly, taking up slack and retying bow, spring, and stern lines.

RAFTING COURTESY

Being on a raft is like staying in an apartment building, with your neighbors in their own places. Respect their quiet times and resist the urge to leap aboard to chat or join a party without an invitation.

If you have to walk across other boats in the raft to get off or onto your boat, take off your shoes and walk as quietly as possible. Usually, going around the deck via the bow is the least disruptive during daytime hours.

Try not to run the generator or engine to charge batteries when people are still sleeping, have retired for the night, or are in the water swimming. If you need your head pumped out, hail the marina pump-out boat. Do your best not to be doing the dirty deed when folks are enjoying a meal or during cocktail hour.

Be a good neighbor by offering to help with tasks, like putting an engine on a dinghy or hauling your neighbor's trash to shore along with your own. When you are invited to another's boat, always ask what you can bring. At minimum, arrive bearing your first cocktail, along with a bottle of wine or a six-pack of beer or soda to share.

CHAPTER 12

Have Fun

You're settled at your destination. Now what? Why, it's time to party of course. Relax, enjoy yourselves. Maybe you want to hang out aboard, or head into shore to see what's going on. It doesn't matter as long as you and yours are doing whatever you want to do. This is your time. No work, no school for the kids, just pure pleasure.

If you've had a long cruise in an open-cockpit boat, your first move before joining shore festivities, visiting friends, or just relaxing is probably washing off the day's grime. Once in port, you'll likely need to tend to a few essential tasks, like finding a hardware store, reprovisioning, washing down the boat, and walking the dog. Concentrate on the most urgent chores—not taking Fido for his constitutional could get messy. If you've chosen a slip, a step off the boat will get you in position to do just about anything. In an anchorage, you may need to go ashore to complete some of these tasks.

GET CLEAN

Where, when, and how you and your crew wash up depends on what facilities are available to you and whether it makes sense to take advantage of them. The old-fashioned sponge bath consumes very little time and water. Wiping down your skin with a lightly soaped washcloth will leave you feeling relatively clean and refreshed.

Just need a refreshing rinse? If the anchorage waters are clean and not too cold, dive in and take along a bottle of combo shampoo/body wash. Some products will lather in salt water, enabling you to get the job done with the prospect of following up with a freshwater rinse. Save precious boat tank water by using room temperature bottled water. Should you be at dock and the marina has a pool, well, jump in. Obviously you can't soap up, and I assume you wouldn't befoul the waters if you are grimy from engine work.

SHOWER ON DECK

In hot weather, showering on deck is much more pleasant than fighting off the heat and humidity in an indoor shower of any kind. The downside is you will have an audience, so you will need to shower wearing a swimsuit or the shower police may drag you off to jail. Seriously, nudity is illegal in the United States.

If your boat has an outdoor freshwater source—a shower nozzle and hose set into your stern, or even the boat wash hose for the anchor—this will suffice to get you clean and refreshed.

Try a solar water bag, a water bladder equipped with a hang-up loop and a hose with an on-off control nozzle. This can be a godsend if your boat is not equipped with a built-in shower and you want to conserve tank water. Purchase one at marine stores or through catalogs.

Fill the bag with water and secure it topside while underway. Unless it's freezing cold and dreary, you'll have enough warm water for a quick shower or two by the time you reach port. If it's warm enough for an outdoor shower, hang the solar bag from the mast or boom. If it's cool, as it might be in the evening after the sun has gone down, use a solar water bag in the privacy of your head. Simply erect the bag in the head from a high hook. If this won't work for you, try mounting the bag outdoors near the head's hatch or porthole, and then snake the spray nozzle through the opening.

A solar bag uses gravity as water pressure, so you won't get the stiff stream common to traditional showers. Use shampoo and soap sparingly because it may not rinse off easily. Check around for accessories designed to boost water pressure and provide a modicum of privacy.

SHOWER IN YOUR BOAT'S HEAD

My husband and I never used our very adequate shower until the summer we attended a 60-boat regatta and needed to get ready for the evening events. The weather was scorching, and the lines for the two lone shower stalls at the marina were miles long. Desperate, I cleared out the gear stored in our shower so we could enjoy a private shower in our own surroundings.

While the typical cruising boat is equipped for showering, many people overlook using this convenience for the same reasons I did.

Try these ways to compensate for common issues:

➢ If the entire head gets wet and it's a nuisance to wipe up afterward, install a track to hang a shower curtain arranged to protect the toilet area from being soaked.

➢ If you are using the area to store bulky gear, organize and pack gear in such a way that it can be easily removed and replaced. I use duffel bags.

> ➤ If you must bring water up and through the shower head using a hand or foot pump, learn to coordinate pumping and washing as part of your shower routine.

> ➤ If you have no hot water, deal with it in hot weather. Otherwise, take a whore's bath using water warmed on the stove.

> ➤ If you need to conserve water, insist your crew take a boater's shower. If a crew member is prone to extra-long showers, shut off the pressurized water switch after a reasonable amount of time has elapsed. (You will hear a squawk.)

Boater's Shower: *Quick rinse. Shut off water. Lather up. Turn on water. Quick rinse. Shut off water. Towel off.*

USE MARINA SHOWERS

Some marina showers are nicer and more spacious than others. You may find them sparkling clean and beautifully equipped, or you may need to resort to a stall with no bench and only a single hook for your belongings. If you are a paying marina customer, use of the showers is free. If not, you may not be permitted to use them or you may be charged per shower.

Taking advantage of the marina's shower and head facilities can be a godsend if you have a boat crowded with people who need to wash up; crave toilets that flush without a hassle; want a long, hot shower; need a place to shave or dry hair without worrying about draining your boat's batteries; or have teenaged boys or girls who are water hogs and will suck down boat batteries running hairdryers, curling irons, and grooming whatnots.

Here are some tips on getting that marina shower with the least hassle and without annoying fellow boaters:

> During peak times of eight and nine o'clock in the morning and four and six o'clock in the afternoon, the wait is long, the water may turn cold, and the room will be steamy and hot. Choose an off-time to take your shower.

> Pack your necessities—soap, shampoo, towel, and change of clothes—in a waterproof, handled boat tote that can hang on a hook and withstand a splash or two.

> If you know space will be limited, wear your bathing suit to and from the shower to prevent getting your change of clothes wet.

> Wear flip-flops to the shower, in the shower, and back to the boat to save worrying about keeping shoes dry and to avoid contact with the shower floor, risking athlete's foot.

> If people are lined up behind you, keep your shower short. The hot water disappears quickly and all those nice people may get a cold shower.

> Before leaving the marine shower room, make certain you have all your gear with you and clean up after yourself. No one wants to deal with discarded soap wrappers and empty shampoo bottles.

FLUFF SHORE CLOTHES

Once you are on shore, ready to explore a new place or a beloved, familiar one, you are no longer a boater. Save your ratty boat clothes for cleaning the boat or the beach. If you will be shopping, touring, or going to a restaurant, put on clothes that don't look as if you've used them as cleaning rags, and wear shoes.

If you will be taking the dinghy to shore, chose lightweight pants or shorts made of a quick-drying synthetic fabric to avoid arriving with dinghy butt, an obvious water marking on a boater's rear end caused by sitting in a wet dinghy or being splashed by a wake or wave while in said spot. A hooded jacket long enough to cover your rear end when seated will also prevent arriving with soaked clothes.

Get started on fluffing by taking the shorts or slacks and shirts you plan to wear out of your duffel or locker. Give them a good shake-out to relax folding and squishing creases, then assess what needs to be done to make them shore worthy.

> ➤ If you need to have the garments ready quickly, use a hairdryer to blow out the wrinkles or shake items vigorously and hope.

> ➤ Spritz lightly with water or a wrinkle-relaxing spray, then hang in an airy spot on the boat or outdoors in the sun or a light wind for ten to thirty minutes.

> ➤ Lay the clothing out on a flat surface and place a slightly damp towel directly on top. Smooth with your hands. Remove towel. Allow clothing to dry for about ten to thirty minutes.

> ➤ If you have time, place clothing under something heavy, such as a mattress, and leave it for about an hour.

> ➤ Iron the clothes. Keep a small low-voltage AC or DC travel iron aboard and use with a folding ironing pad.

GO ASHORE

At some point you will want to get off the boat and explore your surroundings. If you will be out of sight of your boat for a while, make sure your boat is secure and set for your return, especially if it will be dark or you expect limited visibility. If this is a designated anchorage in the United States, you are not required to have an anchor light lit at night. In a foreign port, check the rules. When in doubt, flip the switch and let your anchor light shine. An anchor light makes your boat more visible to other boats.

Before you leave, double-check your dock lines and mooring to be sure they are secure. Is there enough slack to accommodate tidal changes? Are you certain your anchor is set? Close overhead hatches and ports that will allow rain and dampness to permeate the interior of your boat. A wet berth is hard to dry out.

Pack a shore bag with extra sweaters, rainwear, hats, sunglasses, and anything else you might need. If it will be dark when you return, take along a high-intensity flashlight. This is helpful for reading the numbers on a combination boat lock, as well as finding your way to and from shore without running over any vacant mooring balls or anchor lines. Remember to take the boat keys, unless you have a combination lock.

Don't invite theft by leaving hatches open that are large enough to permit entry, and by failing to lock your boat. The average marina provides little or no security to mariners. A visitor may need to ask for a key to use the restroom but is free to stroll the docks and may be tempted to board a boat that appears vacant. This happened to us one night when we were asleep. Awakened by strange sounds, we found a couple necking in our cockpit.

Leave a light on inside the boat or in the cockpit so you can find your boat in the dark. Doing so will also make your boat appear to be occupied, even with its dinghy gone.

Locating your boat in a strange marina can be an issue, especially if it is dark, rainy, or foggy. Note the dock and slip number, mooring number, and the names and kinds of nearby boats, as well as any landmarks.

GO BY DINGHY

Is your dinghy ready to take passengers on a shore jaunt? Before you set off, take a few minutes and run it through these checks:

➢ If your dinghy has an outboard, do you have enough fuel? Are the oars aboard in case the engine fails?

➢ Do you have enough PFDs for however many people will be aboard? Children under twelve need to wear theirs.

➢ Do you need a whistle or air horn? State regulations for boats less than 16 feet in length may require you have aboard a whistle or air horn in addition to a bow light.

➢ Is the dinghy repair kit aboard? If you have not done so already, put together a few items you might need for repairs and store them in a dinghy locker or in a portable tote you bring along whenever you use the dinghy. The bag should contain spare parts, such as cotter pins. If your dinghy is rubberized, include a patch kit and an air pump.

➢ Do you have an anchor? An anchor will keep you from drifting if the engine fails. Also, it will help secure your boat if you need to beach the dinghy.

➢ Can you find your way back? A hand-bearing compass is small and tucks easily into a tote bag. If you have one, take it along in case you need to find your boat later. Note the course to shore, and then reverse it by 180 degrees to return to your boat.

➢ Will you need a handheld radio? A handheld VHF radio is handy if you need to hail the launch or harbor master when you are away from your boat.

➢ Is your dinghy ready for passengers? Do you need to bail out water or mop up slippery dew from the floor and seats? Is the floor relatively clear of obstacles that could cause someone to trip and fall?

BOARD PASSENGERS

Most dinghies are unstable and relatively lightweight. They will move with the waves and current. If the dinghy is sloshing around like a kid having fun in a bath tub, decide whether to delay or cancel your trip to shore or to tolerate a messy, uncomfortable ride. Under such conditions, boarding and debarking are dangerous. Agile passengers seem to have no problem hopping into a dinghy from the primary boat, but not everyone is fleet of foot, has good balance, and can time the leap so they don't slip and fall.

Here are a few means of simplifying the boarding process:

➢ Having a sugar scoop or some other sort of boarding platform at the stern of your primary boat would provide a good base for getting off and onto a dinghy.

> Dropping the swim or boarding ladder from the transom would give people something to grab onto and use as a step to access the primary boat.

> Attaching one or two sturdy pull lines to the stern would give passengers something to grab onto for leverage when hopping onto the boat. These also can be used to control the position of the dinghy for boarding once the painter has been released or until it is fastened.

> Installing a boarding ladder in the gate area on the port or starboard side of your primary boat would eliminate the need for passengers to make the grand leap from the stern. They would climb down backward and step in. On the return, someone need only grab the ladder to stop the boat, and then climb up and into the boat.

POSITION THE DINGHY FOR SAFETY

Dinghy 101 involves these steps in positioning the dinghy for embarking and debarking and assisting your passengers aboard:

1. Pull the dinghy as close as possible to the stern or side of the boat where it will be boarded. It's easier to board with the dinghy placed sideways against your primary boat, rather than bow facing.

2. Tie the dinghy lines in place to keep the boat as stable as possible.

3. Hop aboard.

4. Start the engine in neutral.

5. Extend a helping hand (or shoulder) to passengers.

Upon returning, coast slowly to the stern or side ladder, grab onto the primary boat by a handhold or pull rope, then situate the dinghy in position to debark. The first person off takes the line and ties up.

DRIVE SENSIBLY

While the coast guard may perform random harbor checks, the harbor master is usually out and about checking for problems. If you are not a rule follower, don't be surprised if you get slapped with a fine. Be sure to heed the speed limit. Going too fast will create a wake and disturb other boats— and may earn you a stern talk or fine. Beware of driving under the influence of alcohol.

Don't zip across the channel in front of a moving boat. A dinghy sits low in the water and is not always visible. When using a dinghy, keep the red auto shutoff wire linked to the engine start button. One quick pull will stop the engine. This safety feature can keep a person falling overboard from being overrun by the engine and badly hurt.

TIE UP AT THE DINGHY DOCK

Most marinas have a small dock or pier set aside for dinghy tie-ups. While a few fancy marinas may charge a tie-up fee, it's usually free. During heavy cruising times, like weekends and holidays, many dinghy docks are jammed. The object is to find a spot where you can wedge your dinghy in close enough to dare leave it.

Resist the urge to tie up alongside a dock reserved for the marina launch, a ferry, or a large boat. If the spot is vacant and you see no incoming vessel, it's okay to borrow the space for a minute to drop off passengers.

Once you have spotted a space, keep these issues in mind:

> Snubbing your dinghy close to the dock makes it an immovable object, hogging space and shutting out others looking to tie up. Despite what you have witnessed, the proper way to tie up to a dinghy dock is to allow 6 to 8 feet of painter. This allows your boat to move more freely, giving other dinghy captains more leeway to squeeze in beside you. A side benefit is boaters tying up after you may not have to step into your dinghy to reach the dock.

> If you tie your painter under the lines that precede you, it won't be necessary for another boater to disturb them to free his or her dinghy.

> Never tip up the outboard engine at the dinghy dock. The propeller will stick out and is apt to tear or scratch neighboring dinghies—and could get damaged.

If your dinghy is stacked behind others, the vertical version of the raft, it's permissible to step over other boats to reach the dock. In cases where the dock is jammed full, it makes sense to drop off crew while you find a spot, and then toss them your painter to cleat.

When you return to the dinghy dock, your dinghy will be waiting to ferry you back to your vessel unless you neglected to wire and lock it and someone "borrowed" it, it's a rowboat and the oars are missing, or you botched up the tie-up and it is now sashaying through the harbor.

TAKE THE LAUNCH

Not all marinas offer launch service. If your chosen marina does, a ride may be free or you may be assessed a few dollars per person each way. Bring cash, and if the driver has gone out of his or her way for you, be sure to include a tip. Using the launch allows for diversity in plans when not everyone wants to go to the same place or plans to leave the boat or return at different times. For example, your spouse might take the launch in to shop, while you take the kids to the beach in the dinghy.

While taking a launch may cause you to reach into your pocket for a few bills, in certain situations it can be well worth it. The launch driver is familiar with the harbor and well trained at traveling in all weather conditions. If visibility is poor, a launch will have a better shot at finding your boat than you would by dinghy. In heavy sea conditions, it will be easier to get off and on a launch than to deal with an unstable dinghy.

A launch provides a safer, more efficient means of getting a crowd of people large enough to sink a dinghy into shore. With a launch, chances of getting splashed are reduced because a launch does not sit as low in the water as a dinghy does. Most often, there's a small cuddy cabin in the bow, with dry seating for those who get there first.

When taking a launch, avoid being stranded on your return. Find out the following information:

➤ What are its operating hours? If the launch stops running at 8:00 p.m. and you know the movie, dinner, or event you are attending won't be over until 10:00 p.m., you could be stranded on shore.

➤ How often does the launch run? There may be a specific schedule, such as every half hour, or the launch may take passengers to and from their boats on demand. What VHF channel does the launch operator monitor? If you try to hail the launch on channel 16, I doubt if you'll reach it. The marina can provide you this information, or it may be listed in your cruising guide. When you call, be sure to give the driver an accurate description of your boat and its location within the harbor. If you receive no response on the radio, call the launch by cell phone. If you see the launch coming your way and you need a ride, do your best to wave the driver over. Get on deck, jump up and down, shout, or blast an air horn.

> Where on shore does the launch pick up passengers? A launch may have several places it stops to load on-shore passengers wishing to return to their boats. Usually, the launch will pick up at the same dock where you were deposited when coming into shore.

GETTING AROUND

If you will be on foot, and your chosen location is farther away than you can comfortably walk, ask at the marina about cab service, courtesy transportation, or shuttle service. In popular tourist towns like Hyannis, Massachusetts, and Boothbay, Maine, you'll find trolley, bus, and even ferry service.

Bike and motor bikes offered by shore rental agencies are convenient for zipping about or touring. Some boaters prefer to bring their own bikes for this purpose. Folding models stow compactly and take less space than traditional bikes do.

RESTAURANTING

Most shoreline restaurants are pretty tolerant of the boating crowd they attract and will forgive almost any attire as long as it's clean and neat. If your restaurant of choice won't accept you as you are dressed, ask if it serves in the bar. You'll still enjoy the ambiance, although with a somewhat rowdier crowd. In fact, if your group tends to be rowdy, it may be wise to put your reservation under an alias name to avoid being denied a reservation on your next visit.

It's always smart to inquire about a restaurant's reservation policy. Some will only reserve for large parties, six or more. Many will not accept reservations at all, which could leave you standing in queue on the sidewalk or overimbibing at the bar. In heavily visited areas, the stock wait at a popular restaurant can be two hours on weekends. Many folks put their names in at several places, and then make the rounds to find a restaurant that will seat them ASAP. Instead of roaming, stick around and periodically remind the host or hostess you are waiting. You are apt to get seated sooner than you expect.

Avoid making a reservation under your boat's name, a practice prevalent in harborside restaurants. You are advertising that your boat will be unattended. When chartering in the Grenadines, our boat was robbed while we dined ashore. If a restaurant can't take your reservation until well past your requested time, think hard about going along with it. As the evening wears on, a restaurant becomes backed up, meaning you'll be seated well past your reservation time or it will run out of its specialty dishes.

Should you change your mind about a reservation, do the right thing and cancel it. One of restaurateurs' chief complaints is when large parties become no-shows, leaving them with a beautifully appointed table they might have filled with other guests.

ENJOY THE WATER

Instead of pulling out the computer or your cell phone and playing games or checking e-mail, enjoy the simple pleasures around you. Better yet, share them with friends, old and new.

Take advantage of being on the water. There are so many fun things to do to entertain you and yours. Here are a few ideas:

Play with water toys. Go to any toy or sporting goods store, or to a chandlery, and look around—you'll find all kinds of water toys and flotation devices. The ocean's your swimming pool. Pull the kids along in a giant tube behind your dinghy, or float atop a queen-sized raft with a friend. Tether your flotation device to your boat, and you won't go adrift.

Swim. If you are in a harbor where the water is relatively clean, swim off the back of the boat or take along a floating cushion, and paddle around effortlessly. Sit on it when you get tired.

Go to the beach. Go to the beach and make sand castles, and ride the waves on a boogie board or surfboard. Poling is popular now.

Rent stuff. If your crew is antsy and wants more action than you can provide, investigate renting small craft—canoes, kayaks, sunfish, and windsurfers. If you haven't brought along your own, shore facilities will likely rent you snorkels or scuba gear. Some harbors will set aside an area for sports, such as water skiing.

Catch dinner. Fishing, clamming, and mussel hunting are rewarding activities. Before you drop that hook or set off to the beach with a shovel and bucket, find out if a permit is required. Often permits, especially temporary ones, are relatively inexpensive.

Charter a boat. If your crowd is very adventurous, send them off on a boat to parasail, go deep-sea fishing, or whale watching.

ENTERTAIN YOURSELVES ON BOARD

At times when the weather is a bit cool for swimming and you just want to chill out on the boat, here are a few ideas to help you pass the time:

Scan the waters. Get out the binoculars and scan the horizon, watch a regatta in action, or peer into the backyards of fabulous seaside estates.

Take pictures. Snap some photos to blow up to poster size and tack on the walls of your office when you return home.

Read. Save space and worry about keeping hard copy books dry by reading digital books and magazines on a computer or digital reader. Some marinas have a book exchange, where you can pick up new reading material in trade for the book you've already read.

Make knots. If you haven't learned to make nautical knots yet, get some nylon cord and a good book on the subject, and try. The most fun book we own is a how-to manual on knot making, which comes with bright red-and-blue shoelaces to practice with. This book can keep a restless adolescent fascinated for hours. Learn the functional knots first. If you enjoy doing those, go on to the decorative knots. A good buddy of mine attracts crowds when he laces up a Turk's Head knot.

Play some tunes. Celebrate being on the water with your favorite music. If you don't have a built-in radio or CD player, download your favorite songs onto your iPod, iPad, or smartphone. Use a portable speaker to extend the range of the music.

Watch other boaters make mistakes. Every one of us has at some point experienced the embarrassment of missing the mark. Yet, it's entertaining to watch the contortions that boaters go through to anchor, pick up a mooring, or enter a slip. One boating couple, deciding to sail out of the harbor, forgot to free their mooring ball and another motored over a small powerboat's anchor rode and set it afloat. If you cannot assist when it's clear a boat is having an ongoing problem, hail a launch driver or harbor master to let him or her know a boat is in trouble.

Stand in the cockpit and play traffic cop. Shake your fist and shout at boaters violating the no-wake rule after they've rocked your boat silly, sending drinks and food careening to the cockpit floor. The offenders likely won't hear you over the roar of their engines, but letting off steam will make you feel better.

Watch a movie. Carry along a cache of DVDs to play in the evening when it's raining like mad outside or when you need to quiet down some restless kids. Many DVDs will play on a computer. Likely, your Wi-Fi signal won't be strong or consistent enough to permit you to stream movies and such. In advance of your trip, rent or buy movies you or the kids want to watch.

SOCIALIZE

In the boating environment, the stress of home life melts away, leaving us the fun, sociable people we were meant to be. Few care if you own a multimillion dollar corporation or work at a discount store; all that matters is you are a boater. It's easy to make friends if you are willing to return a wave, a smile, or continue a conversation.

Whether you are in your home port or on cruise, the opportunity to get together with others is there. Invite someone aboard for a drink or to share a potluck-style dinner. The party is casual, the theme is fun, and expectations are low.

TRAVEL WITH A FLOTILLA

Forming a flotilla with friends can make a great trip magnificent. Each summer our group heads off for a week or two in a flock of four to six boats. We stop at many of the same harbors and usually get together in the evening for cocktails or dinner and for lazy days on the beach, sipping cold drinks, and watching our kids have a grand time in the water. Sometimes, we break off in groups to go shopping or to explore.

If it's rainy or foggy, we may sit inside our own boats and read or nap, or buzz around in our dinghies swathed in foul-weather gear, invading each other's boats and begging cold beers. Often, we pile onto one of our boats, make popcorn, and watch movies.

Any cruise becomes a flotilla when several boats travel together, keeping contact along the way, and meeting at prearranged harbors. Typically such trips include an informal group party, so pack up a side dish or dessert to contribute and come prepared with appetizers for the inevitable cocktail hour.

Here are some tips for traveling with a flotilla:

> Agree on a radio channel to monitor and maintain contact throughout your trip.

> There's safety in numbers. If it is foggy, a lead boat with radar can help you navigate through the haze.

> Should your engine fail or you go aground, it's comforting to know that a fellow boater is nearby to assist you.

JOIN CLUB FLOTILLAS

Learn about yacht club events through billboards at your marina or club newsletters. The trip may be a weekend jaunt or a more extended cruise. Such trips involve fewer people than regattas or rendezvous and usually center around an informal event such as a gathering on the beach, a lobster fest or catered clambake, a BYO food and booze communal barbecue, or an out-to-dinner night at a local restaurant.

ATTEND RENDEZVOUS, REGATTAS, AND TOURNAMENTS

It's great fun to attend a planned gathering of fellow boaters, meet new people, test your skills, and learn from talks by experts. Boaters come from afar, and there may be anywhere from ten to eighty boats in attendance.

Most boat manufacturers put on such events in conjunction with a local sales office. You will also find opportunities to partake in fund-raising regattas, as well as fishing tournaments. Once you sign up to attend, you will be provided an agenda that spans the event, usually held over a weekend. Typically, these are based at a major harbor, where restaurants and groceries are available.

COMMUNICATE

Our world has changed. No longer do we sail into the sunset without a care in the world, knowing full well that the boss can't call with an emergency because there's no way we can be reached. In our early boating days, we had no such thing as a wireless phone. To make a phone call on cruise, we had to find a land line or a phone booth. Today, it's common to see folks walking the streets with a cell phone to their ears or plopped in a restaurant using free Wi-Fi.

When you are heading out on cruise with the spouse and kids who expect their digital lives to continue or when you know darn well you'll have to stay in touch with the office, what can you do to make it happen?

CELL PHONE COVERAGE

Cell towers are land based. The farther away from land you are, the weaker the signal. Thus, cell phones are less reliable on the water than they are on land. Most are not water-resistant, and the maximum range between your cell phone and the nearest tower will vary. Note where your carrier's towers are located to determine how much cell phone coverage, if any, you can expect. Some carriers place towers in populated areas, where businesses flourish, whereas others focus on more rural areas. As you cruise, you will come to know which harbors are cell phone friendly.

If you are constantly out of range, even at dock, think about taking on a second carrier, one that services the areas you frequent when you cruise. My husband and I have been able to stay pretty much connected between our two different carriers when cruising the Maine coastline and traveling the Intracoastal Waterway. Because my carrier had few towers in the British Virgin Islands, my phone was constantly in the costly roaming mode, while his carrier offered good, direct coverage.

SATELLITE PHONE

Years ago, when I tried to reach my husband when he was on an extended sea voyage, the only alternative was AT&T's ship-to-shore communication, which requires a phone call to the AT&T operator along with a request to connect. Failure to connect sometimes meant no contact with him for days.

Ship-to-shore communication has improved, thank goodness, with the development of private companies offering mobile satellite communications. With an on-board satellite phone, you can be 200 miles from the nearest point of land and receive and make phone calls to your office, friends, and relatives.

Much the same as with a cell phone or physical hard-wired phone for your home or office, you simply buy a satellite phone from a company such as Globalstar or Iridium, and then sign up for its service. Once you purchase the unit, the service can be turned on and off by the month, thus allowing you to discontinue service off-season. Most satellite carriers offer e-mail messaging as part of the service, a welcome benefit.

When researching satellite companies, find out how many operating satellites they have orbiting the earth. Too few satellites can mean sporadic service. A satellite works by receiving radio signals sent from Earth (uplink) and resending the radio signals back to Earth (downlink). As a satellite rotates in an orbit around the earth, your signal to and from it will rely on where the disc happens to be in respect to the location of your boat. Expect times during the day when you will be unable to send or receive calls or messages because the satellite is out of range.

GET WI-FI

Digital connectivity has become vital to us. Internet access helps captains keep up-to-date on weather shifts and navigation. Wi-Fi service allows boaters to maintain contact with family and the office, even making it possible to work from your boat, as many do. Socially, you can call friends on Skype, or by using a similar service, update Facebook, send e-mails, or play computer games with remote digital friends.

Wi-Fi works on line of sight. In a marine environment, particularly if you are on a mooring on anchor, masts and hulls of nearby boats can block the signal being emitted from a particular shore location. If you are fortunate enough to get a decent signal, it may disappear as you go belowdecks. Also, consider the movement of your own boat as impacting your ability to maintain a signal.

To top it off, moisture, typical of the marine environment, can corrode electronic gadgets needed for Internet connectivity to the point where entire computer networks can crash. In the Caribbean Islands, heavy rain can be a death knell for networks. Lines get wet and credit card transmission comes to a halt, meaning tourists must pay cash for meals and groceries until the rain stops and the lines "dry" out.

Don't be discouraged. People and technology have devised a variety of ways to expand Wi-Fi services and improve connectivity. As you are aware, most customer-oriented facilities offer free Wi-Fi, and some places offer computer usage online as a paid service. It's common for boaters to haul a laptop or other portable digital unit such as an iPad into shore and park at a location offering Wi-Fi. In my travels, I have learned to check with the person in charge to make certain the network is turned on if I'm having difficulty getting connected.

It's also possible to upgrade your vessel's ability to access shore Wi-Fi by purchasing an advanced omnidirectional antenna that will extend the Wi-Fi range of an on-shore location or other nearby signal source. In our experience, using an extension antenna, while less costly than some other options, is also less reliable.

Cell phone companies provide a service called Hot Spot, either as an option on a smartphone or as a stand-alone unit. By activating the hot spot on your cell phone, you can use it to access Wi-Fi from one or more digital devices such as computers and tablets. Should you decide to go this route, understand that your connection will be only as good as your cell phone signal is.

Some Wi-Fi companies sell access to their service through various marinas. Once you sign up, you may find you can use it in many places. For example, we were able to obtain Wi-Fi as far south as St. Thomas, in the Virgin Islands, once we were in our service provider's network.

The most reliable means, I have found, of having consistent Wi-Fi while cruising is to make your boat a mobile Wi-Fi station—that is to say, a hot spot. To do this, pay a visit to a cell phone service company that offers roving Wi-Fi. It will sell you a preprogramed unit set up to connect one to ten devices, depending on the model you choose. These devices can be a combination of smartphones, laptops, and other digital devices requiring an Internet signal to operate. This easy-to-use equipment only needs to be plugged into an AC outlet and turned on in order to make your boat a mobile Wi-Fi station.

As you cruise, be prepared to encounter dead spots and to accept a low signal strength, even with a mobile unit. While the local carrier service we used in the British Virgin Islands was less than perfect, we felt lucky to have almost continuous connectivity. With such excellent carriers in the States, I imagine the level of service you might receive would be higher.

CHAPTER 13
Entertain Landlubbers

Boating has a glamour that few can resist. It attracts all ages and types of people who want to share the experience with you. Yet, making arrangements to share a cruise with friends or relatives can leave you kicking up your heels with anticipation or spending sleepless nights trying to figure out how on earth you're going to manage them. Read on to find out how to prepare yourselves, your boat, and your guests for their cruise, as well as how to make them feel welcome.

   If your intended visitors have been on a boat before, you've cleared the worst hurdle, and nonboaters who are willing and able to enjoy the day with you are always most welcome. The real challenge is entertaining folks like frail Uncle Harry who is enthusiastic but has limitations, or your mother-in-law who detests the sun, the wind, and anything that will mess her hair and makeup.

By taking the time to understand and educate your prospective guests and prepare for their visit, even the most demanding folks will enjoy their time aboard. It's not always easy to share our boats with others, but by planning ahead and doing whatever it takes to make their visit pleasant, we are giving friends and loved ones a gift worth all the salt in the ocean.

PLAN SMART

Begin planning for visiting friends by making decisions about how you will handle your upcoming cruise. Here are a few decisions you might need to make:

➢ Will you have too many people aboard? Beware of overcrowding. The cockpits on most average-sized cruising boats won't accommodate more than six people without restricting their movements or forcing some people to the upper deck or elsewhere on the boat to make some space. This can create a problem when the seas or winds kick up, or if it rains.

➢ What are their expectations? Do they want to catch fish, learn to sail, go fast, get a suntan, go snorkeling or swimming, lie on a beach, simply spend time with you, or do they just want to brag that they've been on your boat?

➢ What kind of trip will it be? Are you taking guests out for a short spin, an all-day cruise, or will they stay overnight?

> ➤ Where will you take them and what will it entail? Resist the urge to take first timers on an extended cruise. Instead, plan a short trip to determine how well they handle being on the water and if they are enjoying the ride.

> ➤ Will you make any stops? If so, what is involved? Do you need to get them in a dinghy to go to shore? Will you be docking for an hour to sightsee and have a meal before returning to your home port?

INTERVIEW GUESTS

Well before their visit, chat with your prospective guests in a tactful, friendly manner. Make suggestions, answer their questions, and try not to scare them off with sea tales. Make it clear to guests whose boating experience is limited to commercial cruise liners that your boat is much smaller and more casual. Define your version of casual to them. Should they ask, "When do we dress up?" say never!

Here are a few suggestions that will help make this visit pleasant for everyone:

> ➤ Insist that guests wear boat shoes or other rubber-soled footwear to protect them from injuring themselves and from marring your boat.

> ➤ Discuss your itinerary so your guests will know to bring along a swimsuit or a fresh outfit for the evening.

> ➤ It's normally cooler and windier by the water than it is on shore, so suggest guests pack long pants and a light jacket or sweatshirt, even if the weather promises to be hot.

➤ Remind guests to pack sunscreen, cover-ups, sunglasses, and a hat of some sort. Unless they're beach bums, they may not be prepared for the intensity of the sun or wind they'll be experiencing.

While you are having this conversation, tactfully find out if any of your guests-to-be get seasick. Have they ever had trouble riding in a plane or the back seat of a car? If so, recommend they bring along a remedy that worked for them. To be safe, keep aboard your cache of motion sickness remedies. It's wisest not to wait until a guest is aboard to ask this question because the power of suggestion can take over.

Inquire about food preferences and allergies so you don't make the mistake of serving ham sandwiches to a vegetarian or cream cheese dip to someone who is lactose intolerant. Needless to say, don't plan on serving an alcoholic beverage to a person who is recovering from addiction or is taking medication that conflicts with it.

Most folks will offer to contribute food or drink. Be honest about what you really need and alert them to your boat's limitations. Let them bring their favorite beverages, salads, or baked goods, but be frank about the amount and type of storage space you have. Many times, people coming for the day will bring their own cooler stocked with contributions to the party. Plan in advance where you might stow it so it won't be in the way. If extra coolers will be cumbersome, say so or you'll be barking your shins on them.

Warn against packaging foods that must be chilled in large containers that will in no way, no how fit in your icebox or refrigerator. I once had a guest arrive with a large glass platter loaded with a luscious taco dip that couldn't be stowed where it wouldn't spill over or break. Such delicate foods require too much babying for this occasion.

When an invite involves an overnight stay, explain it as camping. This way, when you assign a visitor a sleeping bag in the cockpit or expect two folks to squeeze into a single berth, they will accept it without grumbling. Any person who offers to bring his or her own bedding or towels is a godsend.

Be alert to comments from guests indicating they may bring along their dog, kids, or a date, since this will definitely impact your trip plans. If you don't feel you can accommodate additional people or don't want to deal with their children or pet, tell them so up front.

PREP FOR COMPANY

You've done your homework, and your Aunt Tillie and her entourage or your nonboating buddies are due to arrive. Are you ready?

> ➢ Is the boat clean, with everything stowed?

> ➢ Do you have extra gear for guests in case they come unprepared for the sun, rain, or cold?

> ➢ Are life preservers that will fit everyone accessible?

> ➢ Are you supplied with enough food and drink to last the trip?

> ➢ Have you considered potential boarding issues?

> ➢ Are you prepared to deal with motion sickness?

> ➢ Will overnight guests have a comfortable place to bed down?

BOARDING GUESTS

Cater to your guests. Most active, healthy adults can physically manage to board a boat and maneuver about on it. Guests who are elderly or have any sort of handicap may present a problem if you fail to consider how they might deal with ladders and stairs. However, it's difficult to tell someone you love, "I don't think you can manage." Although you want them to share in your joy of boating, they don't have a clue what they're in for. Getting such folks aboard needn't be an issue or an embarrassment for them if you've thought it through beforehand.

AT DOCK

Make boarding easier by securing the boat in a stationary position at a floating dock so guests can climb aboard with the fewest contortions. A small step stool or set of steps will facilitate this task. If you don't have either, perhaps a neighbor will loan you theirs.

If your boat is at dock on a fixed-piling-type slip, boarding can be most difficult. Your boat will be tied to four or more surrounding pilings, which look like telephone poles; it will float up and down with any prevailing tides. In New England, where high and low tide can easily vary by 8 feet, getting aboard at low tide can be treacherous. If this is your situation, boarding anyone who is not agile will be a problem. I suggest locating to an easier boarding location, even if it means pulling up at another marina or begging space at a fuel dock for a few minutes. Do this before guests are due to arrive so they won't be left standing and waiting for you to bring the boat around. Also, you want them to feel that what you are doing is normal boarding procedure. Return to this same spot for disembarking.

IN AN ANCHORAGE

If you keep your boat on a mooring, getting guests aboard from an unstable dinghy requires an intricate dance of timing and synchronization. You may have become expert at the procedure and know exactly how and where to support and balance yourself, and how to swing into the cockpit, but first-time visitors may not. Ask someone experienced to board first to guide others, and don't make a big deal about it.

Use a launch service to get visitors to your boat. Elderly or slightly infirm passengers whom you were unable to board dockside might be able to handle boarding from a launch. Boarding will be much easier because the launch will pull alongside the widest part of your boat and enable guests to easily disembark with a small hop upward. Provide guests your boat's name and location, and tell them where to pick up the launch. Pay the launch driver in advance, or inform guests if any costs or tips are expected.

WELCOME GUESTS ABOARD

Before you get underway, make your visitors feel at home and safe. Assure them that you have enough safety equipment to save a sinking ship, without scaring them into thinking it might happen on this cruise. Designate a life preserver to each person aboard and have him or her try it on, adjust the straps, and either wear it or keep it handy.

If you hope to avoid the nasty task of unclogging the head postvisit, clearly explain its use—without making your guests feel reluctant to use the facilities. A guest in the head-avoidance mode will refuse liquids, thereby risking dehydration. Have your visitor perform a practice flush, and demonstrate the amount of toilet paper to be used—two squares maximum. With women, be explicit: absolutely no sanitary products are to be flushed. A small plastic trash bag placed in the head may discourage sneak flushers.

Reassure your guests that it's perfectly normal to be nervous about using the head for the first time. If going below is a problem for them because they can't handle the motion or manage the companionway, assist them and make sure they are safe.

If you have a sailboat or if you expect much movement, issue cautions about stowing or securing loose items such as glasses and cameras, and taking care not to leave open cups of liquid about.

ENSURE GUESTS ENJOY THE RIDE

Once the engine is on, inexperienced or new boaters sometimes get nervous from all the scampering to stow lines and fenders. Seat guests who don't wish to participate in the action where they will be relatively free of sudden jolts.

Keep guests comfortable and entertained by assigning minor tasks to anyone interested and capable, like tweaking the jib and assisting with docking. Many folks enjoy taking a turn at the helm; it's a thrill to envision oneself as captain and in control of a vessel. Be sure to heap on the praise with each new accomplishment. (You may be training future crew.)

Share the sights you enjoy with your passengers. Use the binoculars to show them points of interest. Point out your position on the chart and show them where you are headed. Instill confidence that you are in control and proceeding safely.

Finally, take a lot of pictures to send to your guests postcruise.

"BABY" ON BOARD

The extra challenge of children can be disastrous if you are unprepared. They get bored easily and they are more active and restless than usual when in a confined area and may run where an adult would tread carefully.

Be clear about what kind of behavior is allowed and what kind isn't. Set rules and urge parents to enforce them. Children new to boating like to spend time belowdecks, where they can get into all kinds of mischief or develop seasickness. As a precaution, suggest children don a pair of acupressure bands.

Ask guests with wee ones to bring games, books, soft toys, and other quiet activities to keep their children safely entertained while they are on the boat. Some of my boating friends who often have children aboard keep a few appropriate toys on hand—just in case.

IT'S A NASTY DAY

No matter how hard we plan for a cruise, it's always going to be dependent on the weather. If you awaken the morning of an impending visit and the wind is howling like a coyote in pain and rain is coming down in sheets, your first thought is to cancel. If you have a cell phone, it's easy enough to call and reschedule (assuming the cellular network is functioning and you're within range).

Oftentimes, visitors want to come regardless of bad weather. The date was on their schedule and they're not sure when they can make it again. We once had a young couple insist on visiting us aboard the day after a hurricane struck our area, even though there was no way we could go sailing. The important thing is to relax. You can't control the weather.

Use the unexpected downtime to enhance your friendships and get to know your family again. We've had some of our best times with people on bad-weather days. Like sloughing off work, we have an excuse for not performing and wind up relaxed, enjoying a great visit.

While you are awaiting your visitors' arrival on an iffy day, devise a default cruise to an area where you are certain the waters will be calm. In our area, we motor up the Mystic River. Often, we'll tie up at a town dock and stroll the main avenue before returning to port.

If taking the boat out will be a problem, turn a miserably rainy day into a sightseeing jaunt. Collect ideas for entertaining those visitors you know won't be content to stay put. Keep local tour guides on your boat or consult the "near me" application on your computer or smartphone. One nasty day, we toured a submarine at Groton, hit the Mystic Aquarium, ate lunch at an Italian restaurant, and then capped the day with a visit to a local winery.

Guests who have come to relax may be content to go with the flow. If you are at dock, where it's easy to get off and on the boat without getting slammed by wind or water, divide up. Let the women go shopping while the guys talk boats, read, or take naps. Some folks are happy to just hang out. Keeping warm and dry inside your boat is far superior to being at home and much more fun for visitors who might enjoy the novelty of "camping." Years ago, nasty weather foiled our plans to sail to Newport with good friends from afar. We spent a blustery weekend on our home-port mooring and ended up having a better visit than we would have had in Newport, with no sunburn to boot.

PART FIVE: KEEP ALL SYSTEMS GO

The fun is over for now, because here comes the hard part: keeping the critical systems on your boat in top notch condition. Does the engine cough and sputter each time you turn the key? Is your water system making grinding sounds? How come the refrigerator isn't getting cold? *Awk!* You smell propane! What do you do? Having such problems sure would put a cramp on your vacation cruise, so let's talk about how to keep everything running smoothly and troubleshoot any problems.

CHAPTER 14

Maintain Critical Boat Operation

Anything with moving parts needs to be maintained to keep it in top operating condition. This is the reason it's wise to run your engine frequently to keep the fuel and oil circulating. Maintain your battery by using it often and keeping it charged. Environmental factors — salt water, humidity, heat, and cold — combined with the stress of moving through the water impacts the amount and type of maintenance your boat will require. Read on to learn what you need to do to service your engine, how and why you should perform routine engine service, how to isolate engine and system problems, and how to charge and maintain your batteries.

PERFORM ROUTINE CHECKS

Make it a point to frequently walk around your vessel and inspect all aspects from the condition of the hull and the lines to the internal components of your engine room. If you have performed this check at the beginning of boating season, you already have an idea of how various parts of your boat should look and operate, so issues needing attention should pop out at you.

Double-checking that everything is in A1 condition is especially important before you set out on that cruise. It's much easier to make repairs or to obtain service when you aren't stuck in a strange port or out on the water.

BE PREPARED TO FIX IT

Once you have the necessary tools and manuals aboard, it will be a snap to make repairs or perform maintenance chores, even when you are on cruise. You should already have a basic tool kit aboard. Add any items you bring from home, borrow, or buy to perform specific tasks. Doing so will provide you or anyone who helps you the wherewithal to fix problems not complex or serious enough to require a professional. Carry spare fuses, filters, extra oil, transmission oil, spare impellers, and some spare fuel in a jerry can.

Take time to review your system manuals. It's easier to fix things if you understand how they go together. Always have your engine and system manuals on board for reference. Organize these in files or in three-ring binders.

It's wise to keep a maintenance log of all service performed on your boat. This is helpful not only when selling your boat, but also to alert you to any developing issues. For example, if you notice you are adding oil or changing filters more than usual, you need to check further for a problem.

MONITOR CRITICAL GAUGES

Use the readings on instruments and gauges to measure the performance of engine-related systems. Reference your owner's manuals or ask a professional service technician what settings or range of settings are normal for your boat.

Here are a few tips on monitoring gauges for essential systems:

Fuel gauge: A full fuel tank is a happy one. If fuel is getting low, schedule a fill-up.

Engine temperature: When you are running your engine, keep an eye on the temperature gauge to be sure the engine is not overheating.

Oil pressure: An oil pressure gauge measures how oil is circulating through your engine. If the number falls below the normal level, per the operator's manual for your boat, check the oil level, and add more oil if needed. If the gauge still reads low, schedule service.

Battery voltage meter: This instrument measures the amount of voltage your battery is emanating and will verify your alternator is charging the batteries as it should be.

Engine hours: Monitor your engine hour meter(s) to make sure you do not exceed the time between oil and filter changes.

PREVENT AND ISOLATE ENGINE PROBLEMS

It's no fun to get stuck with a dead engine while out and about. Keep ahead of problems by managing your fuel and maintaining the associated systems used to run the engine on your boat. Most problems can be avoided or solved by regular routine maintenance and taking the time to learn how to make basic repairs. Even if you customarily have your engine serviced, it is good to know how to flag and prevent problems, perform simple chores like changing the oil and filters, and bleeding the fuel system.

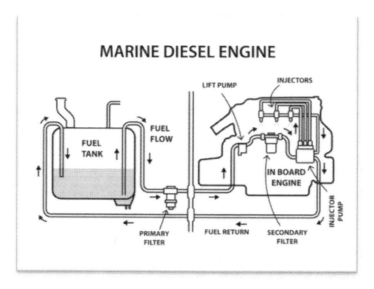

Undertaking these chores at dock will ensure you have the correct spares, tools, and know-how to handle emergency situations on the water.

HAVE ENOUGH CLEAN FUEL

Keep fuel tanks as full as practical to prevent engine problems. When you are traveling and low on fuel, debris from the bottom of the tank is likely to get sucked into the fuel system, blocking the engine fuel filters and starving the engine. Another problem with dead space in the fuel tank is the formation of condensation. If you aren't using your boat frequently, water will build up and algae may form, adding water and ick to the problem. Prevent this by adding an algaecide when refueling.

Dirty fuel can turn to jelly and ruin your entire fuel system. For the most part, the fuel you obtain from reputable fuel pumps within the United States is relatively free of debris or gunk. In other parts of the world, this may not be so. As a precaution when obtaining fuel from a questionable source, filter the fuel as you fill your tank by using a funnel with a filter. If the fuel already in your tank looks dirty, treat it with a fuel additive and replace the fuel filters.

PREVENT OVERHEATING

Check that water is cooling the engine. On raw water-cooled engines, the surrounding sea water is used directly. Most modern diesel engines use raw water to cool the freshwater, which in turn cools the engine.

When the normal heat produced by the burning fuel is not being removed from the engine quickly enough, the engine will overheat. To avoid damaging your engine, stop the boat immediately and isolate the problem.

Check for these issues:

➢ Is the thermostat stuck?

➢ Is the raw water strainer (seacock) blocked with debris? Raw water passes from the seacock below the waterline through a filter in the strainer. Most strainers are cleaned by turning off the seacock, opening the strainer, and removing the filter. If the filter is in good condition, wash and replace it. Once you are finished, be sure to reopen the seacock before starting your engine.

➢ Is the freshwater pump for the engine working? If the pump impeller fails, water will no longer be forced through the heat exchanger, which will stop water from circulating through the engine and cooling it. Check the impeller for cracked or broken blades. If it appears to be clogged, you may need to remove and clean the whole assembly.

➢ Is the heat exchanger blocked? Good preventive maintenance involves inspecting the heat exchanger each season and, if necessary, removing it and rinsing it out to clear debris.

➢ Does the zinc need to be replaced? Often heat exchangers have their own zinc anodes to minimize electrolysis. If your zinc has decayed by more than 50 percent, it's time to replace it.

Should you experience frequent problems with overheating during the summer, when the temperature of the raw sea water is already high, installing a larger heat exchanger may alleviate the problem.

heat exchanger = a component used to transfer heat from freshwater to raw water in a freshwater system.

seacock = a valve on the hull of a boat that permits seawater to flow into the boat for cooling the engine, or to run through a faucet, sink drain, or toilet.

CHECK AND CHANGE ENGINE OIL

Don't put off oil changes. Expensive problems result when your engine is not properly lubricated or has old engine oil. Accumulated dirt and sludge in your engine oil can act as an abrasive on bearings rather than a lubricant. Over time, this will cause wear in your engine.

Use the dip stick to check the engine oil level. If it reads low, add the manufacturer's recommended type of oil to the fill level indicated on the dip stick. Manufacturers vary on the intervals for oil changes. The most commonly suggested interval is every 100 hours; but the range can vary between 75 and 200 hours. Check your engine's manual.

The process for changing the oil in a gasoline or diesel engine is similar to changing the oil in a car, except you will need a catch bucket.

Follow these steps:

1. Remove the oil filler cap or the dipstick.

2. Insert the extractor tube from the pump into the dipstick tube.

3. Pump out the oil into a throwaway container such as an empty water jug.

4. Set the old oil aside to dispose of per marine regulations.

5. Refill the engine with fresh oil.

CHANGE FILTERS

It's a good practice to replace your engine's oil and fuel filters with each oil change, or at least once each season. This will head off potential engine problems. When you do so, be sure to top off the new fuel filter with clean fuel.

Air entering the engine is usually filtered to remove particles that may cause damage. Air filters for marine engines are normally the same kind used in car engines. Some need to be cleaned at regular intervals. On each filter, make it a practice to mark the engine hours and the date on which they were changed. Enter this information in your maintenance log.

ELIMINATE AIR IN THE FUEL

Air in the fuel can cause your engine to fail when you are out on the water. In most cases, bleeding the system to remove air will allow the engine to restart. If you changed the fuel filters yourself, you probably learned then how to reconnect the system and bleed air from the secondary fuel filter or injection pump intake.

Try these methods to get rid of air bubbles:

➢ Once all the fuel filters are on and tight, bleed the fuel system. Some engines are equipped with electric fuel pumps that make bleeding either automatic or much simpler. If your engine has an engine-driven fuel pump, you will need to use the priming pump either on or next to the filter.

➢ Track down leaky seals. Leaking seals on the suction side of the tank can cause air to be sucked in; on the pressure side, leaks cause fuel to be sprayed out.

To manually bleed the fuel system: Open the bleed screw. Start the pumping process until fuel begins spitting out of the bleed screw hole. When you are finished, close the bleed screw.

INSPECT BELTS

Belts on the engine are used to connect pumps, alternators, and compressors. Periodically inspect the belts for wear from misalignment or cracking due to old age. Adjust belts to the correct tension for their use.

CHECK ALTERNATOR OPERATION

With the engine running, check to be certain your alternators are operating and charging your batteries.

REFILL TRANSMISSION OIL

Using the dip stick, check your transmission oil levels to be sure they don't run dry. On an inboard engine, the process is similar to checking the oil. Some transmissions use plain oil, whereas others use standard transmission fluid. Read your manual and make sure you have what you need on board.

Clear Air Intakes

Check to see how your engine receives its air supply to be sure the intake valve or area is not blocked. A diesel engine needs an adequate supply of air. Special air intakes may be installed to force air into the engine room of boats with large engines. With smaller engines, air is usually provided to the engine through cockpit lockers or the bilge.

Replace Damaged Metal Parts

Watch for signs of corrosion, rust, or electrolysis on metal fittings and wire terminals in contact with water. Bronze parts that have turned pink indicate a stray current problem. Discolored wire terminals or insulation are signs of excessive heating or corrosion.

Inspect Motor Mounts

Check motor mounts to make sure they are tight and have not broken. Damage to the stuffing box and cutlass bearing may result if they wear or engine vibration allows them to come loose.

Check for Leaks

While you are working in your engine compartment, check for oil or antifreeze drips. Make certain there isn't water where it is not supposed to be. Move oily rags and any garbage that doesn't belong. Be sure any and all supplies are stored and secure, with nothing touching the engine or in the way of moving parts.

Troubleshoot Engine Start Problems

If your engine starts and dies after maintenance, it could be caused by an air lock in the system, especially if the engine has just been serviced. When you start the engine after changing its fuel filter, don't let the engine idle. Rev the engine up for a few minutes to ensure that any lingering air in the system works itself through.

A major cause of a sluggish or nonfunctioning engine is weak or failed batteries. Blocked air filters can also be a factor in poor starting, as can overly cold air that has caused failed glow plugs or impacted compression.

Maintain Battery Power

The engine may be the heart of your boat, but your batteries are its soul. Without them, none of your boat's systems will work unless you are plugged into shore power. By keeping them charged and performing simple maintenance, your batteries will keep your boat moving and operating smoothly.

Battery Bank

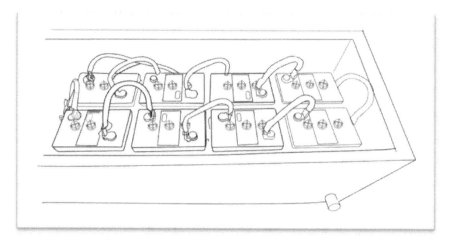

Monitor your battery level on the voltage meter. Normally, if the battery level dips below 11.5 volts, it needs to be charged. However, you should check the level requirements in the documentation in your boat owner's manual or the battery brochure.

At dock while connected to shore power, your batteries will get a good, hard charge. In an anchorage, running the engine or a generator periodically will keep your batteries strong and your boat's systems operating properly.

Wet-cell batteries need to have their water levels checked regularly. If water level is low, fill them to the full line with distilled water. Periodically check batteries for loose connectors and corrosion. Tighten fittings and clean off green coloring or white powder around posts with anticorrosion grease.

If your batteries are taking longer than usual to charge, you may have a bad battery. Even one bad battery can strain the system. Neighboring batteries in the bank must work harder to make up for the loss, and they too will wear down. If batteries are not charging at all, check for an alternator problem.

Test for bad batteries: Test each anode using a voltage meter to determine which, if any, are low. Replace low-voltage batteries with the correct size for your boat.

STOP, LISTEN, LOOK, STAY AWARE OF CHANGE

Strange noises, funny smells, and anything that looks or feels odd can mean loose parts or that something is broken or defective. Investigate. Ignoring a potential problem can be expensive later on and may even cause you to be stranded in a place where no help is available.

ALARMS

If a system alarm sounds while you are underway, slow down or stop. Hand over the helm to a capable crew member while you investigate the source.

UNUSUAL EXHAUST

On a normally running engine, the exhaust should be clear. Any smoke indicates a potential problem.

White smoke results from water vapor and can occur when an engine is first started. Continuing white smoke may indicate water in the fuel. White smoke accompanied by loss of engine power could mean that one of the cylinders has failed to fire due to cooling water entering via a cracked or leaking cylinder head gasket.

Black smoke is the most common. It indicates that unburned fuel is being ejected with the exhaust gases. Gas engines smoking for more than ten seconds at startup indicate a problem with the fuel mixture. A diesel engine emitting black smoke may mean it needs a new air filter. Billowing smoke might mean new injectors. Another cause is a blocked exhaust elbow where cooling water is injected into the exhaust.

An excessive load on the engine due to a badly fouled propeller or boat bottom, or an overly large propeller will cause the injector pump to deliver maximum fuel to the engine. Because of the load, the engine will be turning slowly and will not be able to use all the fuel, resulting in black smoke. Continuing to overload the engine could cause major damage.

A *sheen on the water* near the exhaust when the engine is running indicates poorly burning fuel caused by bad injectors, timing, plugs, or poor compression from valve or ring problems.

Blue smoke indicates your engine lubricating oil is finding its way into the combustion chamber and is being burned. If this occurs, the engine needs decarbonizing and perhaps an overhaul.

FUNNY SMELLS

Abnormal odors can signal problems in various areas of your boat, so don't turn up your nose at them.

Keep tuned in to these odors:

> ➤ A change in *bilge smell* indicates leaking condensation from the air conditioning, refrigeration, or a shower sump.

> ➤ *Fuel smell* means a problem is developing. Often a fuel leak is caused by the vibration of a fuel line against another part of the engine. Leaking of high-pressure fuel could cause a fire.

> ➤ A *burning rubber smell* can be caused by a slipping belt. This can create friction and overheat an alternator, or freeze the bearings in an alternator or water pump, and lead to equipment problems.

> ➤ If the odors of *steamy water or antifreeze* emanate from the engine compartment, check if the engine is running hot. With an antifreeze odor, you may have a cracked head or block in the cooling system.

> ➤ A hot *lube oil smell* indicates an oil leak. Shut down the engine at once.

> ➤ A *burned oil smell* could mean serious internal problems. Have the engine checked stat.

> ➤ *Burning electric insulation smells* indicate a terminal is overheating and about to short out or arc. It also could mean there is too much load somewhere in

the electrical system and an electric component is having an internal meltdown. To isolate the source of the odor, turn off the suspected component at the breaker, or shut off AC and DC power for the entire boat. Turn on circuits one at a time to determine the problem area.

Unusual Sounds

Like odors, abnormal sounds can indicate serious, as well as minor, issues with your boat.

Keep your ears perked for odd sounds like these:

➢ *Cracking or creaking noises* made by the hull while you are underway are indications of stress. Check the hull for signs of delamination, failure of the structural bonds between bulkheads or supports, the potential for the transom detaching, and other serious problems. If a structural part of your boat begins to flex or move while you are underway, it is about to fail.

➢ A *gravelly noise* could mean the bearings on a component, such as an alternator or freshwater pump, are about to fail. Check that the fan belt isn't too tight, because this could speed up deterioration of the bearings.

➢ Abnormal *change in tilt-lift motor noise* on an outboard means the pump may be ready to fail or there is air in the tilt motor fluid. If the sound indicates a drop in voltage, there may be a problem with the charging system, corrosion on connections, or wiring.

➢ *Variation in engine noise* indicates there may be impurities in the fuel, or you may have an air leak in the suction line, a clogging filter, a failing fuel pump, or a failing injector pump.

➢ A *heavy thunk* when you push the start button for the engine may be caused by a hydraulic lock due to standing water on a piston. A lighter thunk indicates a bad solenoid, engagement gear, or starter.

➢ A *squealing noise* is a sign of a loose V-belt or that one of the components—alternator or freshwater recirculating pump—is freezing up, or that there are bad bearings. In the alternator, it could be caused by an overload or deteriorating parts.

➢ A *bilge pump running* more often indicates a possible leak. Check the propeller shaft seal, freshwater system, cooling system, pop-off valve in the hot water heater, and the hoses on the engine.

➢ Unusual *noises in the transmission* are a sure sign of a developing problem. Get service.

CHAPTER 15

Maintain Water Systems

Whew, that engine chapter was a bear to get though, but you did it. Now, we'll move on to water. Whether you are using the water from your boat's tanks to wash dishes, shower, or to drink you'll want it free of bacteria and odors. Read on to learn how to keep your pressurized water system in good operating condition, how to use salt water to boost your freshwater supply, and how to obtain clean, free-flowing freshwater from the water surrounding you.

BUILT-IN WATER SYSTEMS

A permanently installed water system provides a functioning sink and faucet. Water is brought up through the system and is controlled either by manually pumping a hand or foot pedal or by using the boat's battery or electrical power in a pressurized system. Should boat power fail, most boats with pressurized systems have a manual pump to use as backup.

PRESSURIZED WATER ISSUES

A pressurized system is turned on and off via a switch on a boat's control panel. When water is turned on at a tap somewhere within the boat, the system makes a grinding sound as water is being drawn.

If your system continues to groan long after you've stopped drawing water, check the water gauge, if you have one, to see if you are getting low on water. If so, get out the hose and fill up. If this doesn't resolve the problem, there is likely air in the system. Burp a bubble out of the line by running water from one or more of the faucets until air spurts out and the water runs freely.

If you are having trouble coaxing water from the tap, check to be sure the water tanks are full enough for the pump to operate without the added stress of digging deeper to get at the water.

Follow this process to isolate the issue:

> If the tank is full and the pump is not turning on, check the control panel to be certain the water pressure breaker is turned on.

> If the breaker is on and the tanks are full, yet no water is flowing from your tap, look for kinks in the plumbing or obstructions in the tank vent.

> If all else fails to resolve the problem, search further for electrical problems, corrosion, or faulty connections.

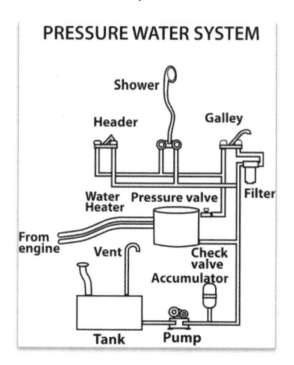

MAINTAIN CLEAN WATER TANKS

Mineral buildup will clog the pipes if tanks and lines aren't flushed and cleaned properly. Standing water grows nasty things if left in your tanks for long periods and may become contaminated. If you have clean tanks and keep the water in them moving and refreshed, you should feel comfortable drinking the water on your boat. If you have more than one water tank, be sure to switch over to the second tank once the first one is empty so you use up the water in both tanks. Bear in mind that all metal tanks must be bonded to prevent electrolysis. If you notice pitting on the exterior of your metal tanks, a defect in your grounding may be causing a chemical reaction.

Follow manufacturer instructions and warnings for cleaning additives, particularly with aluminum tanks. New tanks, especially fiberglass or plastic, may smell of the material of which they're made. Often, adding baking soda to the water will help sweeten the water and help prevent other odors later. The amount depends on the severity of the problem and volume of the tank. Typically, about a cup of baking soda mixed into a gallon of water will suffice for a ten-gallon tank. As with any large quantity of additive, flush through the system and drain the tanks, then refill with freshwater.

DISINFECT WATER TANKS

If the water in your tank has been standing for some time or you suspect it may be contaminated, follow this procedure to purify the tank and all distribution lines being served by it. For a unit with an installed water filter, remove the cartridge before disinfecting.

To disinfect your tanks:

1. Add 2/3 cup (6 ounces) of chlorine for every 10 gallons of water in a full tank of water. Adding a commercial brand of chlorine, such as Clorox or Purex, is fine as long as it is unscented and does not contain any other active ingredients or deodorizers.

2. Run water from each tap or outlet until you smell heavy chlorine.

3. Close off the taps. Allow the chlorinated water to sit for two to four hours until the chlorine smell disappears. I recommend evacuating the boat during this period since inhaling chlorine gas is not a good thing.

4. Drain tank(s) completely and refill them with freshwater.

If, after completing this procedure, your water retains a slight chlorine odor or taste, try flushing water through again and again until it dissipates.

You won't need to repeat this disinfectant process as long as the water system remains intact, doesn't get contaminated, or isn't interrupted to install new equipment.

MAINTAIN POTABLE WATER

Once you've ensured your tanks are clean and sterile, help them stay that way. Always fill tanks with water drawn from the cleanest, most dependable water source available. Each time you refill your tanks, add a chlorine compound to the water-storage tank. Allow 1 teaspoon of chlorine for every 10 gallons of water. If you have not done so already, install a water filter to remove bad tastes, odors, and disease bacteria that may still be viable.

SALTWATER SOLUTIONS

If you will be cruising on the ocean and want to eliminate having to repeatedly tie up in port to refill water tanks, take advantage of the availability of salt water by substituting salt water for freshwater whenever it makes sense. For this to be a viable option, sea water must be relatively clean and not brackish.

Here are some ways to take advantage of salt water:

> Plumb your galley, and possibly your head, with salt water. Installing a diverter valve on the water inlet to the pressure water pump will allow you to switch between using salt and freshwater.

➢ If your boat is not equipped with a pressurized system, save on the amount of freshwater used by installing an extra foot pump to bring salt water into your galley sink. You can also have a dual pump set up to handle both fresh and salt water.

➢ Cook with salt water. Substitute a mix of salt water and freshwater for all freshwater in dishes requiring boiled water, such as pasta. Use salt water to rinse vegetables and clean pots and pans. Save freshwater for drinking, sensitive recipes, and a final rinse of dishes.

INSTALL A WATERMAKER

A watermaker is made up of a motor/drive assembly, a pump, and a prefilter. As mentioned earlier, a watermaker converts salt water to fresh by the process of osmosis. Watermakers are designed for use in clean sea water, not harbor water or tap water.

If you already have a watermaker on your boat, skip over to the section on maintaining and troubleshooting. If not, read on for tips on installing a new watermaker.

➢ Install the motor drive assembly in a dry, accessible area of the boat that does not get overly hot or exude potentially explosive fuel fumes. Because the unit is not waterproof, it can corrode. Excessive heat, such as in an engine compartment, can damage or destroy the motor or membrane, and a spark could start a fire.

➢ Be sure not to install the pump assembly above anything that could be damaged if the pump leaked or near quiet sleeping quarters.

> For easy testing, removal, and servicing, use properly sized ring terminals and a terminal strip near the pump to connect electric power.

> Use a total dissolved solids (TDS) meter to test the quality of the water before it diverts into your tanks.

> For ease of routine inspection and maintenance, find a convenient, accessible spot to install the prefilter assembly for your watermaker.

> Don't use a thru-hull installed high on your vessel's hull for the watermaker's seawater intake, especially on a sailboat. Under sail, a normal amount of heel can cause the thru-hull to be out of the water, allowing air into the intake system. A rolling anchorage can do the same.

> Provide a shutoff valve (seacock) in the seawater intake line along with a coarse strainer.

> Installing two Y-valves on the watermaker intake makes it easy to draw in water from the freshwater tank for daily flushing, or to take in biocide when preparing for longer-term storage.

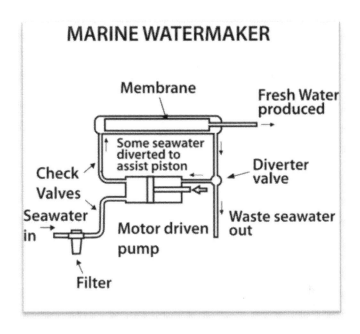

MAINTAIN YOUR WATERMAKER

By regularly managing and maintaining your watermaker, clean-smelling water will flow freely through your system. Here are some ways to keep your system operating properly:

> ➢ Run your watermaker when the batteries are being charged to ensure the voltage is high and that the energy goes directly into the water-making load without being stored in the batteries.

> ➢ Operate the watermaker between two and eight hours, depending on the capacity of your unit and the amount of water you intend to make.

> ➢ Use your watermaker every day to prevent biological growth. If possible, flush the system with unchlorinated freshwater after each use.

➤ If you haven't used your watermaker for a week or more, are in a tropical climate for three days, or will be putting your boat in storage, flush or pickle the system with a biocide. After each biocide treatment, discard the water produced during the first 20 minutes of the next session.

➤ During regular use, rinse the prefilter at least once a week to prevent silt from accumulating and entering the watermaker.

➤ Once the prefilter loses its rigidity, replace it with a polyester 30-micron prefilter, instead of a paper filter that will break down.

➤ After every 1,000 to 1,200 hours of use, replace all O-rings (seals) and check valves with parts from a seal repair kit.

➤ At least once a year remove biological growth and mineral scaling using acid and alkaline cleaners.

➤ When operating your watermaker in areas with high silt content, install a more elaborate prefiltration system to ensure that the watermaker gets enough water flow.

➤ Periodically inspect and test the entire seawater intake system to assure that all joints and fittings are airtight, especially the connections at the prefilter assembly.

➤ Remove any silt or sand during prefiltration to prevent damaging the components of the high-pressure pump.

➤ Avoid operating the unit in harbor water, which may contain pollutants that can eventually destroy the membrane.

SOLVE WATER-MAKING PROBLEMS

Like any system with moving parts, there will be issues needing your attention. If there is no or little freshwater output, air may be entering the seawater intake system. A small amount of air can keep the pump from producing enough pressure to produce freshwater.

Sea water that is cold or has high salinity will cause a slight increase in amp draw, which can result in diminished output of the water being supplied. Air bubbles caused by a leak in the intake line or turbulence around the intake thru-hull can destroy the membrane.

Stinky water is usually caused by decomposing organic materials, such as seaweed, trapped in the prefilter housing or strainer bowl. As these materials break down, undesirable chemicals pass through the watermaker system along with the freshwater being produced.

CHAPTER 16

Safe Propane Systems

Propane gas is kept aboard a boat to fuel the stove, and sometimes a grill. If you have an all-electric stove and are using a portable canister for your barbecue grill, you can skim over this section. The beauty of having a propane system is you can cook whether or not you are at dock. As a fuel, propane is explosive, which is why it's critical that your system is correctly installed and well maintained to prevent dangerous gas leaks.

THE PROPANE SYSTEM

Propane or natural gas-fueled cooking systems are typical to sailboats and some powerboats. Both gases light instantly. Of the two, propane gas is the most popular but also requires more caution. Because it is heavier than natural gas, it will sink. This means if there is a leak anywhere in your system, escaped gas will accumulate in the bilge and create a fire hazard.

By having your system installed by a professional in a cool, well-ventilated area of the boat, and by taking simple precautions when using it, you can enjoy the convenience of propane cooking with little concern.

Several components make up a propane installation. Each has a unique function and must be installed as indicated in the following section.

PROPANE LOCKER

The propane assembly needs to be contained and installed in a vapor-tight compartment separated from the interior of the boat, or outside of the boat in a spot where leaking gas will not drain to the bilge. If your boat does not have a built-in propane locker that vents directly overboard, you can purchase one ready-made. On the bottom of such lockers, a vent line allows fumes, water, or any accumulated liquid to drain overboard and above the waterline.

PROPANE TANK

The traditional propane tank is metal, usually stainless steel or aluminum. If you will be installing a new system or replacing an existing tank, consider opting for a tank constructed of fiberglass. Although more expensive than metal tanks, the new fiberglass propane tanks are lightweight and won't rust or corrode like metal. Because fiberglass is translucent, it's easy to tell how much gas is in the tank. On the average metal liquefied petroleum gas (LPG) tank, there is no fill-level gauge. Most folks try to estimate how much fuel is left in a tank by lifting it. (An empty tank will be lightweight as compared to a full one.)

Propane tanks should have intact collars and be up-to-date and UL listed. Without the protective collar, a propane cylinder is unfit for continued propane use and illegal to fill. The bottoms of all propane cylinders are required to have a foot ring, which ensures the LPG cylinder stands in an upright and level position while keeping the storage container off the ground. Cylinders without a foot ring are unfit for LPG use and are illegal to refill.

Liquefied petroleum gas (LPG) is a clean-burning fossil fuel. It consists of a mixture of propane, ethane, butane, and other gases that are produced at natural gas processing plants and refineries.

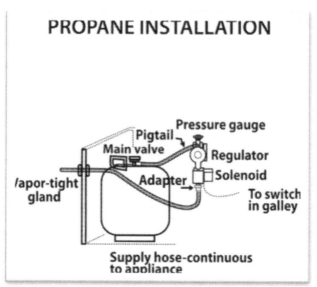

PROPANE INSTALLATION

SOLENOID VALVES

The fuel supply should have shutoff valves called solenoids both at the tank itself and at an electrical panel. The manual propane solenoid switch is usually installed in the galley area, away from the stove. Flip this switch on when you are ready to use the range and off when you are finished. As a reminder, a red light glows when the propane valve is open. For safety, solenoids close in the event of a power failure.

Post instructions in a visible location so anyone aboard will know how to perform a hard or soft shutdown. With a hard, or complete, shutdown, the propane valve at the tank is turned off, totally isolating the supply to the stove. A soft, or partial, shutdown involves turning off the solenoid switch on the boat, usually located in the galley.

FUME DETECTOR

While not required by American Boat & Yacht Council (ABYC) specs, these inexpensive, easy-to-install detectors can save your life. In the interest of safety, shut down the propane system whenever you are through cooking or plan to be away from the boat. Depending on how long the system will go without use, you may choose a partial or complete shutdown.

> *The ABYC was created in 1954 as a nonprofit organization to develop safety standards for the design, construction, equipage, repair and maintenance of boats.*

PRESSURE GAUGE

A pressure gauge is a separate or built-in unit used to detect leaks in the propane system. Install this immediately after the main valve on the LPG tank. The pressure remains relatively constant in a propane system until the fuel runs out. However, this gauge will not measure the amount of fuel.

REGULATOR

The amount of pressure issued through the propane system to provide a flame to a burner is controlled by a regulator.

CONNECTING HOSES

Lengths of hose connect the gas supply to the marine stove. On gimbaled stoves, the gas-supply line needs to be flexible as well as fire resistant. Here are some tips on installing hoses:

> ➤ Hoses must be UL-approved for propane. Do not substitute hoses meant for other uses.

> ➤ Use one continuous length of hose between the supply and the stove. Keep the number of fittings minimal because every connection is a potential leak.

> Gas lines for each appliance should originate at the tank, preventing a junction inside the boat. No junctions means fewer opportunities for leaks.

Hoses that pass through bulkheads need to be well supported and have chafe protection. Constant movement and vibration on a boat causes hoses to wear against a hard surface and leak.

MAINTAIN YOUR PROPANE SYSTEM

As mentioned earlier, if your system is properly installed and maintained, you shouldn't have any issues. Nevertheless, wear and tear on a system can create problems.

Here are some ways to prevent dangerous gas leaks:

Avoid plugged vents in the locker. If the vent is blocked in any way, leaking propane can accumulate to dangerous concentrations in the locker. To prevent this, periodically remove the tank, pour water into the locker, and verify it drains directly downward with no pockets of water remaining on the floor of the locker. While you are doing this, check the gaskets on the lid of the locker for wear and a tight seal.

Keep the propane locker clear of other gear. The only items that should be in the propane locker are the propane tank and its assembly. During a rough ride, heavy objects, like anchors, will shift and can damage the regulator or gauge; sharp objects, can cut the hose.

Replace rusted tanks, regulators, and solenoids right away. A rusted tank could fail at any time, as can one of its components, even if the date stamped on it is still valid.

Check that the protective collar on the tank is intact and undamaged. Hit hard enough, an unprotected valve can break off, allowing liquid propane to escape at a dangerously fast rate. The escaping propane can act as propulsion for the cylinder, allowing it to become a dangerous projectile.

Within the compartment, check that the tank is locked in place. If the foot ring on the tank is missing or damaged, the bottle will fall on its side and roll around. If this happens while you are using propane from the system, liquid may enter the service valve and hose, creating a dangerous situation.

Make certain the pressure gauge is in place and working properly. Without a reliable gauge, there is no way to test the system for leaks that have occurred due to certain repairs, running aground, or collision.

Test the sensor on your propane fume detector periodically by holding a flame from a butane lighter nearby. Detectors have a life span of about five years, so also check the date of manufacture.

Store tanks and cylinders away from potential fire hazards, such as a gasoline-fueled engine or hot exhaust pipes. Store spare gas cylinders of any kind, including portables, in the same manner as your primary propane tank—never inside your boat—and in a vented locker or on deck.

Don't tie an electrical wire to a propane line. If there is a short, the wire can become hot enough to melt through the hose.

Check hoses and fittings periodically for cracks and wear. Hoses won't last forever, especially if exposed to sunlight or heat. Watch for and replace rusted or corroded fittings.

WHAT IF YOU SMELL GAS?

If a *strong gas odor* permeates the boat, it could mean an explosion is about to occur. Human life is worth more than your boat is. Get off the boat, opening as many hatches as you can on the way. If you are underway, stop the boat, jump in the dinghy (or swim) as far away from the boat as possible. Warn others to clear the area, and phone the fire department or the coast guard, depending on where you are.

In the case of a *slight propane odor,* open up everything on the boat and turn on the blowers. Don't run anything powered by electricity, including fans, or turn on an inverter or a breaker: the start-up spark could ignite the propane. If you are underway, stay on deck (far from the source) and steer for shore. Keep the boat with its opened hatches pointed in the wind.

CONTROL A GAS FIRE

Should a small gas fire erupt, grab the nearest fire extinguisher and aim it at the tank to douse the fire. If you don't have an extinguisher handy and are waiting for the fire department to arrive, contain the fire by hosing it down with a continuous stream of cold water to keep the gas tank as cool as possible. When you do this, be sure to stand as far from the tank as possible.

In the case of an explosive or major fire, evacuate immediately, get as far away from the fire as you can, as fast as possible. Then call for help.

DETECT A PROPANE LEAK

Once the boat has been vented, is free of gas fumes, and deemed safe to enter, get to work finding the source of the leak.

Begin by verifying there actually is a leak. Open the manual and solenoid valves, note the reading on the pressure gauge, and then close them. The pressure should remain constant for at least ten minutes. If it doesn't, there is a gas leak in the system.

Next, isolate the source of the leak by performing the bubble test. Do not, under any circumstances, use a lit match or butane lighter to test.

To perform the Bubble Test, follow these steps:

1. Make certain all the burners on the range are shut off.

2. Mix some detergent in water.

3. Apply this mixture to all connections and other suspect points.

4. Check for areas in the hoses and connections where soap bubbles appear, indicating leaks.

Finally, repair the leak using an approved patch or by calling in an LPG service professional. Make certain the leak has been repaired by reopening the manual and solenoid valves. Note the reading on the pressure gauge, and then close the valves. If the pressure remains constant for at least ten minutes, the leak is repaired. If not, repeat the bubble test to find additional leaks.

CHAPTER 17
Maintain Heating and Cooling Systems

Having a means of heating or cooling your boat will extend your time aboard by allowing you to move comfortably about the interior despite the temperature or humidity level of the outside air. Reverse cycle heating and air-conditioning, diesel heat, and air conditioners will keep the interior of your boat dry and prevent the formation of mold, rot, and mildew. This chapter details how to maintain your reverse cycle heat and air-conditioning systems, how to find potential sources of problems with a diesel heater, and how to keep your marine refrigeration system charged and maintained.

REVERSE CYCLE HEAT AND AIR-CONDITIONING

Reverse cycle heat and air-conditioning systems, also called heat pumps, use a refrigerant as a cooling agent. A heat pump works much like the compressor on a refrigerator. It draws in outside water, and cycles it through the unit causing refrigerant gas to expand and compress. Depending on whether heat or air-conditioning is called for, the system dispels or sends hot or cool air through a ducting system within the boat. When heat is called for, the blower releases the warm air into the boat instead of to the outside as it would when in air-conditioning mode.

KEEP REVERSE CYCLE SYSTEMS OPERATING

Reverse cycle systems are temperature controlled. If your system is pumping cold air when it should be pumping warm air or vice versa, or if it simply isn't working, here are a few things to consider to resolve issues and to keep your system operating as it should.

First, understand that due to the nature of a reverse cycle system, the colder the water the boat lies in, the less heat the system will be able to deliver.

If this is not an issue, perform these checks:

➢ Find out if you are low on refrigerant. If so, have a technician refill your unit with the correct product for your system.

➢ If you find ice on the coils, look for a clogged air filter.

➢ With seawater-cooled systems, debris can clog the system, reducing water flow to the heat exchange and leading to system failure. To avoid blockage and maintain peak performance, regularly check the seawater strainer between the intake valve and the pump for accumulated debris. To loosen debris, flush with freshwater.

➢ Periodically check hoses. Remove the hoses leading from the thru-hull to the pump, and flush them with pressurized water, such as from a hose, to clear out any accumulated mud or algae.

➢ Check the filter. Ensure the proper amount of air is circulating freely by cleaning and changing the system's air filter with a good-quality, correctly fitted air filter if needed.

Resolve Air-Conditioner Issues

The cooling system in an air conditioner is identical to a refrigerator's. Neither enjoys being restarted. Don't turn the unit off and then back on without giving the unit enough time to equalize the pressure. By holding off restarting for about ten minutes, your air conditioner will be less stressed and will last longer.

Whereas some of the same problems with a reverse cycle system are common to a built-in air-conditioning system, others are more specific.

Here are some ways you can prevent or isolate problems:

➤ Check cooling coils for frost or ice build-up. If the room becomes too cold (60 degrees Fahrenheit or lower), the coils on the front of the air conditioner may ice up. Turn off the air conditioner until the air in the room gets warm enough to melt the ice.

➤ Tend to the filter. During the cooling season, clean or replace the electrostatic filter located in the front grille area of your unit.

➤ Check the condenser pan. The condenser pan catches the water the air conditioner has extracted from the humidity in the air during the cooling process. If the water in the pan feels overly hot, you may have a blockage in an upper area of the system. The pan should be free of any debris that could prevent water from draining out of it.

➤ Clean the condenser coils. A condenser is a device used for changing a gas into a liquid. Over time, condenser coils accumulate dirt, which causes the system to be inefficient. Once or twice a season, remove the cover of the air conditioner to access the coils. Vacuum out the dirt or wipe it off with a soft brush. While you are performing this task, also clean any dirt build-up at the bottom of the air conditioner.

PRECHECK DIESEL HEATER ISSUES

Diesel heating systems differ according to their capacity, model, and use. If your system isn't working properly or fails to start, check for these issues before phoning a technician:

➤ Is the heater receiving power?

➤ Are all switches and thermostats on?

➤ Is the motor fuse working?

➤ Is the control box defective?

➤ Are there any loose connections or corroded parts?

➤ Are the fuel hoses and fuel filters clear of blockage?

➤ Is the exhaust pipe obstructed?

Once you have performed these actions, you will be able to provide your service person information that may lead to a speedy repair.

MARINE REFRIGERATION SYSTEMS

Some marine refrigerators are driven directly by the boat's engine; others are powered by the boat's batteries, which, in turn, need to be amply charged by the engine or a generator. Still another source of needed power can be provided by 110-V AC shore power. As long as the power source is consistent, your boat's refrigerator and freezer will be operating as smoothly as the one you enjoy at home because it is simply designed. All parts are sealed, and its operation is straightforward.

> *Refrigeration is the process of removing heat by taking heat from one place and transferring it to another. The compressor pumps refrigerants (liquid gas) through the system, which allows the heat in one area to be absorbed and carried to another area to be released.*

USE YOUR REFRIGERATION SYSTEM

If you are in a slip, you can simply plug into shore power and reap the joys of refrigeration. You will be able to leave the refrigerator on when you go home. When you return to the boat, it will be to perfectly chilled beverages and firm sticks of butter. If you have a steady source of dockside power, switching off the refrigeration at the electrical panel at the end of a stay is inefficient, unnecessary, and puts undue stress on the system.

If you are on a mooring or frequently at anchor, you may find refrigeration is less of a boon because it is a challenge to maintain consistent temperature. Unless you have a generator to provide additional power to maintain the operation of a refrigerator without draining your batteries, you will use it sporadically and do most of your chilling with ice.

Do you routinely shut off refrigeration when departing the boat for home? If so, tend to your unit to avoid a snootful of moldy stench upon opening it days later. Once you've packed all perishables in cooler bags, prevent the growth of mold. Wipe down the interior of the refrigerator to remove moisture, and then leave the lid propped open to allow in air.

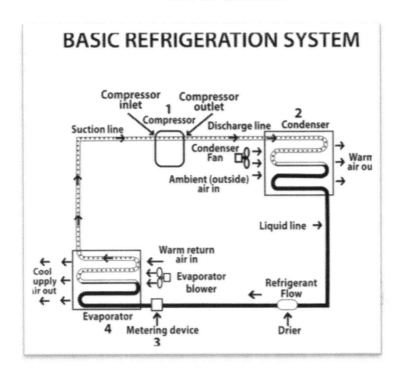

BASIC REFRIGERATION SYSTEM

KEEP CHARGED

When on cruise or in an anchorage, keep your refrigerator charged to prevent spoilage. While you are charging your batteries, flip a switch or do whatever is necessary to have your refrigeration system charge along with them. If your boat has a timer and a refrigerator charge switch, turn them on before charging the unit and off when finished.

Refrigerators normally need to be charged twice a day, morning and evening. A well-insulated box will hold its temperature during the period in-between charges, even in hot weather. Allow the refrigeration system to charge until its thermostat reads 40 degrees Fahrenheit, the safe temperature for keeping perishable foods well chilled without freezing them.

The size of the box, amount of insulation, and the burden of any warm or room temperature foods and drinks put inside during charging will affect the amount of time needed to complete the charging process. Figure out the average number of hours it takes to bring your refrigeration to its ideal temperature so you will know how much time to allow for charging it.

RESTART A WARM REFRIGERATOR

If your dock is prone to power issues or you are in an anchorage and need to shut down the refrigeration and pack up perishable foods and drinks each time you go home, you will need to perform a hard restart on your return. Flip whatever switch is necessary to turn on the unit. Avoid putting unchilled items inside until the refrigerator has become sufficiently cool. Doing so will extend the time it takes to cool down your refrigerator and, if the items are perishable, they may spoil. To hasten the chilling process, add bags or blocks of ice, as well as already cold, nonperishable beverages. Leave milk, meats, and other perishables in their cooler travel bags until the unit has reached the desirable 40 degrees Fahrenheit.

KEEP YOUR REFRIGERATION HUMMING

Refrigerators are happiest when they are running continuously. Yet they are energy eaters and may consume between 100 and 300 amp hours daily, the equivalent of running an engine or generator for one to two and a half hours a day.

Under normal conditions, a refrigerator will last for years with no more maintenance than a periodic washing and seasonal vacuuming of the condenser. The problem is that a boating environment is seldom normal due to exposure to moisture, movement, and the need to turn the system on and off.

Here are some ways to care for your refrigerator:

> Avoid unnecessary restarts. Each time your refrigeration has to be restarted from ground zero, it uses two to three times as much current to reach the optimum cooling temperature to keep foods fresh.

> When power to the refrigeration is cut off or reduced, condensation forms and the icebox gets warmer. This creates a secondary problem as the condensation refreezes on the surfaces of the coils or the metal holding plate, leaving it coated with ice.

> Keep the drain switch shut when not in use to prevent warm air from entering the box, thus raising the temperature and making the compressor work harder.

> Know what kind of refrigerant and oil your particular unit requires. Servicing your unit with the wrong product can cause the compressor to fail.

Heat is a by-product of the cooling process. Be sure your unit is located in a ventilated area that will allow any heat to exit.

TROUBLESHOOT PROBLEMS

If your refrigeration system is running all the time, attempting to reach a prescribed temperature or simply refusing to do anything at all, check out these potential causes:

Intermittent power: If you usually leave your boat plugged into dock power and you are concerned that food in your freezer may be thawing and refreezing, perform this ice cube test. Before you leave for a few days, set a cup holding one or two ice cubes inside your freezer box or compartment. When you return, look at the contents of the cup. If the ice is intact, power has been continuous in your absence. If the ice has melted and refrozen, something is going on either with shore power or within your system.

Blocked vents or filters: If your system radiator vent is clogged or blocked; or in the case of sea water, if the raw water filter is choked shut with sea grass or debris, hot air cannot vent efficiently and the system will slow or shut down completely. If you know a particular harbor is notorious for sea grass, stay ahead of the problem by checking and cleaning out the raw water filter on a daily basis.

Blocked circulation: Proper circulation of airflow is key to the operation of a refrigerator or a freezer. One of the most common causes of blocked circulation is built-up ice on the coils or holding plates. When the frost forming on the coils or cold plates is over 1/4-inch thick, it's time to defrost the unit.

Leaky seals: If your unit is accumulating an undue amount of frost, it could mean outside air is coming into the system through a poorly sealed lid, door, or liner joints. Check also if the drain has been left open.

Leaking coolant: A determined amount of coolant is needed to properly operate the system. If there is seepage, efficiency goes out the porthole. Check for a coolant leak by looking at the moisture sight glass. If you don't see bubbles or some sign that there is fluid present, you likely have a leak. Repair gauges, used by professionals, are more accurate.

WHAT IF YOUR REFRIGERATION DIES?

Murphy's Law deems your refrigerator will go kaput on a Sunday or holiday, when technicians are as scarce as $1 million bills, you have a boatload of people, and it is chock-full of food.

Don't go berserk. Remember, your refrigerator is an icebox. It is insulated, much like a good cooler. Send someone out to purchase several bags of ice and a couple of blocks, which will last much longer than cubes. In the meantime, offload extra beverages into a spare cooler to make room for ice in the box, taking care to keep the door (or lid) shut as much as possible.

Once the ice arrives, rearrange the contents of the refrigerator so you can place a block or two of ice at the bottom and some bags of cubes on top of your perishables. If you are plugged into dockside power and accustomed to leaving your refrigeration on, remember to remove everything, leave the box open to dry out, and take home the perishables.

PART SIX: OFF-SEASON

If you're lucky enough to be situated in a year-round boating climate, you may not have to deal with the sad task of winter storage, as many of us do. It seems that just as the boat becomes an integral part of our lives, weather or situational changes force us to put it away for a couple of months or more until we can once again enjoy it. We'll discuss your storage options, and optional ways to keep on boating even as you're experiencing a blizzard in your home cruising ground.

CHAPTER 18
Put the Boat to Bed

Week after week throughout boating season we transport what seems to be all our worldly possessions to our boats, and then, just as we have everything perfectly stowed and our procedure down to a science, the air has the audacity to chill and toast the green leaves of summer crispy brown.

Instead of joyously charting our next boating jaunt, we are saddled with making tough decisions about the preparation and storage of our boats during off-season. In areas where temperatures dip below 32 degrees Fahrenheit, boats are prone to mold, mildew, and corrosion caused by condensation and moisture, as well as cracked components caused by expansion from the cold.

This chapter covers ways to protect your boat and any gear left aboard before storing it, how to choose a winter marina, and the procedure for land or in-the-water storage.

MANAGE END-OF-SEASON TASKS

The sordid task of temporarily moving out of your boat does not necessarily mean taking the entire contents home. Begin by removing and storing the dinghy outboard. Next, store the dinghy. A portable style can be taken home or stored in a garage, but many boaters find it easiest to stow their dinghy on the bow of the boat and under a winter cover.

If you have a sailboat, remove the sails and either wash and dry them yourselves or transport them to a professional sailmaker for cleaning and winter storage. (Off-season is a good time to have sails repaired, recut, altered, or replaced.) Otherwise, you can store the clean sails belowdecks on the boat or in your basement or garage at home.

Next, methodically go through your boat, opening each locker and cabinet, and determine how best to handle items you wish to leave aboard or take home.

Here are my suggestions:

➢ Take home any metal tools that are apt to rust, or coat them lightly with oil and seal in plastic to leave aboard.

➢ Interior cushions in berths or in the saloon can stay as long as you tip and lift them off the berths to allow air to circulate around them.

➢ Store cockpit cushions and outdoor canvas windows and covers inside the boat.

➢ Leave aboard dishes, pans, and other cooking utensils.

➢ Hard liquors do not freeze, so leave them aboard if you wish.

➢ To avoid cleaning up exploded messes in the spring, take home all liquids and creams, such as canned goods, beverages with no or low alcohol content (including beer and wine), cleaning supplies, toiletries, and medications.

➢ Check the expiration dates for pills, sun lotions, and boxed foods. Take home and use up any items that will expire before spring launch, otherwise these are safe to leave aboard as long as they are stored in moisture-proof containers.

➢ Dry goods, such as tea, coffee, soup mixes, and spices can handle the cold as long as they are stored in moisture-resistant packaging such as glass, plastic, or foil.

➢ Sun lotions lose potency when frozen and they also expire. Take these home and use for sunny winter vacations.

➢ Decorative pillows and bed pillows can stay aboard if protected. I suggest vacuum sealing these in moisture-proof bags. Add a fabric softener sheet to retain a fresh smell.

➢ Give clean towels and bedding the sniff test. If they smell fresh, these can be vacuum sealed in bags and left aboard, otherwise take them home to wash and store.

➢ Clothing and shoes should go home, unless you prefer to vacuum seal them. Keep in mind that you will need tank tops, shorts, sandals, and hats if you plan to vacation somewhere warm over the winter.

➢ Foul-weather gear will not be harmed if left aboard but usually needs to be washed by the end of the season. Do this by machine and hang to dry completely before storing.

Once the boat is under a snow-covered tarp 20 feet off the ground, it will be difficult to retrieve items you want to take on a winter charter vacation, such as the blender, sailing gloves, and snorkel gear.

Winterize the Boat

Along with packing and organizing supplies, you also need to tend to the boat's main systems, especially if you live in a freeze zone. Avoid corrosion and prevent freeze damage over the winter by running antifreeze through all systems, especially the motor flushers or intake pumps and each engine. The antifreeze process displaces any standing water, coats the water jackets and heat exchanger with a corrosion inhibitor, and distributes a coat of clean oil inside the engine and transmission.

The exact steps for winterizing your boat's engine, water system, refrigeration, head, and other operating systems will be detailed in your owner's manual, but these general procedures apply to the average boat system.

Service the Fuel System

Take the boat for a final spin and refuel. Top the tank with gasoline or diesel fuel. Doing so will help prevent bacterial and fungal growth that can plug filters, create starting problems, and damage engines. Once you have done this, take the following actions:

> ➢ Treat the fuel with a biocide.

> ➢ Install new primary and secondary fuel filters.

> ➢ Bleed the fuel lines to eliminate air pockets.

Change the Oils

Letting the engine sit over the winter with old oil will cause acids and other corrosives to damage interior components. Follow this process to change the engine oil, and then repeat it for the transmission:

1. Warm up the engine, then shut it down.

2. Pump out the old oil from the crankcase.

3. Replace the oil filter.

4. Fill the crankcase with fresh oil.

CLEAR RAW WATER SYSTEMS

Remove the raw water impeller to prevent damage to drains from freezing temperatures, and keep it clear of antifreeze residue. Now, open all drain plugs to purge the raw water cooling systems, clearing any sediment from the drains with a stiff wire. Next, clear water from the pumps (start the engine to do this, if need be), and then replace the drain plugs.

CIRCULATE ANTIFREEZE

To prevent freezing and cracking of components, replace fresh or raw water with antifreeze using these procedures:

> ➤ Pump out the holding tank for your head and drain all water from your water tanks. Do this by turning on all the taps (galley, heads, and shower) and running the water until no more comes out.

> ➤ Pour antifreeze into water tanks according to directions on the bottle.

> ➤ Pump antifreeze through your freshwater system by turning on all taps until the pinkish antifreeze emerges.

> ➤ For raw water heads, pour antifreeze into the toilet and pump it through the system.

> ➤ For freshwater heads, which draw water from tanks, flush the toilet several times until the water is pink, indicating the antifreeze has pumped through the vacuum system.

> ➤ To prevent frozen pipes on refrigeration systems with holding plates, circulate antifreeze through the seawater circuit until the antifreeze discharges.

PREPARE THE REFRIGERATOR

Wash out and defrost the refrigerator and freezer, being certain all water has been drained from the box. Leave the door or lid propped open to allow air circulation and prevent mildew. Spray the condensing unit with light oil to prevent rust.

SEE TO THE BATTERIES

If your batteries require water and you plan to store your boat on land, remove them and take them home to prevent cracking from freezing temperatures. Otherwise, keep them active by either putting them on a trickle charger or charging them frequently.

SEAL THE VALVES

Prevent moist air from entering the combustion chambers of the engine via an open exhaust or intake valve by sealing the exhaust outlets on the hull and the air filters on the engine with heavy-duty duct tape.

VENTILATE THE INTERIOR

Cold temperatures breed condensation, which makes a fine playground for mold and mildew. Prevent this by ventilating the boat before you step off it for the last time. Leave the dorade vents open and drawers and cabinet doors ajar. Hang moisture-absorbing packets throughout the interior.

PLAN FOR SPRING

If you are looking for an excuse to hang out at the boat a little longer, get a jump on spring maintenance by checking the zincs, belts, electrical connections, and the O-rings on the fuel filters. Inspect all physical connections at the transom and along the exhaust outlet. Replace, repair, and service anything that appears worn.

CHOOSE A WINTER MARINA

For many of us poor souls living in cold weather climates, a boatload of decisions arise as to where and how to berth our boats for the winter season. The safest place to store a sizable boat is ashore. Unless you have a trailerable boat, you will store your boat at a marina. Although indoor storage is the least stressful on boats, space is limited and costly.

The typical boat is stored outdoors either in the marina yard or in the water, although some marinas offer indoor, heated storage. Boat owners don't necessarily store their boats at their home port marina. Some want to store their boats closer to their homes, or they may have found another marina that is cheaper and has better facilities and contractual terms for hauling and storage.

If you choose to relocate your boat for the winter, evaluate the marina much the same as you would your home port marina with some additional considerations.

LOCATION

Consider the location in regard to water and land access. You will need to get the boat to the second marina and move it again in the spring, as well as drive there to check on your boat and perform spring maintenance before its launch.

COST

Marina payment plans vary. In lieu of paying slip fees, you will pay storage fees. Look for perks like discounts for early payment, priority consideration for an in-season berth, or an invite to the marina's annual customer appreciation party. Indoor storage rates are based on the square footage (LOA x beam or width) of a boat. Outdoor storage is based on the size of the boat in terms of cost per foot and whether it will be hauled and stored in the yard or kept in a slip.

Winter storage typically includes hauling, washing the hull, and launching the boat in the spring. Other procedures you request such as shrink-wrapping or winterizing are billed at the marina's hourly rate or by time and materials.

Before you sign the contract, to avoid surprise invoices, obtain an estimate for any extra work you want done. If this yard will be doing major work such as painting the boat or installing major components like refrigeration systems, generators, and watermakers, obtain a separate written quote detailing the work to be done and the cost breakdown.

SAILBOAT MASTS

For sailboats, many marinas require unstepping the mast when hauling the boat due to windage, which can tip the boat off-kilter in high winter winds and induce the rig to vibrate if it is up, leading to cracked fittings. Extreme temperatures stress the rig by causing dissimilar metals in the spars and rigging to expand and contract at different rates. Aluminum masts, in particular, are affected by this problem and should be taken down.

While having the mast down makes it convenient to clean, check, and wax the spars and replace lights, it also means disconnecting the VHF antenna and the wiring for lighting. If everything isn't properly reconnected in the spring, it can mean several trips up the mast in the bosun's chair once the mast is stepped.

The yard normally stores the mast as part of the hauling process. Ensure that your mast is set on well-padded supports with no weight on top of it and that any attached rigging is tied off.

Manufacturers claim there is no harm in leaving carbon fiber masts (which are not impacted by temperature changes) in place through the winter. We have left our mast up for several seasons without incurring any problems. Should you opt to leave the mast stepped for the winter, you have two choices: relax the entire rig by loosening the turnbuckles for shrouds and stays, then tie off the halyards so they don't slap against, and thus nick, the mast; or take down all lines and store them inside the boat or at home, then rerig when you erect the sails in the spring.

WINTER LAY-UP CONTRACT

When you sign up, you will need to provide the marina a date you'd like your boat launched in the spring. While you are in this mode, discuss with the service manager the location of your boat in the yard. If it is tucked behind several other boats that won't be launched until a later date than you've requested, you may incur an unwanted delay.

As with any contract, make certain you agree with the terms and liabilities presented by the marina. Some contracts absolve the marina of blame in the event of damage to the boat while under its watch; others may require you to have all-risk insurance coverage.

If the marina requires you, as a sailboat owner, to have the mast unstepped for hauling and your mast is the type that does not react to cold, phone around to find a marina that will agree to your terms.

Some marinas have regulations regarding work by outside contractors, such as charging outside vendors a percentage of their bill for work done on the premises. If you have a favorite rigger or teak man, either negotiate this term or go elsewhere.

Dry Storage

Once you have chosen a marina that meets your requirements and have set a date, the marina will haul out your boat, place it ashore in a cradle, and then pressure wash the bottom to remove barnacles and other debris.

Be certain the keel rests solidly on the main beam of the cradle, since the vertical risers are only stabilizers. Boats that sit on a soil or gravel surface, which softens when it gets wet, should have plywood placed beneath each poppit stand. The stands should be chained together to assure the assembly will remain balanced and in place.

Wet Storage

If you enjoy puttering around your boat off-season, consider leaving it in the water. If you decide to do so, you will need to check your boat frequently, especially if it will be exposed to winter storms or radical temperature changes. If your winter marina is not convenient to your home, ask someone you trust to keep an eye on your boat for flooding, chafing, and other issues. Even though a boat is at home in the water, its engine and other systems still require winterization of all systems as indicated earlier in this chapter.

To safeguard your boat against high winds and heavy seas, batten it down using these same protective measures as if preparing for a hurricane:

➢ Use additional lines to secure your boat to the dock, crisscrossing them in a web fashion to allow for rising and ebbing tides.

➢ Protect dock lines with chafing gear.

➢ Remove external canvas and other items that might take flight in heavy winds or seas.

➢ Remove or protect outdoor electronics: compass, GPS, radar, and VHF microphone.

PREVENT FLOODING

In addition to following the aforementioned procedures, it's necessary to ensure water will not enter your boat and cause it to sink. Be sure to close all openings to the water, seacocks and gate valves, except for the cockpit drains. (Store your boat ashore if it has thru-hulls below the waterline that can't be closed.)

Make certain that the bilge pumps work, that float switches activate the pumps, and that no debris blocks the exit openings.

Batteries need to be fully charged to operate the bilge pump automatically. Service the terminals and check the electrolyte level monthly. In cold weather, add water sparingly so it won't freeze.

WARD OFF ICE

If the water in the area where you plan to store your boat is prone to freezing, you risk damage to inner ducts and thru-hulls caused by expansion.

Here are some ways to prevent problems:

➢ Install a deicer, or bubbler, at your slip. A deicer is a DC-powered unit that continually churns the water around a boat. It works by sucking up warmer water from the bottom to prevent ice from forming on the surface. Some units also prevent water pollution, which helps keep debris from forming on the propeller.

➢ Some boaters add heat to prevent ice formation by placing lightbulbs near thru-hull openings, or by leaving a space heater in operation. Untended heaters are a fire hazard, and experts say they aren't necessary if the boat has been properly winterized.

➢ Frozen water will lift a poorly secured hose off a fitting. It is critical to double-clamp all thru-hulls using stainless steel hose clamps at each end.

➢ To avoid rupturing, replace lightweight (or PVC) tubing with heavily reinforced hose, especially in the cockpit drains.

➢ Plug all exhaust ports. Snow and ice add weight and can push exhaust ports underwater, allowing water to invade the exhaust system and rust engine components.

WINTER COVERS

Covering the boat with a winter blanket is the final step in protection for a boat stored on the hard or afloat. This added protection will keep gelcoat and bright work from fading and will shield your boat from ice, snow, sea salt, and the effects of pollution. In cold climates, it will prevent water from collecting in deck drains and freezing.

Various materials and methods are used to cover a boat. The key issue is to provide ventilation. Whatever type of winter cover you choose, don't forget to create a flap so you can exit and enter to steal a winter boating moment.

DECIDE ON A TARP

Tarps are usually either synthetic (plastic) or canvas rectangles, which are draped and tied down to fit over a wooden or metal frame that extends the length and beam of the boat. A frame is helpful in keeping the tarp off the surfaces of the deck, allowing air to circulate, and preventing water from pooling. If you really love your boat, treat it to a custom canvas cover, which can be made to accommodate mast, rigging, and extraneous equipment left up during the winter.

SHRINK-WRAP

Many marinas offer shrink-wrapping, which involves applying heat over a thin coating of disposable plastic to conform to the shape of the boat. Although convenient and protective, shrink-wrapping can trap moisture under the cover and invite mildew unless the cover is vented to allow air to circulate. Beware of shrink-wrapping hulls finished with AwlGrip or other linear polyurethane paint systems, as covers and tie-down lines may cause abrasion.

CHAPTER 19
Extend Boating Season

The time of year when the cold weather moves in and boating season moves out means different things to every one of us. If you enjoy winter sports, you might be looking forward to the cold weather. And, admit it, there is a certain relief from the packing and unpacking cycle. But no matter what your life outside of boating is, I guarantee the day you put your boat to bed for the season will leave you with a feeling of loss.

But cruising doesn't have to end. Extend your boating season by vacationing in a warm place, or by having your boat there for visits throughout the winter season.

WINTER BOATING OPTIONS

Today there are many more options than ever for extending the boating season. If time and funds are limited, the least costly option is chartering. But if you have the kind of job you can perform almost anywhere or are joyously retired, consider transporting your boat somewhere warm for the winter. You can sail it yourself or have it shipped, an option that is becoming increasingly popular with owners of midsized boats. One of the side benefits of taking your own boat is that all of your belongings can travel with the boat, minimizing packing between visits.

CHARTER A BOAT

Charter companies have locations all over the world, including at shore points throughout the United States. Off-season, it's common to head south to seek warm weather in boating-friendly waters. For the price of a plane ticket, chartering a boat offers a fabulous opportunity to cruise exotic waters, such as the Fiji Islands or Tonga, or to enjoy popular boating meccas, such as the Caribbean or the Bahamas.

Many charter companies focus on sailing vessels, but several have added power cats, trawlers, and traditional powerboats to their fleets. If you are worried about navigating an unfamiliar boat in strange waters, or you just want to relax, the charter company will outfit your boat with a local captain—and even a cook, if you prefer.

Peruse your favorite boating magazine or check the Internet for performance ratings on companies offering the type of cruising you wish. You'll find the best deals at fall boat shows, where there will be an opportunity to speak directly with various charter company representatives who will gladly help you create a personal package for your trip. They may have boats on the premises for touring.

As you consider the concept of chartering a boat, you will have decisions to make. By you, I mean the collective you, which includes others who will be going along with you. It may be your spouse and kids or a few friends.

Ask yourselves these questions:

> ➤ What kind of boat do I want to charter? Sail or power?
>
> ➤ Where would I like to go?
>
> ➤ Do I want a crewed charter or to captain the selected boat myself?

> ➤ Who and how many will go with me?

> ➤ What time of year will I go?

> ➤ What is my vacation budget?

COST

It costs more for the best: a new model boat in good repair from a charter company that is fastidious about maintaining its fleet and providing good customer service. First-echelon companies charge more because they turn over boats every four or five years, often to second-tier companies offering bargain charter rates or to private buyers.

While the lowest rates may entice you to charter off-season, be aware that this can mean cruising in stormy weather or fighting off buggy humidity. Signing on for a Tahitian charter during rainy season might mean enduring the tail end of a cyclone, as we did one year. In the Caribbean, the Christmas winds come in December and last through most of February. During that time you're apt to encounter squalls, high winds, and rolling swells.

Usually, airfare is not included in a charter company's package, but some have arrangements with a travel agent for special rates. Ask about this as well as flight schedules. We nixed chartering out of Grenada when we found there were so few flights that it would have taken us a day and a half to get there.

SERVICE

Many companies and private charterers are vying for your business. It pays to beware by learning from the experiences of others. Contact former charterers who have traveled out of the charter location you are considering.

Ask these specific questions and to verify information advertised by the charter company:

How much time does the company allow between charters? A good company will allow sufficient time between charter drop-offs and pickups to completely clean and overhaul the boat. One prime company has its staff members strip a boat of cushions and wash them all down, hose out the entire bilge, scrub out lockers and cabinets, sterilize the galleyware, sand down teak cockpit seats, and lubricate and test all working parts.

What did the charter company do for provisioning? If it provided food, how was it? Were the vegetables and breads fresh (and free of mold), and what about the meats and seafood?

Were there any service issues? A first-rate charter company understands customers don't expect to lose valuable vacation time waiting for a bad part to be replaced. When our dinghy engine sputtered and died, a working engine was delivered within four hours. One company provided same-day service the time we clogged one of the heads; and once, when the CD player was stolen from the boat (that's another story), the next ferry brought its replacement.

CHOOSE A BOAT

When sharing, it's customary to divide the costs between families or couples, so involve the key players in the boat selection decision. Be prepared to spend more money for the *right* boat to accommodate your family, two families, or friends. It's vacation, right?

Match the boat style and size to your crew. If you have gourmet cooks in your group, as we did one year, be sure the galley has enough space to accommodate multiple delicacies-in-progress. Whenever we've skimped on size, we've paid for it by tripping over duffels, gear that had no home, and fighting to share a tiny head.

Some monohulls and powerboats are designed for chartering, with cabins of equal size and comfortable facilities. We've found catamarans work well for a large group, especially if some are nonboaters. There is more deck space and the boat won't heel underway and tip over glasses of liquids left about.

If at all possible walk through a boat similar in layout to one you are interested in chartering. Determine whether it will work for the number and needs of people you intend to share the charter with. If you do not have this opportunity, be sure to study those tiny layout diagrams in the Boats Offered section of the company's brochure. The brochure for a boat we once chartered claimed it slept eight, which seemed perfect for four couples; we arrived to find the eighth "berth" was the floor.

Family is more forgiving than friends when it comes to sharing accommodations. Check that each person or couple has a berth, a small area to stow belongings, and access to a head. If you are splitting the cost of the charter with other couples or single friends, we've found it's only fair to provide a separate cabin with a private head for each person or couple.

DECIDE ON PROVISIONING

Charter companies offer several options for provisioning, but you may opt out and supply your own food. Incorporated into provisioning are items like paper towels, toilet paper, trash bags, and a few cleaning supplies.

The means you choose for provisioning may depend on how well you all like to eat, whether you can obtain dietary necessities, how much you are willing to pay for food, and how much cooking you want to do yourselves.

The split provisioning option is most common. However, full provisioning is normally recommended when chartering in areas where restaurants are sparse to nonexistent, or if dietary issues make dining out difficult. Often, the charter company has a store on its premises, which makes it easy to swap out food once you arrive.

If you are trying to cut costs or have special food requirements, you may prefer to buy your own food and have it delivered from a local market to the boat, or go shopping once you arrive.

Taking food along with you on airplanes has become difficult or impossible, especially with liquids or perishables. If need be, it may be possible to ship foods and supplies directly to the charter company for it to hold for your arrival. Before you do this, check on how the company receives packages and what the time frame is for delivery.

Full provisioning = you will be provided the ingredients to prepare three meals a day for the length of time you will be aboard for the number of people to be fed.

No provisioning = you are entirely on your own to supply the foods and beverages needed for the length of your charter.

Split provisioning = you will be provided the ingredients to make breakfast, lunch, and half the dinners needed for the number of days you will be aboard for the number of people to be fed.

ENSURE SAIL-AWAY CONDITION

It's generally cheaper to charter an older boat rather than a spiffier new one. No matter the age of the boat you choose, what's important is that everything is in good repair when you leave dock. Not only can a breakdown cramp your travel plans, but the company may try to charge you to replace a previously frayed anchor line that broke loose while you were in charge, for example.

Arrange to have repairs made for malfunctioning engines, refrigeration systems, stoves, and toilets before departure. With a top-notch company, everything will be working (save for the occasional blowfish caught in the engine intake pipe) and you'll cast off at noon, when most charters actually begin. With lesser companies, you may waste a wonderful afternoon hanging about the dock waiting for last-minute repairs to be completed.

Read the chartering agreement carefully to avoid unexpected or erroneous charges. Check over the boat thoroughly when you inventory it, and report deficiencies and potential problems, such as a shredded anchor line, bent stanchions, torn sails, or missing supplies.

Keep in mind that you are responsible for any mishaps that occur during your charter period. Once, a passing boat ran over and cut our anchor line. If my husband hadn't harangued the evildoer to replace it, we would've owed the charter company a new line (as well as an anchor if we had been unable to retrieve it).

TAKE YOUR BOAT

Whether you want to ship your boat, which is all the rage right now, or sail it, you first need to make decisions about where you will go and where to keep the boat once you arrive.

If you need access to the Internet and telephone service, it makes sense to stay within the boundaries of the United States. The Bahamas and the Caribbean have gained in popularity. With the ease of boat transport, offshore sailing conditions, fuel consumption, and boat stress are no longer concerns. We have seen more privately-owned powerboats from the States in the Caribbean than ever before.

In conjunction with all this, you should be hunting down a secure berth at your destination. This is more of an issue if you plan to leave the boat for weeks at a time and fly home. In the British Virgin Islands (BVI), where we used to keep our boat for the winter season, a yacht service handled needed repairs or maintenance while we were gone, and cleaned and readied the boat for our return. What a godsend it was to arrive after flying all day to find the interior cool and neat, my wine iced, and the bed made up.

Choose a reputable marina with docks that are in good repair. If you opt for a mooring, be sure it is sufficient to hold your boat. We have seen boats left on anchor, which is usually free. If you care about your boat, though, don't risk it. Lastly, hire a trustworthy person or service to keep an eye on your boat while you fly home for holidays and the like.

SHIP IT

Many owners of midsized boats have found shipping their vessel cheaper and more viable than sailing it themselves. As with chartering, investigate companies beforehand. Talk to people who have used a particular service to find out if they would sign on again and if any delivery problems were encountered.

A variety of carriers have taken on private boat transport. By land, smaller boats can be trailered or trucked, but new oversize-load restrictions have made commercial land transport more costly. One transport company hauls boats up to 60 feet in length on a trailer anywhere throughout the United States, but mainly to shore points along the

Eastern Seaboard and as far west as Texas (which may include traversing the Erie Barge Canal).

Most commonly boats are shipped to a destination by sea. Since 1990, many commercial shipping companies have added private yacht transport to their services. Now, it's a booming business. Quotes to ship boats are based on the boat's dimensions—obviously the larger the boat, the more costly.

The typical carriers are semisubmersible, which means they sink the deck just enough to permit boats to float on their decks and be secured in place. The loading and unloading process is heavily supervised, and trip insurance is included. Early sign-up is rewarded with a discounted price.

You, or someone you trust, should be around when your boat is being loaded and unloaded. When our new boat was being shipped to Florida from Sweden, the carrier went aground. Its arrival was delayed for several days while the crew was replaced and the boat was towed out. And friends of ours who routinely shipped their boat between Newport, Rhode Island, and the BVI were stunned when their shipping company canceled their return and they had to scramble to find an alternate means of getting their boat home.

TRAVEL THE INTRACOASTAL

If you think you'd like to take your own boat south, you have a few options for doing so. Where you travel, and how far and under what conditions, depends on the type of boat you have—its seaworthiness and fuel capacity—as well as your capabilities.

The popular Intracoastal Waterway (ICW) has long been a favorite route. This navigable toll-free shipping route extends for about 3,000 miles along coasts of the Atlantic Ocean and the Gulf of Mexico in the southern and eastern

United States and utilizes sounds, bays, lagoons, rivers, and canals. Some portions can accommodate deep-draft vessels. Although it is federally maintained, lack of funds have caused some portions to be so badly shoaled that they are closed to through traffic, which means taking the outside (ocean) route to bypass those areas.

> *The ICW was originally planned to form a continuous channel from New York City to Brownsville, Texas, but the canal link through northern Florida was never completed; hence, it is now in two separate sections—the Atlantic and the Gulf. The Gulf Intracoastal Waterway (GIWW) is the nation's third busiest waterway. The 423-mile Texas portion handles over 58 percent of its traffic. Find out more online at http://www.txdot.gov/inside-txdot/division/maritime/gulf-intracoastal-waterway.html.*

With its two separate water routes, the ICW is fairly comfortable to travel. The passage you choose depends on your home port location and your destination.

Here are a few tips on navigating the ICW:

➢ Stock up on the necessary travel guides and charts.

➢ Keep a bridge information sheet handy. Check the bridge height at mean low water to be sure your mast isn't too tall to travel underneath, causing you to take a circuitous route to avoid the area. On the GIWW, sailboats may need to travel with the mast taken down.

➢ Be alert to shoaling and blocked areas that will set your boat aground or render an area impassable. The depth is supposed to be maintained at 12 feet, but since the reduction of commercial traffic, the Army Corps of Engineers isn't as good as it used to be about keeping it dredged. (Check online at http://www.waterwayguide.com/waterway-updates/nav?area=5 for updates on the Atlantic ICW.)

➢ On the Atlantic ICW, if you cannot navigate past a section of the waterway, you will need to bypass the area by going out through an inlet and traveling on outside waters until you have bypassed that portion and can reenter the waterway. Read up on the inlets in your waterway guide's navigation section. Not all of them are safe passage.

OPT FOR LONG-RANGE CRUISING

If you have a seaworthy boat with long-range travel capability, such as a substantial sailboat or a large power yacht, you may enjoy the challenge of an offshore passage. Bear in mind that such a trip requires several days of round-the-clock travel on a safety-equipped boat. If you are cruising 1,500 miles or more, fuel replenishment and costs can easily become issues, even on a sailboat.

Check with your insurance company beforehand because you will need extended coverage. Most policies have restrictions on travel in certain areas during hurricane season, which runs from June to November. This also applies to southbound travel on the ICW.

TEST YOUR METTLE

Have you ever been out of sight of land without freaking? Before "running" on longer, more involved passages, learn to "walk" by cruising short offshore passages that won't take you into known turbulent waters or hundreds of miles from land. If you have never completed an overnight sail, try this in familiar boating grounds before committing to a longer passage so you will be familiar with night navigation, watches, and more.

The first time my husband took our boat to the Caribbean, he hired a delivery captain who had made the trip before, and then convinced two friends to go along as well. Professional captains charge a daily rate, plus expenses. Friends can be had for the price of airfare and unlimited rum on arrival.

Once you are comfortable with your ability to cruise for several days without landfall, consider these other factors:

> ➢ Who are your crew members? Experienced sailors looking for adventure? Your spouse? Has at least one crew member made the passage you envision?

> ➢ Will children or pets be included? Will they be able to tolerate the rigors of an offshore adventure?

> ➢ What are your goals? Do you want a challenge, a learning experience, or a fun family vacation?

> ➢ How much time can you spend away? One week? Two years?

> ➢ Where do you want to go and what sea conditions can you expect?

TRAVEL WITH A RALLY

Traveling as part of a rally is a safe and fun way to sail to parts beyond. Some rallies are geared to coastal cruisers who want to try offshore sailing; others are intended to satisfy the thirst for challenge common to intermediate and veteran sailors. Understand that when you are out on the ocean, you are on your own. In the larger, more expansive rallies, one can travel for days without seeing another boat on the horizon. The ultimate responsibility for the boat and crew lies with the skipper, not the rally organizers.

A rally provides education, hard information, and resources that would otherwise take weeks to assemble on one's own. Organizers choose the optimum season and safest routes for their wards, usually provide educational seminars in preparation for the trip, and may negotiate discounts for berths, food, and other necessities at departure and arrival destinations.

The boats in a rally are linked electronically via daily SSB radio chats, updated weather routing, and satellite tracking. Traveling with a knowledgeable group can be an on-the-water safety net for assistance with mechanical or medical problems.

All rallies aren't created equal. Choose one that will be well tolerated by your boat, your crew, your boss, and your bank account. Talk to former rally participants and follow chats on rally web pages. Find out if transportation to and from the rally start and finish locations presents a problem for you or potential crew members. See the Appendix for a partial list of rallies. For a full listing of worldwide, established rallies consult http://www.noonsite.com/General/Rallies.

GO AS CREW

Crewing on someone's boat is a great way to get offshore experience without having a boat of your own that is up to the task or taking on the responsibility of captain. If your boating experience qualifies you, many rally organizers will gladly put your name on a crew list to provide to short-handed boat owners.

Boaters looking to spread their wings use crewing as a chance to gain confidence sailing offshore before trying a passage on their own boats or to solidify an extended cruising plan. Adventuresome men and women who do not own a seaworthy boat or who want to learn the skill of boat handling under challenging conditions find crewing rewarding. Often they do it for sport, but many positions are also paid.

It's easy to be tempted by opportunities to crew on ocean passages advertised in sailing magazines or over the Internet. Who wouldn't want to head to an exotic location, sail under the stars, and forget responsibilities of work and family? Nothing is as pretty or as simple as it seems, though.

If you have decided to try crewing, make your dream a reality by doing due diligence to the expectations of the trip, the seaworthiness of the boat, and the personality of the person who will captain the boat.

Here are a few things you can do:

> Prepare a sailing resume, being honest about your skills and level of experience. Are you a good cook, navigator, expert sail handler, engine mechanic, electrician, equipped with medical know-how, or fluent in the language spoken at the destination? Include the names and contact information for several people who can attest to your skills and personal characteristics.

> Make personal contact with your potential captain by phone or in person, not over the Internet. Be enthusiastic and show flexibility, especially if the trip seems interesting.

> Ask the captain for a written resume of his or her sailing experience, including names and contact information for former crew. Check references to avoid signing up for an unsafe or problematic situation. (You are "trapped" on this boat with this person for the duration of the trip.)

- ➢ Ask a lot of questions, including how capable the captain is in situations when electronics fail.

- ➢ What, when, and how much money, if any, will this trip cost you? Settle on a price in writing up front, not during or at the end of the voyage. Who will pay transportation? The owner is legally obligated to pay your passage back to the point of origin of the passage. If asked to sign an agreement, be careful not to sign away your rights.

- ➢ If you have purchased a nonrefundable ticket home from your intended destination and are delayed or wind up at a different destination, as can be the case, how will this owner resolve it for you?

Once you have checked references and spoken with the captain, if you are still interested, schedule a visit to get to know him or her and to check out the boat. Decide if you like the captain enough to spend a lot of time in close quarters with him or her, and if you trust that person is interested in the welfare of the crew.

Find out the following information:

- ➢ How committed is the captain to this trip? If he or she is wishy-washy, *run*.

- ➢ Is he or she a straightforward, flexible person who exudes confidence? Do you trust this person to be in charge of your well-being?

- ➢ How many other crew members will there be, besides you, and what are their experience levels? A crew of four with experience is ideal; everyone is rested, and if one falls ill, three others can compensate. If you will be one of two people aboard, think hard about taking on the stress of overly long watches with little sleep.

Crap happens fast offshore, and being wide awake and alert is critical.

➢ Check the boat to be sure it is seaworthy. Even though it may not be neat, due to preparation for the trip, you can still look over its critical components. What is the state of the engine compartment? Are the galley and cooking apparatuses clean? What does the electrical wiring look like where it is exposed? Is it neat, or is there a rat's nest of wires around the navigation station? What kinds of thru-hulls are present; are they operative and in good condition? Are there rust blooms on rigging terminals? What is the state of the running rigging? Are the sails in good shape?

➢ Request a copy of a recent survey, if one is available. If the captain puts you off, assume he or she is hiding important information, so bow out while you can.

➢ Compare expectations and arrive at compromises. Are you living on a schedule whereas the skipper has none? How far along is he or she in planning the itinerary and the provisioning? What measures has the captain taken for crew safety? Is there an offshore life raft and medical bag aboard?

➢ Ask how the captain deals with heavy weather or storms. How well does the boat handle under such conditions?

> ➤ Is alcohol permitted underway? If it seems that drinking booze will be the norm, back out. Alcohol dulls reflexes, and it's not worth putting your life in the hands of a drunken crew.

CHAPTER 20

Sell Your "Baby"

Selling a boat you love can be tough, even if you've purchased a new, bigger, more luxurious boat. As a finale to this book (boo hoo) we'll discuss what's involved in selling your boat or trading it in for a new one. Information is provided on choosing and dealing with a broker, preparing your boat to sell fast, and negotiating the deal.

My husband and I have bought and sold several boats during the course of our 35-plus years of boating, but the memories of the good times we had on each one of them remain with us still. Whatever your reason for parting with your baby, I hope it will bring you pleasure and new adventure.

TRADE IT IN

When purchasing a new boat, the dealer usually offers to take your existing boat in trade. While doing so may mean giving up your boat for less than you think it is worth, it also means reducing the amount of the loan for the new boat by the trade-in value and relieves you of all the responsibility for it. When you perform your calculations on trading in your boat versus selling it, keep in mind that you won't be paying sales tax on the full price of the new boat, only on the amount less your traded value.

According to one dealer I interviewed, if he were to take a boat in trade toward a new one, his average offer might be 70 percent of the boat's retail value. While some boat owners may consider this a loss, they should keep in mind that the dealership takes the boat as is, so the owner is relieved of the expenses associated with getting the boat prepped to show and the continuing costs of yard storage and upkeep.

SELL THROUGH A BROKER

Depending on the market, a boat can take from three months to a year (or more) to sell. If the loan for your existing boat is still outstanding when you contract for another boat, you could be stuck with double payments. If you opt to sell your boat, your choices are to go through a broker or dealer or to sell it on your own.

Consider these tips on selling your boat fast at the highest price, with the least amount of hassle:

➤ Advertise heavily.

➤ Price it to sell.

➤ Store it in a location convenient to buyers.

➤ Keep it in top-notch condition.

If you have a smaller boat and don't want to deal with a broker, you may be able to strike an informal agreement with a local boat dealer for use of yard space and inclusion in its advertising.

HOW A BROKER CAN HELP

Broker commission on used boats is typically 10 percent, depending on the boat and its location. A broker earns his or her keep by handling advertising, showing the boat to prospective buyers, performing sea trials, and dealing with surveyors. A broker will negotiate an acceptable offer for you, and then arrange all closing details.

OPT FOR A GO-GETTER

Choose a reputable broker who represents boats similar to yours and operates his or her business close to where your boat is located. You will want someone who has closed a lot of sales and has happy customers. Be sure this person is licensed and bonded by a professional organization and carries credentials from the Yacht Brokers Association of America.

It's helpful if this individual is part of a skilled team that can take over when he or she is out of the office. For maximum marketing coverage, choose a person who works for a company that markets beyond its location and through the Internet, boat shows, and social media.

Decide on a brokerage agreement. There are three types of agreements from which to choose: open listing, exclusive, or central. Avoid signing a long-term agreement that will prevent you from switching to another firm in case you are not pleased with the one you chose.

These terms are associated with brokerage contracts:

Open listing: the owner can sell the boat him or herself commission-free, while listing the boat with a number of brokers.

Exclusive listing: this is given to a single broker who can earn a commission, even if the owner sells the boat.

Central listing: commission is split between the listing broker and the broker who actually manages the sale (similar to the Multiple Listing Service in real estate).

DON'T SUGARCOAT SALES INFORMATION

Think of your broker as a lawyer in a criminal case. In order to show your boat's best qualities, your broker needs to know the truth. A prospective buyer will want to know everything possible about your boat, and the broker needs to be able to answer questions with confidence and accuracy.

In addition to providing the general specifications of your boat, which can come from an old brochure or be looked up, offer your broker specifics concerning your boat's history and current condition.

Here are details you should include:

➤ Builder information, especially if the boat was custom built or is not a well-known make or model

➤ Revisions and upgrades to the hull or design

➤ Engine hours

➤ Any accidents the boat's been in, details of the repairs, and its current condition

➤ Brands and ages of the electronics

➤ Cruising areas (how it has been used)

➤ Previous owners, if any

➤ Items coming up for repair and your intentions

➤ Current problems with leaks or systems

➤ Items to be sold along with the boat, such as the dinghy

SELL ON YOUR OWN

You may make more money selling your boat yourself, but until it's sold you will own the boat and continue having the responsibilities that go along with ownership. By omitting the middleman, you take on the responsibility of keeping your boat in saleable condition, being available to show your boat, and doing your own marketing and paperwork.

Once your boat is in top condition, here are a few ways to let people know it's for sale:

> Pass the word around to fellow boaters and ask them to share the news.

> Make up flyers to post on bulletin boards in yacht clubs and marinas, and anyplace boaters frequent. (Ask permission before posting.)

> Post For Sale signs on your boat. Beforehand, check your slip or storage agreement. Some marinas automatically charge commission for selling your boat in their yard.

> Place ads in local newspapers, national boating publications, yacht club and marina bulletin boards and newsletters, and anyplace else you can think of—including Internet social networks.

SET A PRICE

If you are working with a broker or dealer, he or she will be able to help you set a reasonable selling price for your boat; otherwise you will need to do the necessary market research. Keep in mind that some boats hold their value better than others.

The saleable price for your boat is based on the following conditions: the current sales market, the boat's condition, the boat's year of manufacture, the configuration of the boat, and where it is located.

Before establishing a price for your boat, consider these factors:

> Check classified ad listings to see what similar boats are selling for.

> ➢ Reference used boat price guides such as *BUC Used Boat Price Guide*, National Automobile Dealers Association (NADA), and *ABOS Marine Blue Book*, found at boat dealerships and some libraries.

> ➢ Obtain a report of recently sold figures for boats like yours. Why did they sell at that price? How are they different?

> ➢ Based on loan payoff amount, if any, and improvements you may have made, establish a minimum price you are willing to accept for your boat. Understand that every upgrade you make will not necessarily translate into increased value.

> ➢ Consider depreciation and obsolescence. For example, digital technology has changed electronics and instrumentation. If you still have a LORAN, it is obsolete and will not add value to your boat.

> ➢ Set an asking price. To allow room for negotiation, sellers often advertise at a price 10 to 15 percent higher than the minimum they will accept.

LOCATION, LOCATION, LOCATION

Make it convenient for prospective buyers to have access to your boat. Ideally, it will be in the water in a slip, but that isn't always possible or to your advantage. Many boats are displayed in dealers' yards, set on poppits with a ladder for access to the cockpit, deck, and interior. While boarding isn't as convenient, this allows buyers (and any surveyors) complete access to the entire boat, including the keel and its hull. If you are getting few hits on your boat, consider moving it to a more popular location.

PREPARE TO SELL

The sales appeal of your boat not only depends on price, but also on appearance, condition, and seaworthiness. Like selling a home, a boat has to be kept in show condition. It has to look good, operate smoothly, and smell clean. Appearance matters. Many will not see a messy or dirty boat as a diamond in the rough.

Take a critical look at your boat, much the same as a buyer would (see "Evaluate a Used Boat" in Chapter 3), and be objective about what needs to be spruced up or fixed. A serious buyer will want to look in every locker, examine the engine room, and test the operation of all systems and electronics.

Put on your company-is-coming glasses and check these things:

> ➢ Is the boat sparkling clean? Have the boat professionally waxed and buffed, and have the propellers and bottom cleaned. Afterward, arrange to have the boat cleaned weekly to rid it of water spots and dirt from the yard.

> ➢ Repaint the insides of dirty or mildewed external or internal lockers. Check the bilge for odor and cleanliness.

> ➢ Are there signs of rust, hull blisters, peeling paint or varnish, previous repairs, cracks, or corrosion? Have the engine room detailed. Remove all rust and replace corroded parts.

> ➢ Remove all clutter. Keep aboard items you will sell with the boat and remove the rest. While you are doing this, make a detailed list of items to be sold with the boat. Be sure to specify any items left for show that will not be included in the sale.

> Get an expert's opinion—your broker's, if you've hired one—for problems that need to be corrected for the boat to sell quickly. Decide whether to make repairs or reduce the price accordingly. Understand that broken parts will show up as a negative in the survey.

> Check operating gear: winches, steering systems, running and standing rigging on sailboats, lights, head and galley equipment, electronics, and instrumentation.

> Start up the engine and take your boat out for a shakedown cruise to determine any operational issues that need tending to.

> Top off the fuel and all engine fluids, and change the oil.

> Check that all required safety equipment is up-to-date and in good condition, because this will go with the boat.

> Keep the boat ventilated with any fans running to eliminate stale odors, a definite turnoff. If onshore power is available, run the air-conditioning to keep the boat's interior cool and dry.

> Maintain batteries to keep all systems operational. If you have no access to shore power, charge the batteries as needed by running the engine or the generator.

ANTICIPATE A SURVEY

A serious buyer will want to have your boat inspected by a marine surveyor and possibly have the engine looked over by a marine mechanic. The buyer's insurance normally requires that a used boat be surveyed, thus the buyer pays for the survey, any haul-outs, or other costs associated with its completion.

Should negotiations occur after the survey, it's helpful to know the problems and the surveyor's advice on the best way to resolve them. Plan to be around when the boat is being surveyed to answer any questions, explain operations, and examine any potential defects the surveyor points out.

PHOTOGRAPH YOUR BOAT

Great pictures and videos will entice buyers to schedule time to visit your boat. Before a photo shoot, be sure to remove all clutter and stage the interior to make it as inviting as possible.

If you are not a good photographer, ask the broker to take photos of your boat. As a salesperson, he or she will know the best angle to shoot various areas to show them at their best. Be sure to include photos of the engine, engine room if possible, and the exterior. A photo of the boat under motor or full sail is essential. It's nice to know how it looks on the water as well as on land.

One of the latest trends is a walk-through video, which can be done professionally or simply with a smartphone or video camera. One of the advantages of a video over still photos is the ability to speak about the various areas as you move through your boat.

YOUR DUTIES AS A SELLER

While there is no obligation on the seller's part to volunteer information the buyer doesn't ask for, withholding information about a known defect or other condition that could make the boat unsafe, or any liens or other debts that could hold up the transfer of title or ownership, is illegal. Should a serious accident occur, a boat sold in as-is condition may not be exonerated if such information had been withheld.

Share information. Be prepared to show prospects your original bill of sale, certificate of documentation or state title, as well as maintenance and repair records. If asked, provide cost-to-own details. Buyers may also be interested in seeing invoices for insurance, taxes, and storage so they can estimate how much it will cost them to own your boat.

Keep yourself available to meet with the prospective buyer and answer questions. Be prompt about returning messages from your broker, dealer, or the prospective buyer. Be sure to keep records of who you talk to and to follow up on inquiries.

NEGOTIATE THE DEAL

Your broker will handle the paperwork and be the go-between for accepting deposits from the buyer, checking that financing and insurance are in order, and managing the closing.

Here are some ways you can help the process move along smoothly:

> ➢ Be nice. If you get an offer, you can accept it, reject it, or negotiate. If you are upset by a low offer, just refuse to counter it. Upgrades you've added may not have increased in value as you had hoped, and market conditions may have deteriorated. Be prepared to renegotiate the sales price when it comes to items that need repair when the boat has a less-than-satisfactory marine survey or if buyers aren't showing much interest in it.

➢ A deal sealed with a handshake won't hold up in court, so make the sale legal. Have a sales contract drawn up by a lawyer.

➢ Set a closing date agreeable to all parties and hold to it.

➢ Once you have accepted an offer, pay attention to details about transferring the title.

➢ If you agree to make repairs prior to the sale, spell out your obligation in terms of exactly what is to be done and how much you will spend. It's smart to get a written estimate.

➢ Attach a list of all the accessories that will stay with the boat to the sales agreement, and have it signed by both parties.

➢ Make certain the buyer has financing and insurance. Unless you can afford the loss, don't offer to finance the boat.

➢ Ask for cashier's or certified checks for both the deposit and the final payment.

➢ To expedite the closing process, remain in easy reach by phone, e-mail, or text message. If you are traveling, be sure to have access to a fax machine in case documents need to be signed and returned.

AFTERWORD

Okay, my friend, you are now armed with the soup-to-nuts info to manage all aspects of your boat and to cruise wherever your dreams take you. I hope you will find, as I have, that the self-confidence you have gained has balanced and improved other portions of your life—that your family bonds are stronger and your boss respects you even more.

Most importantly, my wish is that you have learned to relax and enjoy being on the water with the wind kissing your face, the sun warming your soul, and the night sky showering you with twinkling starlight. Enjoy your boat and the new challenges cruising continually casts before you. You can handle them.

Go for it!

Appendix

Boating Courses

These are some physical and online organizations that offer various levels of online and classroom boating classes throughout the United States:

American Boat Operator Course (www.boatcourse.com/) offers online boating safety courses with online certification tests for a number of states.

American Sailing Association (www.asa.com/) offers courses for long-range sailing. You can sign up for passagemaking classes at Blue Water Sailing School (www.bwss.com/) in various locations, and participate in guided ocean sailing events.

BoatUS Foundation Courseline (www.boatus.com/courseline/default.asp) is a searchable database of current boating safety courses around the nation.

BoatEd (www.boat-ed.com/) offers online boating safety courses with online certification tests for a number of states.

BoaterExam (www.boaterexam.com/) offers online boating safety courses with online certification tests for a number of states.

Boatsafe (www.boatsafe.com/) offers an online basic boating certification course approved by the National Association of State Boating Law Administrators, and a coastal navigation course.

Commander Bob (www.commanderbob.com/) is an award-winning website that advances boating education.

The National Association of State Boating Law Administrators' online directory (http://nasbla.org/i4a/member_directory/feSearchForm.cfm?directory_id=3&pageid=3335&showTitle=1) provides contact information for state boating agencies that offer boating safety courses.

PWC Safety School (pwcsafetyschool.com/) offers online courses and certification for PWC operators in several states.

Safe Boating America (www.safeboatingamerica.com/) classes meet the educational requirements for operating a boat or personal watercraft and the requirements for a youth operator in accordance with individual state regulations.

United States Coast Guard Auxiliary (www.cgaux.org/) has boating courses for boaters of all ages and levels. These include basic introductory boating safety courses, navigation, sailing, and personal watercraft safety, among others.

US Sailing (www.ussailing.org/education/) programs offer instruction for small and large sailboats, windsurfers, and powerboats. All levels of instruction are available around the country for beginner to advanced skills.

United States Power Squadron (www.usps.org/) offers an online boating course that can be used for certification, if your state requires it. As the education arm of the USCG, the USPS also hosts a series of advanced courses designed to be taken in sequence. Each course builds on previously learned skills and awards titles such as Seaman, Pilot, and Navigator. Its America's Boating Course 3rd Edition is the most comprehensive boating safety course and is available as a classroom, home study, or online course. It includes a course book, a narrated student CD, and a digital charting DVD.

BOAT REPAIR

Keep these basic tools and repair supplies aboard to handle minor repairs wherever you are:

Wrenches of several different sizes

Screwdrivers or an 11-in-1 screwdriver set

Multitool such as a Swiss Army knife

Socket set in various sizes

Spare flashlight with fresh batteries

Canvas repair kit, which should include small pieces of canvas, needles, and string (for sailboats)

Duct tape and electrical tape

Plastic ties

Superglue

A clogged filter or oil leak can put a major cramp in your cruising plans, especially if it occurs while you are underway or mooring in a strange harbor. Be prepared by keeping these items in a handy spot aboard, such as in the engine room:

Air filter

Fuel filter
Power steering fluid
Transmission fluid
Hydraulic fluids
Engine oil
Lubricants
Stainless steel hose clamps and rigging tape
Caulking
Anodes
Seawater impellers

CLEANING, GENERAL

Basic cleaning materials to keep aboard:
Dish detergent
Baking soda
Chlorine bleach
White vinegar
Multipurpose cleaner
Wood polish
Glass cleaner
Metal cleaner/polish
Sponges, cleaning cloths, and paper towels
Small bucket

GALLEY NECESSITIES

Stocking your galley with the following items will equip you
for general food preparation:
12-quart stockpot with cover
10- or 12-inch nonstick skillet with cover
1-quart saucepan with cover
Coffee or teapot, manual or electric
Toaster, manual or electric
Large spoons, 1 slotted

Cooking spatula for nonstick pans
Paring knife, carving knife
Kitchen tongs
Rubber spatula
Can opener
Foil or metal baking pans sized to fit oven
1-gallon plastic drink container
Plastic storage containers (nesting)
Assorted plastic food bags for mixing, storage, and trash
Aluminum foil, plastic wrap
Corkscrew
Ice pick
Scissors
Paper towels
Potholders and dishtowels
Barbecue fork and spatula
Igniter or waterproof matches
Dish detergent
Dish sponge or cloth

MEDICAL SUPPLIES

The following list will help you amass medical supplies to treat common ailments:

Prescription medications
Ibuprofen or aspirin-based products to relieve headaches, fevers, and soreness (add children's strength if you have kids)
Antibiotic cream to prevent infection
Chewable pills for seasickness
Acupressure bands to prevent and alleviate seasickness
SPF 15 or greater waterproof sun block and lip balm
Aloe to soothe sunburn

Antihistamine for sun poisoning, allergies, colds

Medication for diarrhea

Antacid for upset stomachs

Anti-itch cream for bites or allergic reactions

Soothing ointment or powder for wet bathing suit irritation and rashes (monkey butt)

Bandage strips and patches in assorted sizes for minor cuts and scrapes, stored in small plastic bags or a moisture-proof container

Alcohol or other antiseptic for cleaning minor cuts or cooling an itch

Petroleum jelly

RALLIES:

Here is a partial list of major rallies held annually throughout the United States. Be sure to check locally for less extensive rallies in your area of the country.

Bermuda Cruising Rally: The Bermuda Cruising Rally sails in June from Greenport, New York, to Bermuda. Tania Aebi, record-breaking circumnavigator and author of *Maiden Voyage*, is an organizer of this event.

Salty Dawg Rally: A friendly, nonprofit rally geared toward the veteran sailor with all the bells and whistles of the traditional paid rally. Travel to two different destinations is supported. The rally departs from Hampton, Virginia each fall for the Bahamas and the British Virgin Islands and returns to Bermuda in the spring, where participants can easily reach homeports located along the upper half of the eastern seaboard.

NARC: The North American Rally to the Caribbean departs from Newport, Rhode Island, stops in Bermuda, and then continues to Saint Maarten. Although this rally is put on by the Swan Sailing program, it is open to ocean-worthy sailing vessels of any make.

Caribbean 1500/Atlantic Cup: For the novice or veteran off-shore sailor, the Caribbean 1500, run by the World Wide Cruising Club, represents one leg of the Around the World Cruise (ARC). Leaving from Virginia each fall, it supports travel to the Bahamas and the British Virgin Islands. Its return leg, the Atlantic Cup, goes to Bermuda in the spring.

Worldwide ARC: Each year participating boats meet at Los Palmas de Gran Cania to join the Atlantic Rally for Cruisers (ARC) to kick off its around-the-world sail. Cruisers can sign on for all or some of the legs of the journey.

The Baja Ha-Ha: A fun, casual two-week fall rally from San Diego to Cabo San Lucas, Mexico, with stops at Turtle Bay (Bahia Tortugas) and Bahia Santa Maria. The event is open to sail and powerboats over 27 feet that were designed, built, and have been maintained for open ocean sailing.

BOATSPEAK GLOSSARY

A

Air draft: is the measure of the boat from the waterline to its highest fixed point, such as the top of the mast of a sailboat.

Anchorage (harbor): a place suitable for anchoring in relation to the wind, seas, and bottom.

Anchor rode: a nautical term used to describe the anchor line.

B

Batteries: A 12-volt system used to charge the engine as well as any other house systems, such as lighting and refrigeration.

Beating: a term used to describe a boat traveling directly into the wind, seas, or an opposing current.

Biocide: a chemical used to inhibit biological growth in the reverse osmosis membrane during storage or extended periods of nonuse.

Bimini: sometimes called a surrey top, this is a cover positioned over the cockpit for overhead protection from rain and sun.

Bitter end: the tail end of a line.

Berth: a sleeping area or bed. A dock slip is also referred to as a "berth."

Boom: a spar (pole), along the foot (bottom edge) of a fore and aft rigged sailboat that greatly improves control of the angle and shape of the sail.

Bosun's chair: a collapsible seat and harness combination used to haul a person up a mast.

Bridge clearance: see air draft.

Bung plug: a tapered softwood plug with the ability to swell.

C

Cabin: an enclosed sleeping area, which may include a head.

Canal: a man-made waterway connecting two bodies of water.

Canal lock: a marine "elevator" within a canal used to move a vessel from a body of water at one height to a body of water at a different height.

Certificate of Documentation: a form of national registration that clearly identifies the nationality of the vessel.

Certificate of Number: a document that includes the vessel identification number, the registered owner's name and address, and the name of any lienholder.

Coaming: the raised section of the deck surrounding the cockpit or other opening.

Commissioning: a process performed by the boat manufacturer or dealer before handing the boat over to the customer.

Cook-aboard harbor: an anchorage with no restaurants on shore or within walking distance from shore.

Cradle: a structure constructed of metal or wood, or a set of metal poppits, meant to support the critical areas of the hull—the bulkhead, keel, and engine of a boat.

Cuddy cabin: a closed deck over the bow that creates a protected sleeping area and usually includes a toilet.

D

Davit: a crane-like apparatus used for supporting, raising, and lowering boats, dinghies, or other such devices.

Dinghy (or tender): any small boat carried or towed behind a vessel large enough to carry one or more people.

Ditch bag: a duffel packed with survival supplies that will not already be present on your dinghy or life raft.

Dock: the water area immediately adjacent to a pier or wharf.

Dock, fixed: a slip where lines are attached to heavy wooden or steel pilings driven vertically into the harbor bottom. A finger pier may or may not be available for ease in getting off or on the boat.

Dock, floating: a slip supported by metal pipes on which it can move up and down with the rise and fall of the water level.

Dodger: a hooded canvas or hardtop cover meant to deflect sea spray from coming into the cockpit from the bow.

Dorade: a type of vent that permits the passage of air in and out of the cabin or engine room of a boat while keeping rain, spray, and sea wash out.

Draft: the amount of hull that is underwater.

Drogue: similar to a sea anchor, except is towed astern to slow forward movement and hold the stern steady.

Digital Selective Calling (DSC): allows a marine radio to broadcast an encoded distress call that can be picked up by nearby vessels equipped with similar capability.

Dunnage: inexpensive or waste packing materials used on ships during transportation to protect and secure cargo from chafing or moisture or to provide ventilation.

E

Emergency Position Indicating Radio Beacon (EPIRB): a device that transmits repeated signals from your location.

Engine room: an enclosed area that contains the mechanical workings of a boat equipped with an inboard engine.

Eye splice: an "eye" shaped loop used to secure the line to the boat by slipping it onto a cleat.

F

Fathom: refers to the depth of the water. One fathom equals 6 feet.

Float plan: a collection of pertinent information about your travel plans that includes methods of contacting you.

Flybridge: an open deck on a cabin cruiser located above the bridge on the cabin roof. It usually has a duplicate set of navigating equipment.

Freeboard: the distance from the waterline to the upper deck level at the point where water can enter the boat.

G

Galley: the kitchen of a boat, equipped with a sink, cooking and cooling appliances, and possibly a freezer.

Generator: an external battery unit that converts mechanical energy into electrical energy.

Global Positioning System (GPS) a system of satellites, computers, and receivers that is able to determine the latitude and longitude of a receiver on Earth.

H

Halyard: a line (rope) that is used to hoist a ladder, sail, a flag, or a yard. The term comes from the phrase, 'to haul yards.'

Head: a bathroom with sink, toilet, and possibly a shower.

Heat exchanger: a component used to transfer heat from freshwater to raw water in a freshwater system.

Helm : the navigational station, which includes a tiller or steering wheel and necessary electronics.

Horsepower: the power exerted by a horse in pulling. One unit of horsepower (hp) equals 745.7 watts or 33,000 foot-pounds per minute.

Hull beam: the width of the boat at its widest part.

Hull length: the length of the boat when measured at the waterline.

Hull speed: the term used to describe the fastest the boat can move given its weight and proportions, even with the assistance of an engine.

Hurricane: a storm having 74 mph winds or greater.

Hurricane warning: sustained winds of at least 74 mph are expected within twenty-four hours.

Hurricane watch: You could experience hurricane conditions within thirty-six hours.

IJK

Inverter: a device connected to the battery banks to convert DC power to AC electrical power.

Jackline: a line or strap used to help keep a crew member on deck.

Knot: the equivalent of 1.5 mph.

L

Lake: a controlled environment that is typically surrounded by foliage and residences.

Lee cloth: a canvas hammock or set of straps designed to prevent a person from falling out of his or her bunk on a boat when the boat is heeled over or bouncing about with the waves.

Lifeline: a wire or cable supported by stanchions that runs along the outside of the deck and is used to help restrain passengers.

Lightning arrester: a device used in preventing damage to radio, telephone, or other electrical equipment.

Lightning rod: a rod-like metal conductor installed to divert lightning away from a structure by providing a direct path to the ground.

Line: a term used to refer to any length of rope having a function on a boat.

MNO

Microburst: a sudden and intense downdraft within a severe thunderstorm that produces powerful winds.

Mooring: a semipermanent anchorage installation that consists of a heavy mushroom anchor, chain, mooring buoy, and a length of rope.

Mooring mast (pickup pennant): enables you to grab hold of a mooring without using a boat hook.

Nautical mile: a distance on the water equal to 1.5 statute (land) miles.

On the hard: a term meaning a boat is on dry dock (or land) in the boatyard.

Overall length: the total length of the boat, from stem to stern.

P Q

Painter: a line with one end affixed to the bow of the dinghy and the other end tied onto the stern of your boat or to a dinghy dock at shore.

Pickling: a slang term for the process of flushing the membrane with a biocide solution before storage.

Prefilter: a filter placed in a desalination system to remove suspended solids from the feed water before it reaches the high-pressure pump and reverse osmosis membrane.

Pressure relief valve: a component that relieves pressure in a watermaker system to prevent damage to the pump and membrane.

Pontoon: a buoyant cylindrical tube that acts as the basic hull to support a heavy load such as a houseboat structure. Often, it is constructed of marine-grade aluminum.

Poppits: temporary supporting braces for a boat while being stored in a boatyard or other land facility.

R

Radar (radio detecting and ranging): a system that transmits microwaves in a focused beam. Some of this microwave energy bounces off objects and returns to the radar to be measured.

Refrigerant: a substance, usually a fluid, used in a heat pump and refrigeration cycle.

S

Safety harness: is an assembly worn by a person to enable him or her to hook securely onto a lifeline or jackline when moving about the deck of a boat.

Salinity: a measure of the amount of salts, minerals, and other dissolved solids contained in a water source.

Saloon (pronounced "salon"): the living area, which includes a dining area and possibly a chart table and an indoor helm station.

Sea anchor: a cone of heavy canvas that acts much like a parachute that creates drag by keeping the bow of the boat pointed into the wind and seas.

Seacock: a valve on the hull of a boat that permits seawater to flow into the boat for cooling the engine, or to run through a faucet, sink drain, or toilet.

Sea trial (shakedown cruise): the testing phase of a watercraft. Shakedown cruise: a short trip on a boat that has been dormant to determine if there are any operational problems. See also "sea trial."

Shoaling: the reduction of depth due to a sandbank caused by silt that has drifted from the shoreline.

Shrouds: pieces of upright rigging which support the mast. Usually, there will be more than one shroud on each side of the boat.

Slip: a water-based parking spot between piers or wharves, sometimes referred to as a "berth."

Spar: a pole of wood, metal, or lightweight material used in the rigging of a sailboat to provide direct or indirect support for the sails. A boom or mast is a spar.

Spring line: a line that keeps the boat near the dock by preventing it from moving fore or aft, while allowing for the rise and fall of the tide.

Stepping: a sailboat term for erecting the mast.

Squall: a burst of violent weather accompanied by intense winds.

Squall, white: The name refers to the color of the waves caused by a sudden increase in wind velocity in tropical and subtropical waters.

Stays: ropes, wires, or rods on sailboats that serve to stabilize the masts. On a ship with a single mast, stays that run aft are called backstays and stays that run forward are called forestays. Along with shrouds, they form the primary stabilization for the standing rigging.

Sugar scoop: a curved platform-like extension of the stern of a sailboat for easy access to swimming or boarding.

Surge protector: a small device to protect a computer, telephone, or other electrical device from damage by high-voltage electrical surges.

Surrey top: see bimini.

T

Tender: see dinghy.

Tiller: a lever attached to a rudder post of a boat that provides leverage in the form of torque for the helmsman to turn the rudder.

Tropical depression: a storm with less than 35 mph winds.

Tropical storm: a storm with 35 to 73 mph winds.

Turnbuckle: a device for adjusting the tension or length of ropes, cables, tie rods, and other tensioning systems.

UVW

United States Coast Guard (USCG): the primary federal and lifesaving agency with maritime authority for the United States.

Unstepping: taking down the mast of a sailing vessel.

Vacuum sealing: the process of bagging items by suctioning out air, thereby stabilizing the item and keeping it free from external moisture and bacteria.

VHF: a line-of-sight system, which means the radio waves won't bend to follow the curvature of the earth.

Waterspout: the marine counterpart of a tornado. Most frequent in the tropics.

Weather window: the marine weather prediction for the length of time you will be on cruise for the area you will be cruising.

XYZ

Yacht: the term applies to vessels 40 feet and up, except in sailboat racing when every competing boat is called a "yacht" without regard for size.

INDEX

355

REFERENCES

www.boatsafe.com/nauticalknowhow/buying.htm accessed 8/7/2012

www.discoverboating.com

http://www.discoverboating.com/buying/neworused.aspx

www.sailnet.com ; SailNet Community, The Joys and Pitfalls of Buying a new Boat: Parts 1 & 2 by Lin & Larry Pardy, posted Jan 2000

www.sailnet.com ; Sailnet community; Buying a Charter Yacht by Josephine Williams, Footloose Sailing Charters; posted Nov 2006.

Chapman Piloting: Seamanship and Small Boat Handling, 62nd edition, Hearst Marine Books, New York, pgs. 17-22, pgs 297-327, pgs.

www.boatsdepot.org

Cruising World, Navigate the World of Dollar and Cents by Mark Pillsbury, Sept. 20, 2010. http://www.cruisingworld.com/how-to/projects/navigate-the-world-of-dollars-and-cents

Power Boating for Dummies by Randy Vance, Wiley Publishing, Inc. 2009

Is the Displacement Hull for You? by Eric Sorenson, Soundings publication (online) posted 11/2008. www.Soundingonline.com

Test: Battle of the Power Cats, Popular Mechanics Magazine, May 1998 issue, p. 1, from online site http://www.popularmechanics.com/outdoors/recreation/boating/1276941

Recreational Trawler, from Wikipedia, pulled from website 9/19/12

All About Houseboats website http://www.all-about-houseboats.com/

The Smart Boats by Michael Vatalaro, *Boat US. Magazine,* October/November, pgs. 48-49

Marine Fuel.com website, Types of Boat Fuel Tanks, http://marinefuel.com/types-of-boat-fuel-tanks/

Electric vs Reverse Cycle Heat, Flagship Marine website, http://www.flagshipmarine.com/heat.html

Choosing a Watermaker, West Marine Website, http://www.westmarine.com/webapp/wcs/stores/servlet/WestAdvisorVie

w?langId=-1&storeId=11151&catalogId=10001&page=Watermakers#.UIhOc2_R5WJ

Outfitting for Cruising, West marine website, pgs 1-15, www.westmarine.com

http://www.clubmarine.com.au/internet/clubmarine.nsf/docs/MG23-6+Tender+Tips

Dinghy Decisions, Club Marine website, pgs 1-5 http://www.clubmarine.com.au/internet/clubmarine.nsf/docs/MG23-6+Tender+Tips

Boating Resource Center, Official site of the US Coast Guard Safety Division, download 2 pamphlets on regulations and navigational aids, http://www.uscgboating.org/regulations/navigation_rules.aspx

US Powerboating, Training, Education, and On-water Classes, http://www.uspowerboating.com/?gclid=CNKPr6G307MCFal7QgodBBkAHw

Sound Environmental Associates (SEA), http://www.seadolphin.com/

United States Power Squadron, America's Boating Courses, Boating Laws and License requirements by State, http://www.americasboatingcourse.com/lawsbystate.cfm

United States Coast Guard Auxiliary, Boating Safety Education, http://cgaux.org/boatinged/

Boat US publications and website http://www.boatus.com

Docklines by Don Casey, Revised by US Boat 2012, http://www.boatus.com/boattech/casey/docklines-casey.asp

Boat Fenders, Choosing the Right Fender, boats-heaven.com Anchoring, Safe Boating Card Website, http://www.safeboatingcard.com/Manual/Chapter5/Chapter5_10.jsp

Top Boat Anchors, http://www.myboatsgear.com/newsletter/200788.asp

Do-it-Yourself : Shore Power, *West Marine website*, http://www.westmarine.com/webapp/wcs/stores/servlet/WestAdvisorView?langId=-1&storeId=11151&catalogId=10001&page=Shore-Power#.UM9-FOSACjs

Bottom Paint for Freshwater Boats, Peter Anjou, Mar 16, 2012 http://blog.boattrader.com/2012/03/bottom-paint-for-freshwater-boats.html

Applying Bottom Paint, Don Casey, *Boat US website*, www.boatus.com

Selecting Bottom Paint, *Clean Boat Tip Sheet*, Maryland Clean Marina website. www.dnr.maryland.gov/boating

How to give your Boat that Glossy New Shine!, *LBF website*, www. Landbigfish.com

www.boatsafe.com

National AG Safety Database website, Lightning Phenomena, pgs. 52-55, http://nasdonline.org/document/209/d000007/boating-lightning-protection.html

Squall, *Learn Weather Phenomena*, XWeather website, http://www.xweather.org/squall

Weather proverbs, Boatsafe website, www.boatsafe.com/nauticalknowhow/weather_proverbs.htm

How Does a Barometer Measure Air Pressure by Rachelle Oblack, *About.com Weather* , http://weather.about.com/od/weatherinstruments/a/barometers.htm

Your Spring Fitting-Out Checklist, Practical Boater Section, *Boat U.S. Magazine*, April/May 2013. Pgs. 92-93.

Prevent Sunstroke with 3 Simple Steps by Richard Kuykendall, *Yahoo Contributor Network*

Tips & Techniques for Rafting -Up by Captain Alan Stopko, Pilot Blog, http://www.pilotmedia.us/wordpress/admin/online-exclusives/tips-techniques-for-rafting-up/

Rafting Up Tips & Tricks, *Boat Trader* website, pgs 3-4. http://articles.boattrader.com/rafting-up-tips-tricks/

Wi-Fi in Motion, Singlepoint website, http://www.yoursinglepoint.com/

Diesel engines repair and Maintenance by Jeremy R Hood, HSH Yacht Sales website http://www.hshyachts.com/html/diesel_engines__repair_and_mai.html

Safe Propane Instructions, *The West Advisor: Propane Systems*, West Marine Website, http://www.westmarine.com

Choosing a Watermaker, *The West Advisor*, West Marine Website, http://www.westmarine.com

Basic Refrigeration Systems, Kollman Marine: Boat refrigeration Specialists, http://www.kollmann-marine.com

Refrigeration Hints, *Kollman Marine: Boat Refrigeration Specialists*, http://www.kollmann-marine.com

Espar's Pre-Heaters for Marine, http://www.espar.com/html/applications/marine.html

ESPAR heating systems website; http://www.boatelectric.com/espar1.htm

A Cruising Sailor's Guide to Rallies by Bill Springer, *Cruising World*, Sept 2009 www.cruisingworld.com

Diesel Downtime by Jim Hendricks, *Motorhead section, Boating Magazine*, pgs. 40-41, November/December 2012.

VHF Marine Radio Service Frequency Table , *CSG Network* website, http://www.csgnetwork.com/marinefreqtable.html.

Running Aground, *BoatSafe* website, http://boatsafe.com/nauticalknowhow/aground.htm

Running Aground , Boating Safety Course online

If you run Aground, Emergency Preparation, Boat U.S. Foundation online study guide

Made in the USA
Middletown, DE
03 December 2016